Elizabeth Taylor

Elizabeth Taylor

Icon of American Empire

Gloria Shin

LEXINGTON BOOKS
Lanham • Boulder • New York • London

Published by Lexington Books
An imprint of The Rowman & Littlefield Publishing Group, Inc.
4501 Forbes Boulevard, Suite 200, Lanham, Maryland 20706
www.rowman.com

86-90 Paul Street, London EC2A 4NE

British Library Cataloguing in Publication Information Available

Library of Congress Cataloging-in-Publication Data

Names: Shin, Gloria, 1978- author.
  Title: Elizabeth Taylor : icon of American empire / Gloria Shin.
  Description: Lanham : Lexington Books [2023] | Includes bibliographical
    references and index. | Summary: "Elizabeth Taylor: Icon of American
    Empire examines Taylor's stardom as symbolic of American Empire at the
    apex of its power"-- Provided by publisher.
  Identifiers: LCCN 2022046130 (print) | LCCN 2022046131 (ebook) | ISBN
    9781666907476 (cloth) | ISBN 9781666907483 (ebook)
  Subjects: LCSH: Taylor, Elizabeth, 1932-2011. | Motion picture actors and
    actresses--United States. | United States--Civilization--20th century.
  Classification: LCC PN2287.T18 S55 2023 (print) | LCC PN2287.T18 (ebook)
    | DDC 791.4302/8092--dc23/eng/20220930
  LC record available at https://lccn.loc.gov/2022046130
  LC ebook record available at https://lccn.loc.gov/2022046131

For My Mother—The first beautiful woman I have ever loved.
Beauty colonizes the imagination.

Contents

List of Figures

Acknowledgments

I would like to thank Tara McPherson, Curtis Marez, Akira Mizuta Lippit, Priya Jaikumar, Fred Moten, Sarah Gualtieri, and Miranda Banks for their wisdom, guidance, patience, faith, and support as I was inventing this project. I thank Karen Bowdre, Sandy Garcia-Myers, Judith Lakamper, Carla Marcantonio, Kerri Steinberg, Ethan Kirk, and Robert Stone for helping me complete this book into its final iteration. Finally, thanks to Heather Malcolm, Alexandra Au, and my family for loving me and ET, too.

Introduction

It has been over forty years since the publication of Richard Dyer's foundational monograph *Stars*, and star studies has since become a vibrant interdisciplinary subfield of media studies.[1] As such it incorporates methods and concepts from film studies, television studies, performance studies, cultural studies, theories of new media, critical race theory, queer theory, gender studies, postcolonial studies, transnational studies, and still others to enable the production of fascinating work that solidifies the connections between media, performance, and identity. I assert that the star is not only an essential critical object of contemporary culture, but is the world's most compelling and powerful conceptual model of identity in practice.

With the ubiquity of celebrity culture and the mobilization of star systems in seemingly every commercial industry, not just media and entertainment to evaluate work and hierarchize laborers, it is in part the promise of performative excellence that makes stars captivating and presents the unique opportunity to critically deconstruct and examine the possibilities of the star as either a figure whose labors are a form of genius or an affective object whose formation is relational to genius or the extraordinary in some way. This project works to help shift this field toward the study of the convergence of genius and affective labor beyond the examination of stars as essentially commercially constructed objects by themselves or through the media apparatuses which circulate their images to consider how these textual bodies help inspire and explicate new theories of performance, affect, and identity through their triangulation. Performance is the compulsive meta-text of gestures, expressions, projections, and embodiments through which presentations of identity are discursively formed and visually and aurally realized. As performance is reified through the eliciting of affects which are the emotive experiences constructed through the reception of body narratives both physical and real or incorporeal or imagined, the overabundance of celebrities and famous people forces the continuous reconfiguration of the meaning of stardom for a global and interconnected popular culture whose consumers are obsessed with almost all forms of affective labor.

I argue that audiences are captivated by affective labor because it is always working toward the naturalization of a certain fantasy about identity that registers through a spectrum of pleasure. Race, of course provides the most binding cultural fantasies that gird US social and political history, of which Hollywood cinema is the most ideologically potent progenitor.

So, who is a star? By all cultural accounts, Elizabeth Taylor's fame and celebration is indexical of postwar, postcolonial, and postmodern stardom at its greatest heights. This examination of her iconicity advances the evolution of the field of star studies by deepening our understanding of the multiplicity of meanings that the star in general and the beautiful woman icon in particular embodies. She helps us better understand stardom and its sites of power and allows an unprecedented full-scale investigation of its impact as a global labor and industrial phenomenon in the production of culture in recent decades.

As her legendary career reaches its zenith during the postcolonial period marked by the global nationalization movements of the 1950s and 1960s, I argue that Elizabeth Taylor is both a metaphor for American Empire and an exemplar of postcolonial whiteness. As an international jet setter whose on- and off-screen images during this historical moment are in direct dialogue with the fantasies and anxieties of whites about a burgeoning postcolonial world, I argue that Taylor's image and film work have become a "cognitive map," a concept according to Frederic Jameson whose effect is to symbolize and make visible the various collective forces and conditions that constitute aspects of the world. He writes that the work of the cognitive map "enables a situational representation on the part of the individual subject to the vaster and properly unrepresentable totality which is the ensemble of society's structures as a whole."[2] As such, Elizabeth Taylor as an imperial icon situates viewers to and enables the representation of the vaster unrepresentable totality of American Empire through a vector of pleasure and a logic of consumption.

Therefore, in my work I use the iconicity of Elizabeth Taylor, meaning the indelible narrative scenarios, visual objects, phenomenological effects, and auxiliary actors intimately associated with her, as the lens to examine how postcoloniality as a series of discourses tied to numerous sociohistorical political conditions resets the social relations between former colonizers and the colonized and reconfigures white identity after decolonization. Postcoloniality is used here not as a term of periodization or a chronology that merely marks a time of decolonization but mobilized as a problematic to understand how other forms of domination after colonialism including economic and military imperialisms and Orientalisms emerge. Examining postcoloniality through a logic of American globalism, I map postcolonial whiteness in its seemingly limitless mobility and reach to explain how white subjects after colonization while unmoored from nations and colonies remain powerful nonetheless.

The studying of postcolonial whiteness leads to a greater understanding of the discursive and philosophical cores of not just white freedom but Black oppression during this time which in the United States are not so much diametrically opposed as they are intimately tied. As Orlando Patterson and Toni Morrison have convincingly demonstrated, the very concept of white freedom defined by white self-will is conceived and practiced through the white subject's distanced encounters with the realities of Black forced labor and oppression. As Black liberation movements ignite the globe during the 1960s, the realization of Black emancipation, African statehood, and US legalized racial equality seem so threatening to white freedom to many white subjects since Black slavery has always guaranteed white selfhood in the past. This study of postcolonial whiteness looks closely at the United States's place in the world in the 1950s to the 1980s and its logic of accumulation that collapses white liberation and pleasure onto Black oppression, perhaps best evidenced by the centuries of vitriolic physical and legislative violence of the US state against Blacks in America. The white American fear of Black freedom runs directly parallel to its fear of the Soviet Union and its perceived brutal spheres of influence. Through Elizabeth Taylor, who signifies not only surplus but excess, viewers are given a more feminine, gentle model of imperialism that privileges accumulation through the simultaneous evocation of excessive visual and erotic pleasure through her image that romanticizes imperialism as the site for white freedom during the Cold War.

Imperialism, the highest stage of capitalism (to borrow from Lenin), defines and produces racial difference to succeed. Philosopher Etienne Balibar and sociologist Immanuel Wallerstein analyze racism as a social relation entrenched within social structures including the formation of the axial, international labor relations between core (imperial) and periphery (Third World) nations. Their findings help allow an investigation of the role of racism in the imperial project. Wallerstein in particular asserts that "racism is the expression, the promoter and the consequence of the geographical concentrations associated with the axial division of labor."[3] This logic is at the heart of the depictions of racial Others in Taylor's plantation films, as they are represented as labor whose very value is set by their white plantation mistress, and it is through their exploitation that their overseers fully achieve proper whiteness. The values set over work and skills not only determine the core but allows it to exploit the periphery. I argue that the racial imagery of the postcolonial era which Elizabeth Taylor helps produce through her performative work indicate US imperiality as a race project centered through the racialization of work and bodies. Particularly through scenarios that naturalize white domination and the subjugation of racial others, they in turn present whiteness as a site of unending power.

Elizabeth Taylor is the sui generis star of the postcolonial cycle of the 1950s and 1960s, whose fame, beauty, performative prowess, and infamy as the world's most powerful film actress make her an icon of empire. As an imperial agent in her various filmic guises, embodying characters who work at the service of empire as well as through her off-screen persona as a glamorous jetsetter who desires to see and the experience all the pleasures of a world without borders, she helps magnetize the explicit and authoritative role of the United States in the world after the European loss of empire while presenting American imperial ambitions as an alternate to Soviet communism in the Cold War era. As a white subject whose image on and off screen is re-racialized during the latter postcolonial cycle of the 1960s, Elizabeth Taylor provides the racial signifiers that signaled the United States' rise as the world's most important imperial power. Through Taylor's considerable performative abilities, she evokes American Empire and assures its legacy through the production of numerous and pervasive cultural narratives that have fundamentally shaped US definitions and understandings of whiteness, nonwhite subjects, and the non-Western world through and against each other and projected those constructions as forms of knowledge through cinema and other visual media across the globe.

Advancing the field of star studies, I explicitly read the star body as a conceptual model of identity in practice that configures social formations such as race, gender, sexuality, class, and national identity. In my work, I utilize media performances as meters to gauge the ways Elizabeth Taylor as an affective laborer embodies and narrativizes both cultural idealizations and collective tensions. It is in part her performative excellence that raises the symbolic and emotive values of media objects and provides a multiplicity of significations for an audience. I consider the ubiquity of media and the fascination with stardom in particular to be valuable opportunities to understand the ways popular culture and stars are what theorist Raymond Williams calls "structures of feeling," which help encapsulate the various lived experiences of a culture within the present moment.[4] Not only are they conduits to consider how ideas about identity become naturalized and acceptable or made abject, but in the specific case of Elizabeth Taylor, my work examines how this star uniquely reveals the political economic history of the United States from the 1950s to the 1980s.

Elizabeth Taylor's film work gives viewers access to the colonial past as the United States rises to become the world's most powerful imperial state in the 1950s, and provides the representations that help form the American racial imaginary during the initial global postcolonial era of the early 1960s and the fight for African American civil rights. Through her global body adventures and romantic conquests, she idealizes consumption during the height of the Cold War in the late 1960s and becomes a corporeal representation of US

imperial ambitions during the 1970s when its full-fledged entry into globalization makes the very borders of American Empire less discernible. Finally,
remaking herself into a safe body, she helps mark the sexual polemics of the
Reagan 1980s that accompany the first cycle of the AIDS crisis in America.

Using critical race theory and postcolonial theory I investigate the ways
Elizabeth Taylor's image reflects the dynamism of white identity as it is
linked to the permeability of geographic and cultural borders due to the
realignments of the globe. I argue that Taylor's global adventures bring
into relief the porous boundaries between the domestic and the foreign that
mark the social and cultural shifts of American Empire. Her on-screen and
off-screen images reflect the numerous effects of decolonization, particularly
the emergence of new national movements, the building of new enclosures,
and the US civil rights movement on white subjectivity. For whites fearing
emerging Black freedoms, Taylor illuminates postcolonial whiteness as a site
of liberation and infinite possibility without the burdens of race.

Elizabeth Taylor's virtuosity as a film actor and insistence on consummate
performance spectacularizes her various evolutions, from Fordist worker who
labors at the service of empire in imperialist discourses of various Hollywood
films to ecstatic white oriental and finally stalwart activist that are models
which stand in for the multiplicity of identities that postcoloniality offers
to the white subject. She foregrounds postcolonial whiteness as a renewed
investment in masquerade, a series of performative acts that chart the recalibration of whiteness through its encounters with images of non-white and
non-Western others. In fact, she and her contemporaries and costars point
to postcolonial whiteness as inherently performative. Indeed rearticulations
of whiteness in the postcolonial era are in fact anchored in performance in
numerous cases examined in this work, from Vivien Leigh and Laurence
Olivier to Rock Hudson and her husband Richard Burton with whom Taylor
shares the celestial firmament as a star.

In chapter 1, using theories from aesthetic philosophy I examine Elizabeth
Taylor's physical beauty and visual allure. Reading beauty ideals and the
labor of beautification as ideologically rich texts, I argue that Taylor and
other women stars reveal whiteness itself to be a dynamic and mutable visual
category. What is celebrated as beautiful is closely associated with notions of
proper whiteness that alleviate the anxieties tied to sociohistorical phenomena such as immigration waves and decolonization. As one of the greatest
icons of beauty in the twentieth century, Taylor is the most powerful figure
to legitimate the beautiful woman as a member of a labor class. In the 1950s
and 1960s, she as a beautiful woman works within networks of commodified
visual performance across the globe, most significantly in photography and
entertainment cinema and is relied upon to produce visual pleasure through
both fictive and actual narratives to promote capitalism. Taylor's on-screen

and off-screen images help recuperate the US colonial past and allows view-ers to encounter the imperial and Cold War present by framing the immediate postcolonial moment as a space of pleasure for white viewers.

Differentiating beauty from beautification which has anchored studies of stardom in the past, I read the star body as a canvas for discipline and labor to consider how Taylor's possession of "natural" beauty elevates her performa-tive power through the delivery of a surplus of visual and emotive pleasure and is racially coded to mark Taylor's whiteness as exceptional but also aberrant. I then succinctly map the significations of the beautiful woman in Hollywood film and ocular culture, asserting that beauty remains a traditional site of female power and male anxiety. I am also expressly interested in the notion of Elizabeth Taylor as a possessor of global beauty. This is particu-larly so because the symbolic apparatus of Hollywood films, of which Taylor is a star of the highest order, still and has always privileged, promoted and commodified the "Hollywood Blonde" across every decade of the twentieth century and beyond, starting with Mary Pickford and Lillian Gish, to Jean Harlow, Lana Turner, Grace Kelly, Marilyn Monroe, Jane Fonda, and onto Kim Basinger, Michelle Pfeiffer, Scarlett Johansson, Charlize Theron, and Margot Robbie.

As a nonblonde woman with exceptional facial beauty, a narrow waist, and considerably large breasts, Elizabeth Taylor's beauty represents an archetypal hyperfeminine form that is easily eroticized. Taylor's actual chromatic dark-ness, meaning her very black hair and her legendary hirsuiteness, gives her a transnational appeal that seems more representative of women of the world, a vast majority who are brunettes. After all, she is not a blinding white Nordic figure who plays Cleopatra to confused and jarred global filmgoers. I posit that Taylor's looks closely align with the visual register of a global spectator and maps the contours of a "borderless" ideal of beauty well into the 1960s, which helps her remain an international star even without the direct support of the Hollywood studio system to market her image and her films.

Past scholarship on the female star has put needed focus on body disci-plines and beautification, particularly of the hyperanglicization of women including Marilyn Monroe, Rita Hayworth, and Jane Fonda which has been used to expand knowledge about the various body practices required to produce visual whiteness and sustain it as a social construction. Through various, often painful techniques, many women performers have dyed their hair, dieted, and shaped their bodies to fit Anglo standards of beauty with its requisite demands of lightness and slenderness.

But during Elizabeth Taylor's major foray into explicit beautification, she transforms herself into an extrafilmic Cleopatra and plays the Egyptian queen as an oriental in whiteface, reversing the process of anglicization. Buttressed by her conversion to Judaism in 1959, Taylor visually re-racializes herself as nonwhite, emphasizing her naturally dark hair, tanning copiously, and adopting a non-Western glamour that permanently exoticizes her image, which I discuss at length in chapter 3. But in chapter 1, I note how Taylor's chromatic darkness is a source of distress for some including the famed tastemaker and British aesthete Cecil Beaton and Taylor's own mother, Sara Sothern, whose descriptions of the star are thinly coded expressions of racial anxiety. Ultimately I argue that receptions of Taylor's beauty as natural, strange, and extraordinary make her an exceptional star whose signification of white singularity are symmetrical to the allegorical justifications for American imperial authority especially as they secure the visual pleasure of her imperial films. I conclude the chapter by performing a reading of Elizabeth Taylor's latter-day 1970s fat body to consider the ways she signified power even through a perceived abject and ugly corporeality.

In chapter 2, I focus closely on Elizabeth Taylor's Hollywood films and argue that her role as a plantation mistress in *Elephant Walk* (1954), *Giant* (1956), and *Raintree County* (1957) disciplines her off screen unruliness and her regimentation allows viewers to access the colonial home through Amy Kaplan's notion of "manifest domesticity," the imperial underpinnings of white femininity. By fetishizing master/servant relations and exporting the Fordist modes of production that mints Taylor as a star onto the fictive plantation space, I assert that these films mourn the loss of Ceylon (currently Sri Lanka) and the US South (Texas and Louisiana) as colonial sites through the celebratory representation of archaic modes of production and labor management that help shore up proper whiteness and restore patriarchal order through Taylor's subordination.

In *Elephant Walk*, Elizabeth Taylor as Ruth Wiley becomes the mistress of the titular settlement, a tea plantation in Ceylon on the eve of British expulsion from the island. Much as leaves are manufactured into tea to export onto the colonial market, both Ruth and her husband are inculcated into proper whiteness on the plantation. Through Ruth's coming to proper femininity and filial conduct by her racial domination of her Tamil servants and her husband John's affirmation of heterosexuality and proper masculinity, the Wileys, who have newly attained transnational mobility through their forced exodus, can name decolonization as the reason for their ensuing liberation.

In *Giant*, Elizabeth Taylor plays Leslie Benedict, the proto-feminist devoted wife of a socially regressive Texas cattle baron. As a Northeastern outsider, she embodies the ideals of social progress and racial acceptance that are forcibly transplanted onto Texas. The state's transition from a cattle economy to fully fledged petrol-capitalism also brings modernity, spurring technological advances, and a major economic boom. Most significantly, the progress tied to petro-modernity is symbolized by white tolerance of

Mexicans who are portrayed as loyal servants, capable professionals, and brave soldiers who die while upholding US nationalism.

Lastly, in *Raintree County,* Elizabeth Taylor is Susanna Drake, a beautiful, schizophrenic Southern belle who seduces an abolitionist into marriage. Her husband realizes that Susanna has pathologized her strong attachment to her Black caretaker whom she believes is her mother. Falsely thinking she is mixed-race, Susanna hates her imaginary Black self. Her psychic war, which she sadly loses, is a metaphor for the impossibilities of race-mixing and an explicit argument against racial desegregation. The South is not only the national designated site of American racial trauma but these traumas are fully contained within its borders through Susanna's destruction.

These plantation films mobilize race to guide whites through three specifically desired outcomes of decolonization: the efficient management of the imminent white exodus and global mobility after the loss of colonies, the acceptance of the making of new enclosures—meaning the privatization of public resources for profit which brings about modernity and is fundamentally beneficial to the white power elite but forcibly remakes white relationships with people of color (who are not Black) through various vectors, including labor, domesticity, and marriage—and finally, the heeding of warnings that accompanies the imagined dangers of racial desegregation to whites which spurs their disavowals of race, racism, and Black subjectivities.

To reveal counterpoints to the intended codes of these films, I incorporate analyses of ancillary discourses that detail Elizabeth Taylor's extracinematic signification of domestic chaos and aberrant femininity in my readings to demonstrate how star discourses can be interventional tools against the films' textual fixity. I also use the biographical discourses surrounding stars Vivien Leigh, a fellow Hollywood plantation mistress and Taylor's predecessor in *Elephant Walk,* and Rock Hudson, Taylor's costar in *Giant,* in this endeavor. I perform counter-readings of both stars' official filmic performances through examinations of some of the narratives of their off-screen lives which exist alongside the textual residue of their films. The reading of these often contradictory narratives against each other helps continuously construct meaning which can both override official performances such as films and become the dynamic significations which circulate across media and beyond the screen.

In chapter 3, I argue that Elizabeth Taylor's visual Orientalism, her successful adoption of an explicitly non-Western glamour on- and off-screen evidenced by her influence as "Cleopatra" to set style trends in women's makeup, hair, and fashion in the 1960s visibly inscribes imperial fantasies of the Other onto white American women's bodies. I assert that this Egyptomanic moment in women's style solidifies the linkage of consumerism to new fantasies of embodiment and remakes the white feminine body into a screen onto which collective colonial yearnings are projected. This episode expands our understanding of the gendered dimensions of imperial desire and its presence in the formation of white feminine American identity during the Cold War.

Elizabeth Taylor's performance as an Oriental in whiteface in *Cleopatra* mediates white dissatisfaction with proper whiteness and its strident dictates of self-control, rationality, and discipline. As the Oriental, a European invention of the Eastern Other which Taylor internalizes and projects with ferocious earnestness on- and off-screen, she organizes herself in the pursuit of pleasure and personal fulfillment through expressions of sexuality and ambition which ultimately signify as liberatory. Also through her newly racialized form white spectators can filmically disavow Blackness and Black liberation during this historical moment of large-scale African nationalization in the 1960s. Imagining Black liberation as an impediment to white freedom, the grief over the loss of colonies is expressed through a white appropriation of Egypt, which Taylor's Cleopatra stands in for in the film. Presented as a site for white pleasure complete with images of Black bondage, the film's depictions erase Egypt's historical role in the formation of Black agency, as the space has long been an inspiration of Afrocentrism. Elizabeth Taylor is a symbolic figure who embodies the qualities attributed by whites to the nonwhite body including sexual excess, hedonism, and unruliness that often inspire fear within the white imagination and tinges her image. But those very qualities Taylor performs solidifies her iconicity and assures her star power because they fulfill the white subject's yearning for liberation precisely during a time of danger when whites profoundly fear the loss of their freedom.

In chapter 3, I also explore Elizabeth Taylor's budding romantic relationship with the Welsh actor Richard Burton, reading his masterful elocution of English as a form of colonial mimicry that both secures and temporarily dismantles his claiming of proper whiteness. Through his film performances of masculine imperiality, Burton comes into proper elite whiteness through his vocalization of the English language, whose acquisition allows him to become a professional actor. His rise as a star is a compelling example of the reach of English language dissemination as a form of linguistic imperialism during postcolonialism. But still, he constantly proves that his masquerade of white imperiality is not seamless by reclaiming his Welshness through his storytelling and his nostalgic valorization of Welsh mining. Grueling Welsh mens' work that the actor insists is the crown jewel of skilled masculine labor in the United Kingdom before modernization, he never emphasizes its actual usefulness to the nation or the Commonwealth, presenting it to listeners as a utopian cultural formation that exists outside the service of the state.

Finally, I also theorize the Taylor-Burton on-set union and conspicuous consumption as their responses to the labor alienation that results from the industrial crisis of the death of the Hollywood studio system. These two stars negotiate their flexible position within the logic of capitalist exchange-value as freelance workers through the acquisition of commodities. Of particular interest is Burton's own fixation on the Faust tale, which he helps adapt for the screen twice. In dialogue with the work of anthropologist Michael Taussig and his study of commodity fetishism in South America that links the devil with capitalism I posit that Burton's own repeated insistence on conjuring the devil, not only demonizes his desire for fame and fortune of which he is often accused, but may allow him to symbolically exorcize his subjugation under the demonic, frantic pace of both fame and capitalism.

In chapter 4, I argue that Elizabeth Taylor's AIDS activism, at the forefront of celebrity diplomacy, is a phenomenon of the culture industry that produces a version of what Néstor García Canclini describes as "consumer citizenship." As a successful fundraiser, Taylor has an unparalleled ability to stimulate capitalism through the mobilization of multinational corporations and individual consumers. I assert that the postcolonial neoliberal white subject is both a consumer citizen and a postmodern jetsetter who maneuvers through a world that privileges markets over states and helps reconfigure national cultures within transnational exchanges. This white subject then operates in transnational, transterritorial spaces in which capitalism can be used to initiate a project for social change. I assert that Taylor's activism is compelling evidence of the possibilities for pursuing an embodied emotive politics for the neoliberal white subject who feels entitled to participate in the fight for social progress.

By skillfully mobilizing the tropes of the maternal melodrama in her activism, Taylor helps viewers imagine engrossing examples of social justice occurring in the actual world, which the filmic melodrama cannot do. Taylor's direct interventions during the first cycle of the American AIDS crisis which evolved to encompass her work as a global activist has helped to permanently reset the affective tones and responses to AIDS by the US government. She strongly encourages the humanization of the AIDS patient, most often thought to be white, male, and gay at the time. By framing the person with AIDS to be a sufferer rather than a sexual outlaw, Elizabeth Taylor's work for people with AIDS begins the symbolic process of figuratively reknotting gay familial ties with the nation. For those gay subjects who are estranged from their own families she becomes an all-loving universal mother to the sick, including her own former daughter-in-law, Aileen Getty.

Consequently, Elizabeth Taylor's success as an activist, having raised more than $275 million for AIDS research and care, persuasively speaks to her genius as an affective laborer who has the power to change culture. Her work also presents a fascinating polemic about the redemptive capacities of capitalism while exposing the racial logics that elevate white consumption and its power above others to produce social change.

My interdisciplinary project on Elizabeth Taylor lays the groundwork to allow a move away from a particular bent in the field of whiteness studies that historicizes and frames whiteness as a minoritarian position by mapping how ethnic Europeans became "white." According to Robyn Wiegman this specific impulse in the subfield uses particularity to depict prewhite ethnics. She writes, "whiteness studies reverses the historical processes of white construction, offering for the contemporary white subject a powerful narrative of discursive Black origins.[5] Problematically, these historical framings in turn place focus away from the mediated, political, and ideologically complex processes that allow whiteness to remain as an exclusionary preexisting base of authority that subjugates the multitude who are raced as never white, while others, primarily European immigrants who, to paraphrase James Baldwin, "thought" they were white, can come into whiteness to share in its power. Certainly, my research turns away from the heavily mined fin-de-siècle period used in numerous works that map whiteness as a social construction while also inadvertently presenting whiteness as a site of injury through studies of racialized ethnics or examinations of permanently poor whites.[6] Instead, my work is fully engaged in the nascent study of global postcolonial white hegemony and investigates whiteness as it is configured by capitalism and imperialism through its media representations to theorize its ability to maintain power across borders in the face of various geopolitical events initially considered as lasting political gains for people of color.

By incorporating critical race theory, postcolonial theory, feminist theory, and political theory, this project is in part a spirited examination of the adaptability of American citizenship to the postcolonial world, an investigation of its permutations as it reconstitutes the globe through its mandate of what C. B. Macpherson calls "possessive individualism." By reading Elizabeth Taylor as a modern figuration of the possessive individual, the ideal subject of liberal democratic humanism for whom American citizenship is invented to protect the pursuit of property, this work links star studies, postcolonial studies, and critical race theory in innovative ways that brings new knowledge and critical insights about whiteness and American Empire.

Historically the possessive individual's privileged sanctuary under the laws of the United States make clear that American citizenship is not a universally available subject position under liberal humanism but a racially delineated, gender-specific, and exclusive status.[7] This individual demonstrates that he owns himself through his exercise of self-will as he determines what happiness is worthy of his pursuit. Through his desire for and ownership of property he secures his comfort within the world of a possessive market society.[8] His collection of property is not only an assemblage of the material effects that make up his world, it interpolates his racial, gender, and national identity and privileges within capitalism.

The explicit framing of Elizabeth Taylor as a possessive individual is first shown in a MGM publicity still used to promote her as a preteen star. Putting her proper femininity on display, it makes a direct allusion to her celebrated role as Velvet Brown since Taylor is seen carefully polishing her stable of toy horses placed atop a table. Cloth in hand and eyes fixed she caresses a plastic horse, pacing herself as she will soon inspect the others. Even at the tender age of twelve, Taylor is presented to the public as a collector and a worker. The historically default gender identity of the possessive individual as male is alluded to through the photo itself. Referencing Velvet Brown, the horse-obsessed girl who is forced to masquerade as a boy in order to race in the British Grand National Steeplechase, her presence in the photo reminds viewers that ownership and self-determination and the ability to exercise self-will are historically masculine while the desire for their possession is also feminine.

This earliest iteration of Elizabeth Taylor as the possessive individual configures the trajectory of her performance in the nationalist endeavor while showing the racial limitations of the formulation itself—the possessive individual though initially conceived as male, is now female—but is still white. As the possessive individual is the prototype for American citizenship and its authority is assured all over the world through the expansion of American Empire, its continuous circulation through Taylor as a spectacular global star infamous for her life of accumulation argues to the world that American citizenship is still a white formation precisely when the fight for Black citizenship in the United States and the world threatens white power.

The power of Elizabeth Taylor's iconicity hinges on her performance of white exceptionalism during the American Century in which American global authority was unquestioned through her impeccable performance of global citizenship. She is more than the most famous actress in the century that first worships fame. More than a movie star idolized and adored by her multitude of fans and more than the most beautiful face of American cinema in its last golden age. Her ability to author and adapt her iconicity to meet the emotive needs that form the US racial imaginary across the decades of the twentieth century while always symbolizing the invincibility of American power in the world make her its greatest star and a performative genius. And better than any other affective genius to come before her, her uniqueness as a performer of superlative ability is best expressed through her incomparable power to project, reflect, and mimic the ecstasy of falling in love. Even as her various media projections which overwhelmingly idealize US imperial ambitions inspire both intellectual fascination and numerous interventions, her ability to envelope viewers in the ecstatic is the reason why Elizabeth Taylor is loved so very much.

NOTES

1. Richard Dyer, *Stars* (1979).

2. Frederic Jameson, *Postmodernism, or The Cultural Logic of Late Capitalism*, 51.

3. Etienne Balibar and Immanuel Wallerstein, *Race, Nation, Class: Ambiguous Identities*, 79–80.

4. Raymond Williams, *Marxism and Literature*, 128.

5. Robyn Wiegman, "Whiteness Studies and the Paradox of Particularity," 241.

6. Ibid., 232, 239.

7. Grace Kyungwon Hong, *Ruptures of American Capital*, 4–7.

8. C. B. MacPherson, *The Political Theory of Possessive Individualism*, 55–61.

Chapter 1

Beauty Is a Rare Thing

Pulchritude, Performance, and Elizabeth Taylor's Body

When the overwhelmed J. D. Salinger looked upon Elizabeth Taylor for the first time, he exclaimed, "She is the most beautiful creature I have ever seen in my life."[1] When Taylor was a teenage actress at MGM, Barbara Stanwyck saw her once waiting to be made up with the other starlets and declared, "No woman has any business being that beautiful with her hair up at five o'clock in the morning."[2] An unnamed magazine photographer on the studio lot told Taylor at age fifteen that she was the most beautiful woman he has ever seen and that he had photographed them all.[3] The wonder, the incredulity, and the satisfaction that accompanies a judgment made through passionate convictions speak to the pleasure and the exhilaration that Elizabeth Taylor's beauty brings to the beholder. Simply, her beauty is a part of and cannot be separated from her performative prowess. She is a movie star *firstly* because she *looks* good enough to be one, so beautiful that as the old adage goes, "She should be in movies." Her ravishing beauty makes her cinematic emoting and her affective entreaties powerfully resonant because they are anchored by visual pleasure.

In this first chapter I read Elizabeth Taylor's beauty, its dynamic shifting racial and emotive contours and its role in her iconicity as an exceptional star. I theorize that Taylor's "natural" beauty and perceptions of her ability as a "natural" in front of the camera are not only fundamental to her stardom and but also metaphorical of American Empire and its territorial and geographical purview based on a notion of American exceptionalism that is used to explain and justify US domination in the world. In this chapter I also differentiate beauty from beautification which are often conflated and argue that beauty is an ideological object of formidable affective power while beautification is a set of labors with explicit ideological underpinnings that use feminine bodily discipline to specific cultural ends. Both are inextricably tied to stardom, particularly to the woman star who must excel within a visual register as all stars even those perceived to be naturally beautiful are still beautified before facing the camera. While beauty and beautification often do not exist purely and separately from each other, they do exist hierarchically.

Physical beauty is raised above beautification in classical aesthetic philosophies that link beauty to the divine and infinite and view beautification as deceptive, false, and limited. Furthermore, beautification for the white Hollywood star, with the pointed exception of Elizabeth Taylor in the 1960s and 1970s, means the undertaking of various corporeal disciplines to "anglicize" the body. Stars such as Marilyn Monroe, Rita Hayworth, Jane Fonda, Audrey Hepburn, and Grace Kelly are not only exemplars of white beauty but reveal through their beautification that visual whiteness is both an ocular and discursive construction that helps maintain a visual hegemony by aligning beauty with golden-light whiteness. But the tension between Taylor's dark, erotic, and exoticized beauty and the blonde patrician beauty of her contemporaries means that whiteness as a visual category is rather a dynamic and varied formation whose particular fetishization is a projection of the cultural fantasies and anxieties of the times in which it is celebrated.

Elizabeth Taylor's swarthy and gorgeous looks help her become the greatest movie star during the immediate postcolonial era in which whites are forced to remake their social and political relations with the newly liberated people of the world. Elizabeth Taylor's dark beauty becomes an object of fascination through its visualization of racial liminality in the 1960s. Her geographic mobility and her chromatic anomalies provide a captivating fantasy based on the continued narrowing of the physical distance between whites to people of color, a new pleasurable proximity that her jaunts of postcolonial tourism and exotic glamour further reiterate.[4] Elizabeth Taylor's masquerade as an Oriental in whiteface in the 1960s, a genuine performance of a fetishized Oriental decadence that reveals her actual whiteness to be both suspect and aberrant, signals that postcolonial whiteness must be an adaptable performative and visual formation that while luxuriating in its evasions of Blackness can no longer ignore race completely.

Elizabeth Taylor's extraordinary fame and stardom makes her indexical of the women star as cultural zeitgeist who reflects and spurs the cultivation and the shifting of various cultural sensibilities specificity tied to whiteness and proper femininity. She uses her beauty to produce affective and visual pleasure through a mode of the ecstatic which promotes capitalism in Hollywood films and is symbolic of American Empire at the apex of its power. By subverting the primary trope most closely associated with the beautiful female performer—that of an exploited victim caught within the machinery of popular culture, who then becomes a cultural specter of the patriarchal violence projected against the feminine body—Elizabeth Taylor becomes flesh for the fantasy of white womanhood in the initial postcolonial era who signifies the white subject's carte blanche to pursue pleasure as an inalienable right of white modernity. As an icon of exceptional beauty in the postwar era, Elizabeth Taylor is the most powerful figure to legitimate the beautiful woman as a member of a professionalized labor class who works within networks of commercialized visual performance specifically photography and narrative cinema and is essential to their profitability and ideological potency. Her beauty signals her singular whiteness and is as ideologically rich as it was for her personally enriching, confirmed by speculation that she had amassed a fortune estimated at one billion dollars at the time of her death in 2011.

While Elizabeth Taylor's possession of "natural" beauty elevates her performative power through visual pleasure, and is celebrated for its singularity in the 1950s, it is also racially coded to mark Taylor's whiteness as aberrant, so much so that the celebrated tastemaker and gatekeeper of proper whiteness Cecil Beaton, upon seeing Taylor in 1971, could not contain his disgust, finding her exotic looks and nouveau riche aesthetic to be abject. The symbolic apparatus of Hollywood cinema, even as Taylor is one of its greatest stars still mints and commodifies a "Hollywood Blonde" every decade of the twentieth century, beginning with Mary Pickford and Lillian Gish during the global silent era of the 1910s. As a figure who provides an alternative to that model as well as one who lacks the blinding blondeness that accompanies the honest vulnerability of Marilyn Monroe during the sexually conservative 1950s, Taylor's visual darkness of the 1960s makes her beauty resolutely non-middle

Figure 1.1. Eternally beautiful, unapologetically non-blonde. Source: Photo by George Rinhart/Corbis Historical/Getty Images.

American, but functions symbolically as a voluptuous dream of the transnational white body that indelibly marks the presence of whiteness as a global formation since it already references the body of the nonwhite dark(er) other within itself. While blondness is visual shorthand for whiteness, quite often American whiteness, the fact remains, the vast majority of the women of the world, including white women in the United States and outside its borders are not blondes, but brunettes, since those with black and brown hair globally outnumber others with light hair.[5]

The death of Marilyn Monroe in the summer of 1962 coincides with Elizabeth Taylor's ascendance as a global superstar without rival at the height of her much-publicized reign as an extra-cinematic Cleopatra during the filming of the multimillion dollar epic in Rome. Monroe is the beauty and sexual icon who best represents presexual revolution American femininity who signifies an unequivocal whiteness, as her gleaming hair is dyed so light to resemble in her own words "pillowcase white."[6] Her pale skin matches the whiteness of the satin halter dress that blew up while she was standing under a New York subway grate in *The Seven-Year Itch,* a comedy of manners lampooning white middle-class sexual mores while still reaffirming the very constrictions of white American middle-class marriage in the 1950s. Even though Marilyn Monroe's performance of blonde American feminine sexuality is engrossing, it is eclipsed by Elizabeth Taylor's sexualized racial masquerade as the Oriental in whiteface, suggesting that American audiences and the US film industry were seeking and enamored with the iteration of the mobile, sexually liberated white exotic as played by Taylor. As a counter strategy, Monroe who bemoans her rival's unprecedented one million dollar contract with 20th Century Fox for *Cleopatra* as well as the considerable public interest surrounding Taylor's ongoing affair with costar Richard Burton eagerly tries to generate publicity for herself by putting her pale body on display. With her hair freshly dyed ice blonde—the lightest it has ever been—she shoots a nude photo spread with photographer Lawrence Schiller based on the pool scene from her last film *Something's Got to Give* (1962) from which is she is fired and remains uncompleted.[7]

While Monroe's onscreen sexuality is irrepressibly bubbly and anchors her iconic comedic performance, she deeply resents the fact that she has never been nominated for an Academy Award. She tries desperately to navigate her career toward more dramatic and challenging roles and yearns to be taken seriously as an actress by the studios and critics. As Monroe's life is nearing its end, it seems she is enveloped within the dark insatiable stomach of stardom, as commercial media culture cyclically sustains itself by feasting on beautiful women. And it seems her only source of light at the time was her blindingly white hair.

Elizabeth Taylor, on the other hand, is a sexual and beauty icon of a different ilk whose mammoth appetite for pleasure including alcohol, food, and sex sends her off to exotic locales as she traverses the globe in order to brazenly experience pleasure in new places, as globetrotting becomes a newfound obsession. Her insistent transnational mobility and her extended locational distantiation from the United States mimic the spatial logic of American Empire, and according to geographer Neil Smith, its hypernationalist but deterritorialized globalism that allows global power to not remain within the borders of one nation but be wielded by a small ruling class whose interests lie with those of the United States.[8]

Elizabeth Taylor's black hair, so dark that it often photographs blue on film, frames and sets off not only her beautiful face but also her deeply browned body, the results of her intensive tanning sessions during the making of *Cleopatra* which is evident in various segments of the film, particularly in the scene in which she is seen aboard her golden barge sailing into Tarsus on a diplomatic mission, which also happens to end in her having sex with Richard Burton's Mark Antony. While her dark hair references globalism through a subverted fantasy of global beauty—as a visual sign of the nonblonde, non-white, and non-American woman of the world, who in this case as played by Taylor is actually white, the darker pigment of her sun-bronzed skin marks her as a global traveler. During an appearance with Richard Burton at the Academy Awards in 1968, Taylor's skin is so tan from her international sojourns, often aboard her yacht *Kalizma*, that her skin is deep brown. It is a visual display of both her body's unencumbered global mobility and how her form shows her body literally at play while she figuratively plays with her visual whiteness and visibly becomes lighter and darker on a whim. She does this while pleasure seeking across borders, taking full advantage of the postcolonial promise of global citizenship that guarantees her safe passage throughout the world as white power continues undiminished after the death of empire. Her orange and brown body becomes a marker of whiteness as a site in which the confluence of capitalism and postcolonialism underwrite new white freedoms based on renewed imperatives of unhindered white power to be and to feel whatever it desires. During this time Taylor is not only photographed lounging in a kaftan aboard ship while playing with Richard Burton's hair, but also on safari, in which the meditative star is seen with her arm draped around a cheetah during her extended stay in Chobe National Park, Botswana, in 1975.

Elizabeth Taylor's projection of dark beauty through her embodiment of dark visual whiteness is magnificent as it is strange, so much so that Taylor's passionate conversion to Judaism in 1959 can be partially used to explain her anomalous darkness to viewers as well as herself. She becomes as a Jew not solely because she "identifies with them as underdogs."[9] While Taylor asserts that she "felt terribly sorry for the suffering of the Jews during the war" and that she "was attracted to their heritage," she uses the cultural obsession with her resplendent dark beauty to establish and control a new visual economy centered around her in which she unleashes her hypermediated performance as "the wandering Jew." Repurposing this image to use as her personal Orientalist fantasy she turns this abjected figure into a glamorous jetsetter whose self-imposed exile from US-based Hollywood filmmaking is not punitive but exalting. Taylor's 1960s performance of Jewishness is certainly not the castigating visual exile that keeps her from being seen in *Ivanhoe* (1952) where Taylor's Jewish Rebecca is often veiled, hidden, and mostly forced off screen in order to picture and privilege the Saxon princess Rowena played by a very blonde Joan Fontaine, but is a continuous and unapologetic spectacularization of her strange and beautiful dark(ening) face and body whose very darkness is a visual evidence of the rampant diffusion of newly realized darker pleasures infusing postcolonial white subjectivities.

WHAT IS BEAUTIFUL?

The beauty celebrated in aesthetic philosophy is also fundamentally defined through pleasure. An object, including a face or body, is simply beautiful as Immanuel Kant asserts in his *Critique of Judgment* because beauty is a not a property of an artwork or a natural phenomenon but a consciousness of pleasure that accompanies the free play of the imagination and understanding. While it seems that reason is used to deem what is beautiful, this judgment is not logical nor cognitive but aesthetic, meaning that it is laying claim to not a subjective but a universal validity. This means that everyone knows a beautiful thing after seeing it, and everyone feels good when seeing a beautiful thing. To further clarify, Kant also points to the difference between beauty and beautification, writing, "natural beauty is a beautiful thing, artificial beauty is a beautiful representation of a thing.[10] As an object of beauty herself, Elizabeth Taylor's intimate relationship to beauty through her possession of her beautiful face and body visually justifies and explains her free reign to play and pursue her desires to a global audience who not only feels pleasure through her visual image but also lives vicariously through her excessive body adventures.

Still, the production of "the beautiful representation of a thing," of the ideally feminine face and body can be a form of arduous labor. Certainly it is hard work to stay thin. In the case of contemporary stardom, many famous performers are celebrated for merely being professionally thin people. But producing the level of visual and affective pleasure that Elizabeth Taylor elicits comes from the execution of her ability to interpret and embody a character that then becomes a screen onto which a culture projects a fantasy about white womanhood. This is also because her beautiful form, and its perceived naturalness is a rare commodity, especially because stars of her era are firstly read as studio constructions and objects produced through the Hollywood glamour factory. By default this makes her a utopian body, an impossible index of beauty made possible and visible. In this regard, Elizabeth Taylor's successful transition from child actor to movie star was contingent on her ability to make herself into a cinematic fantasy—an idealization of both femininity and whiteness—heighted by perceptions of her natural beauty.

Popular culture constantly and complicitly affirms Elizabeth Taylor's natural beauty as she is the greater star and cinematic phenomenon because of it. She is capable of signifying grander ideas, including the redemptive essence of capitalism and the justification for American Empire through its exceptionalism if her beauty is God-given—if her effects are celestial rather than results of a kind of mediated manipulation from the film camera and its capacity to turn simple objects into photogenic magic or even worse a commercial product who was wholly a studio construction.[11] The star is photographed for the entirety of the seventy years of her public life and any evidence of the plasticity of her looks is yet to be unearthed. Furthermore the earnestness of her excessive persona debunks any readings of the plasticity of her extra-cinematic image as Taylor continued to play "Elizabeth Taylor" in the numerous offscreen marital and health melodramas that characterized her life since the 1950s. Rather, Elizabeth Taylor is thought to be a natural beauty and a natural in front of the camera through the hyperbolic discourses that construct a collective understanding of her looks and assert that her beauty and poise even as a child are exceptional.

For example, Taylor wears a blue velvet cape during her audition for MGM producer Sam Marx who is casting *Lassie Come Home* (1943), and he claims her clothing gave her a "purple glow that was truly like an eclipse of the sun" that "blotted out everyone that was in that office." He continues, "all you saw was this gorgeous, beautiful, darling little girl."[12] As a preteen working actress, she is considered cute as Velvet Brown in her first leading role but within four years she is cast as the female lead in films opposite much older male stars. She easily transitions from adolescent roles, never having had "awkward years" of unattractiveness, and looks so lovely that she is always filmable. With the exception of 1945, Taylor is cast in a film every year of the 1940s and 1950s since her debut as a child actor in *There's One Born Every Minute* (1942). And her first stint as a sexy romantic leading lady is in the film *The Conspirator* (1949) opposite Robert Taylor (who is thirty-eight at the time of production) at age seventeen. She works steadily in the 1960s, breaking briefly after the release of *Cleopatra* (1963) to focus her efforts in supporting Richard Burton's career. Even so she is often called and described as the "Queen of America" by the popular press at the time.[13]

It is not surprising that Taylor herself takes up passionate claims of her natural beauty as she desires to present herself as a "real" and still vital star who has no need for studio artifice since she began authoring her own image in the 1960s and works to distance herself from perceptions of the archaic and oppressive nature of the studio system. Elizabeth Taylor sometimes recounts how her father, a notably passive presence in her Hollywood career, vehemently refuses to consent to the dyeing of her hair and the changing of her name as the studio began to try to invent her image, but according to her childhood account, fails.[14] After a set of portraits which pictures her with a shaved head are printed in *Life* magazine to celebrate her successful brain surgery in 1997, she gleefully notes that there are no scars around her ears to indicate plastic surgery of any kind. A dominant narrative of her natural beauty also emerges during the days following Taylor's death. Biographer J. Randy Taraborrelli first asserts that the star possesses a genetic mutation at FOXc2 resulting in distichiasis, giving her the legendary "double-row of eyelashes" that startles so many gawkers including childhood friend and costar Roddy McDowall. And stories of Taylor as a beautiful genetic mutant gain a notable momentum, circulating online which express contemporary viewers' fascination with both her strange visual exceptionality and her uniqueness as the last major woman icon of the studio era, even as Taylor herself continually spoke out against the oppressiveness of the studio system during the last quarter of her life. The mutation is also used to theorize why Taylor has the congenital heart problems that are understood to be its subconditions which cause her death, explaining how the film goddess was mortal after all.[15]

Even though ideals of beauty are socially constructed, historically situated, theorized, gendered, and racialized to favor natural beauty (quite possibly to mask its constructed-ness), and privileges a European facial canon in the United States,[16] beauty deeply matters. This is because it gives viewers immediate but mediated pleasure that reveals a collective idealization of race and gender, class and nation as it claims the human face and body and captures the cultural imaginary. Beauty is culturally produced and encoded, but it also appears to just be. Viewers know beauty the moment they see it, and are deeply invested in its naturalness, timelessness, and vitality because it instantly connects them to pleasure.

Psychologist Nancy Etcoff, when speaking of Elizabeth Taylor's visual allure, describes the star as a lavish beauty who embodies the physical attributes that qualify her as a hyperfeminine icon. I argue that Etcoff's assessment shows how Taylor is a physical realization of a cultural ideal of the feminine secured by a sex-based assumption of both proper female corporality and (im)proper feminine behaviors—the enticing and contradictory combination of her beauty with her iconicity as the frequently lovestruck but unruly bride. Etcoff suggests that Taylor's 1950s striking chromatic contrasts, her raven-colored hair, white skin, and violet eyes, make up her pulchritude. Citing psychologist Richard Russell's experiments on beauty, she posits that faces with higher contrasts between eyes, lips, and surrounding skin in various studies are perceived by participants to be more feminine.

She also notes that Taylor's "small gacile jaw" is a further sign of hyperfemininity, noting that male faces grow to develop brow ridges and square jaws and women's faces remain less pronounced in those areas. Finally, she points out that Elizabeth Taylor's beautiful, hyperfeminine face is combined with her large-chested, hyperfeminine sexy body, which she calls an exaggerated super normal stimulus hourglass figure, a biological signal of fertility. Taylor's extremely narrow waist, reportedly twenty-one inches in her studio days, means that her physical dimensions best the ideal hip-to-waist ratio of 0.7 at 0.6.[17] Universal acceptance of Elizabeth Taylor's facial and bodily beauty speaks to the desires for a corporeal form that embodies the culturally legible signs of the feminine that directly correspond to a visual fantasy of female biology through images of fertility. I theorize that Elizabeth Taylor is an archetype of the sexy heterosexual hyperfeminine woman not insignificantly because her visual corporeality ties a sex-based biology to its traditionally culturally designated gender and her spectacular image normalizes the idea of a "naturally" and unequivocally feminine woman. This is ideologically powerful because it diminishes other formations of womanhood through the elevation of a notion of biological truth through beauty—aesthetic perfection as evidence of biological correctness and ultimate superiority.

MANIFEST STARDOM AND MANIFEST DESTINY

Elizabeth Taylor's possession of her legendary "natural" and exceptional beauty makes a corporeal realization of a racial and gender fantasy of white exceptionality which is mobilized in film in the 1950s and 1960s to present viewers with romantic encounters with empire and capitalism as her persona, films, and her beauty reflect imperial desire. Specifically through Elizabeth Taylor's natural beauty and the pleasure it elicits, viewers are directly connected with the primary metaphor of exceptionalism that girds American Empire, a political formation created to protect the rights and privileges of white subjects. And through the spectacularization of Taylor's exceptional whiteness, her combination of natural beauty, poise, charisma, and dramatic talents, Hollywood imperial narratives, particularly *Elephant Walk* (1954) and *Giant* (1956), are created which foreground her white singularity, visually justifying whiteness as a racial formation based on an unquestionable superiority that demands the continuation of white power and the protection of white rights under the law.

The fantasy of preordained greatness which Elizabeth Taylor's beauty projects onto 1950s movie screens across the world also anchors the primary claim of Manifest Destiny, which argues that the United States is destined to expand across the North American continent from the Atlantic coast to the Pacific Ocean because of its exceptionality. It is a nineteenth-century belief which espouses that American exceptionalism, the outstanding greatness of its Anglo-American people and its culture of democratic government makes its expansion across the continent both wise, exorable, and readily apparent.

The Democrats in Congress mobilize Manifest Destiny as a working plan for American expansion during the Polk administration, overseeing the taking of Texas and Oregon for US incorporation. The term "Manifest Destiny" is first used by an influential advocate for the Democratic party, journalist John L. O'Sullivan, in an essay titled "Annexation" in *Democratic Review* (1845) in which he strongly argues for the taking of the Republic of Texas from Mexico by the United States as he believes new republics and independent states should be made a part of the larger democratic American nation. Soon after James K. Polk, who is himself in favor of annexation, is elected to the presidency, Congress approves Texas annexation. Even though the practice of slavery in Texas divides the Democratic Party, it is incorporated into the nation because its area greatly expands the power of the United States across the Southwestern region of the continent.

The Mexican-American War ensues after Polk occupies the portion of Texas that wins its independence from Mexico while the Mexican nation still laid claims to the land. The successful armed conflict waged by the United States against Mexico for Texas and the extension of the United States through military means lead to further arguments for the annexation of the whole of Mexico. These talks end because the US government believes Mexicans as nonwhites are unworthy of American citizenship and is unwilling to grant them such rights, a stance amended in Taylor's film *Giant* (1956) in order to argue for the inherent humanism of petro-modernity which I discuss in chapter 2. The Congressional hunger to annex all of Mexico is sated after the 1848 Mexican cessation of California, Nevada, Utah, and portions of Arizona, Colorado, New Mexico, and Wyoming to the United States.[18]

John L. O'Sullivan then calls for the United States to take the whole of Oregon from Britain in an escalated transnational border dispute that leads President Polk to threaten war with the United Kingdom. O'Sullivan writing about Oregon for the *New York Morning News* in December 27, 1845, asserts,

And that claim is by the right of our Manifest Destiny to overspread and to possess the whole of the continent which Providence has given us for the development of the great experiment of liberty and federated self-government entrusted to us.[19]

O'Sullivan's great disdain for antirepublican and European aristocratic institutions and his unwavering belief in the inherent value of the proliferation of Anglo-Saxon American democracy "to establish on earth the moral dignity and salvation of man" compels him to argue that Britain should lose its claim to Oregon because it does not plan to use the territory to spread democracy.[20] The United States ends its Oregon dispute with Britain in 1846 and organizes the region into Oregon Territory consisting of Oregon, Washington, Idaho, and parts of Wyoming and Montana two years later. This comes to be after Congress is shocked by the news of the deaths of white missionaries in the area, Dr. Marcus and Narcissa Whitman and eleven others who are killed by Cayuse and Umatilla Indians in the Protestant Whitman Mission established in Oregon Country in present-day Washington. The federal government then works to permanently incorporate the region. The Whitman deaths also set off the Cayuse War (1847–1855) between European settlers and the Cayuse people in which the influx of white colonizers, disease, and numerous cultural clashes exacerbate hostilities into armed conflict. This is the first war between Native peoples of the region and white Americans and results in the US government making several reservations to contain the Native Americans of the Columbia Plateau.[21]

HOW BEAUTY SERVES CAPITALISM

The exclusionary logic of American exceptionalism that expands the purview of white authority in the world works to contain and hinder the power of racial Others, including Mexicans and Indigenous peoples of the Western hemisphere in the 1840s. But the celebration of and fascination with Elizabeth Taylor's darker beauty in the 1960s are representative of a recalibrated postcolonial white American hegemony that favors white mobility and globalism. This foundational ethos has been entrenched in American politics and the American imagination long before the Polk administration's leadership of the federal government which bestows onto the US citizenry a vast territorial wealth to pursue its happiness and capitalist endeavors across the North American continent in the era of European high imperialism.

In a similar vein, Elizabeth Taylor's beautiful face and body as they are photographed and mobilized in Hollywood cinema of the 1950s are firstly always at the service of capitalism. Her body is a racial fantasy of white adaptability that ties dreams of empire with capitalism in the cinematic imperial spaces of Hollywood films that point to the actual historical links between capitalist pursuits and imperial ambitions. Also, her film work exemplifies how visual pleasure is a foundational building block of Hollywood cinema and deploys beauty to fortify American films with emotional power and ideological resonance to naturalize white American authority through the positive representations of capitalism via the beautiful white star.

To this end, Paul Newman and Elizabeth Taylor take over the roles of Brick and Maggie in the film adaptation of *Cat on a Hot Tin Roof* from the actors who play them in the acclaimed Broadway production, Ben Gazzara and Barbara Bel Geddes.[22] This is because Newman and Taylor's considerably greater combined erotic and beauty capital could be better utilized in close-ups, a uniquely cinematic tool that helps build intimacy between the viewer and the screen. According to film theorist Hugo Münsterberg, the close-up is the explicit means through which cinema transcends the power of theater by objectifying the viewer's world of perception, capturing the inner mental act of attention which is impossible with actors working on a stage.[23]

Since the film version erases Brick's homosexuality from the original play due to the sexually conservative and moralistic 1950s Hollywood censorship codes that largely dictated film representations, its sexual logic of arousal, refusal, and consummation is rerouted through the accelerated erotic tension between its main male and female star, further demanding that they be beautiful and sexy. Paul Newman and Elizabeth Taylor's sexual reunion after months of abstinence rewards viewers who have sat through hours of dialogue delivered at high volumes. Through Maggie's insistence that Brick investigate the "truth" of his masculinity, he is forced to reconcile with his father and his wife which guarantees the stability and sanctity of heterosexual marriage and primogeniture. The reconsummation of Brick's marriage assures the continual transfer of white wealth within a Southern planter family whose patriarch prepares for death by making peace with his very handsome estranged son and granting his reentry and that of his son's future heirs into the proper cycle of capital inheritance.

While securing capitalism through the sanctification of family and heterosexuality, the beauty of Newman and Taylor show how the visual allure of the male and female leads of a Hollywood movie seem fundamental to the notion of cinematic magic, the movies' ability to provide among other things, an ecstatic experience. Using Greta Garbo's visage, which he describes as an "admirable face-object" as his primary example, theorist Roland Barthes asserts that from cinema's earliest days, the film camera's ability to capture the human face "plunged audiences into the deepest ecstasy." To him, Garbo's "deified" face "represents the moment when cinema draws an existential form from an essential beauty."[24]

Elizabeth Taylor and Paul Newman, as beautiful performers are also professionally beautiful people (to the great consternation of the latter), whose roles as cultural ideals and earning power as top stars are directly tied to the way they look. They promise pleasure through filmic encounters with just their beautiful faces. A trio of Elizabeth Taylor's other notable costars has been deified as the most successful and iconic Method actors in the history of American cinema, namely Montgomery Clift, Marlon Brando, and James Dean.[25] This trinity, I posit, achieves film stardom because all three are considered by producers and audiences to be beautiful on film.[26] Speaking about the beauty and affective power of Montgomery Clift with Elizabeth Taylor in *Suddenly, Last Summer* (1959), film historian Jeanine Basinger says,[27]

> They're a pair of beautiful people who can welcome the camera very close, who can share their passion and intensity very easily in front of the camera. Whatever training was that gave him access to that kind of thing that he could use as performance, she had the same access through some kind of natural instinct. [28]

Independent filmmaker and Method actor John Cassavetes reportedly watched Montgomery Clift and Elizabeth Taylor in their first onscreen pairing, *A Place in the Sun* (1951), every day for a week, enraptured by their beauty which is captured in one of the most gorgeous and well-known close-ups in cinema history.[29] Even though he is put off by the film's moral absurdities, the greatest of which is the condemning of Clift's character George Eastman for not actually having killed his pregnant girlfriend but not wishing fully that she had lived, Cassavetes returns multiple times to the theater, obsessed. He watches this narrative of the American Dream deferred and made tragic not by the death of a hapless and innocent woman but by the fact that the man yearning for social elevation and monetary success could not be united with his true love, a wealthy society girl played by Elizabeth Taylor as Beauty Incarnate, the living embodiment of all of his capitalist fantasies. The affective power of Clift and Taylor's performances are delivered through the intensity of their ravishing close-ups, as the film frames capitalism as a system that brings lasting happiness, empathy, and love while proving that his forced exile from it is equaled to and also accompanied by his physical death.

Paul Newman, sometime after having worked with Elizabeth Taylor and fearing that his good looks are the primary reason for his stardom, once declared, "I picture my epitaph: Here lies Paul Newman who died a failure because his eyes turned brown."[30] Forgiving him for what sounds like ingratitude for having accrued enough beauty capital from birth to become the greatest white American male movie star of the latter half of the twentieth century, Paul Newman's disdain for what he perceives as the viewer's privileging his looks over his technical training as a Method actor of the Yale Drama School and the Actor's Studio speaks to his anxieties about beauty.[31] This is particularly so because as a beautiful performer, he is feminized. Generally, women rather than men are thought to be beautiful, celebrated for their beauty and tied to beauty practices.

While the norm for female stars, Paul Newman's circulation as a male beauty whose looks are explicitly on display and simultaneously admired as he is performing a filmic role for him could be a discomforting gender role reversal. One way he counters this cross-gendering is through his self-induced remasculinization and the adoption of an off-screen role as an avid race car driver which then informs his work in films such as *Winning* (1969) and *Cars* (2006). Still, one assumes he thinks the praise for his looks diminishes his masculinity and his creative abilities cultivated through hard work. The affective value of beauty that helps Newman in his film work, at the very least permits him to transition from regional stage roles to film work and a studio contract. As one of the select few actors to become an international movie star and an icon of eternally cool and boyish American masculinity, Paul Newman proves how much beauty matters in cinema. Beauty is inextricably tied to the positive receptions of the ideological codes embedded in the film narrative as they are delivered through the gestures and emoting visage of the beautiful performer.[32]

What Paul Newman manages to do with his fusion of considerable beauty and extensive technical training is to perform white American masculinity as a social practice based on mildly dangerous antiestablishment rebellion. In films such as *Hud* (1963), *Cool Hand Luke* (1967), and *Butch Cassidy and the Sundance Kid* (1969), viewers are made to closely identify with Newman in his plight for freedom and independence from American institutions. This spirit of liberation, while referencing various global race-based battles for emancipation contemporary to the films' production, is problematically appropriated in these films for white pleasure, most often through the fetishization of Newman's half-naked body. Newman's bare chest and torso are eroticized during its representations of white triumphs over pain in the films previously mentioned, as the tendency to expose his beautiful body has characterized the whole of his career from *Somebody Up There Likes Me* (1956) to *The Hudsucker Proxy* (1994). By eliciting visual pleasure through Newman's body, beauty's hegemonic value is used to reroute any possible sympathy the viewer feels toward the oppression of nonwhites and falsely projects it onto a white male body, whose agency and citizenship are never in danger. In the social world, white heterosexual masculinity's base of power is firmly secure and continues to exist as the default position of power in the United States and all over the globe.

Alluding to the power of the beautiful face and body in Hollywood film and speaking to Newman's cinematic charisma, astute film critic Pauline Kael once wrote about the star, "His likeability is infectious; nobody should ever be asked to not like Paul Newman."[33] Like Elizabeth Taylor, Paul

Newman's power and charisma are inseparable from his beauty and cultural function as a star. Beautiful stars elicit a multitude of affects including excitement, pleasure, and anxiety but never indifference. Paul Newman is aware of the social truths of physical human beauty. Beauty is not a meritocracy; it is undemocratic and unequivocal and if not definitive of proper femininity then conjoined to the inflated ideals of the feminine.

The significations of the beautiful woman in Hollywood film and ocular culture reveal how beauty remains a traditional source of female power and male anxiety, as a disconcerting number of Hollywood female beauties are narratively annihilated on screen, an act which precedes their actual destruction in real life. Lois W. Banner states that beauty practices have played a unique part in the maintenance of women's separate culture outside the world of men even as attempts at beauty's acquisition make for heady competition between women and is often oppressive.[34] The work it takes to be beautiful may be indeed arduous and anguished for those in its pursuit. Banner continues, asserting that beauty is not only a primary concern for many women but varying standards of beauty and appearance both differentiate classes and groups and are key marks of identification pointing to what both men and women consider themselves to be which I think hints at beauty's fundamental place in the formation of identity.[35]

I posit that the beautiful woman in commercial visual media is actually considered dangerous and punitive measures are taken to control her in various cultural projections, most significantly cinema, even as her beauty is used to promote those very mediums and capitalism as a whole. According to avant-garde filmmaker and feminist theorist Laura Mulvey, a gendered system of looking organizes the ocular lives of men and women and is also mimicked in classical Hollywood cinema, an inherently patriarchal system of representation. Using methods from psychoanalysis she politicizes and polemicizes the visual economy of Hollywood films that she asserts works to assuage male anxieties of castration by displacing them onto the female form which, because it is without a phallus, already represents it. She asserts that through the use of several formal techniques including narrative structure and the strategic use of editing and camera angles that objectify and fragment the female body, classical Hollywood films image female bodies in these particular ways to ameliorate fears of the loss of male power and to elicit the pleasure of the idealized male heterosexual viewer. [36]

The ocular-erotic culture of postwar America that names a woman a beauty icon and a sex symbol eventually frames that woman as an object of fear. For example, beautiful women are often represented in Hollywood films as femme fatales who use their good looks to seduce male protagonists to participate in criminal schemes that trespass their moral boundaries and reset their relationship to the law. Often, like in Orson Welles's film noir classic

The Lady from Shanghai (1947), the femme fatale, Elsa Bannister, played by Welles's estranged wife Rita Hayworth, is considered too dangerous to be allowed to live and is killed by the film's end.

In the Billy Wilder film, *The Seven-Year Itch* (1955), a comedy, the beautiful woman played by Marilyn Monroe is only referred to as The Girl, and is still dangerous, to be avoided at all costs and whose excessive naïveté seemingly gives her male counterpart the upper hand as he constantly considers taking sexual advantage of her. Her very presence arouses Richard Sherman's (Tom Ewell) prurient desires so much that he must fight diligently to not engage in an extra-marital affair with her when his wife is away. Because her default primary value is as the maker of erotic desire, no matter the genre of film or the specificities of its iconography, the beautiful woman in representation is a constant threat to patriarchal law and order. She inspires both murder and laughter because she is believed to be the cause of the loss of masculine control. While she often dies at the hands of a jealous lover in film noir, many professionally beautiful women, including Marilyn Monroe who carves an iconic Hollywood career playing hilarious blondes, die tragically in real life, as Monroe succumbs to a drug overdose at age thirty-six.[37]

As the beautiful woman is professionalized to perform and display her body for an eager audience willing to buy the many products which circulate her image including movie tickets, magazines, beauty products, alcohol, vacation packages, and cars, her destruction in film diffuses her power over the men who gaze at her, while her off screen counterpart is frequently also destroyed.[38] Her tragic fall comes from the unique and crushing pressures tied to embodying and performing as a feminine ideal, sometimes even as a sort of whiteness perfected that is always already at the precipice of coming undone because markers of her ethnic difference as perceived imperfections can only be suppressed for so long, as is the case of Rita Hayworth who is famously quoted as saying, "Men go to bed with Gilda, they wake up with me." Having suffered with mental illness for years, which is exacerbated by the strains from film work that she is forced to undertake due to financial problems, Hayworth's Alzheimer's disease remains undiagnosed for so long because doctors and family members believe her symptoms are masked by decades of alcohol abuse.[39] Even though she is a beloved icon of beauty, a sparkling performer, and a brilliant dancer with a rich filmography, she declares that her films with Fred Astaire are the only ones she could bear to watch.[40]

THE BEAUTIFUL STAR AS ANGLICIZED WOMAN

The beautification of the professionally beautiful woman also points to larger imbricated networks of body disciplines and the labor necessary to maintain proper whiteness as a visual category belying this formulation as a dynamic and adaptable sociohistorical construction. Elizabeth Taylor's visual allure highlights the shift in the cinematic presentation of visual whiteness from the Kantian ideal that links moral goodness to lightness, a formula for female desirability in the US cinema of the silent era to the spectacularization of a dark white beauty which actually mirrors the heart of darkness at the center of American Empire and its accelerated rhythms of domination, accumulation, and consumption for postcolonial Cold War audiences.

While admired by so many for her raven hair and violet eyes, Elizabeth Taylor's visual whiteness does not correspond with Richard Dyer's reading of the actress Lillian Gish, who is considered "the light of the world." Dyer's foundational work *White* defines whiteness as a visual category by examining its construction through racialized discourses and technologies that tie its representations to ideologies of purity and moral superiority. This means that in visual media, white women are imbued with an angelic glow through the deliberate brightening of their paleness and blondeness that harkens back to the Christian tradition. For Dyer, Lillian Gish and her contemporary Mary Pickford are put forth in order to celebrate a "Victorian virgin ideal" and to argue for cinema's growing respectability in the early years of the twentieth century. As waves of non-Northern European immigrants come to the United States and more African Americans migrate from the rural South to the urban North, Gish and Pickford's representations on film alleviate anxieties about race and the new proximities of Blackness and undesirable European ethnicities to proper Anglo-Saxon whiteness. (1997, 124–27)

Elizabeth Taylor's looks continue to expand the parameters examined by Dyer in his study of visual whiteness to include the visuality of an "exotic" whiteness that stars Marilyn Monroe, Rita Hayworth, Audrey Hepburn, Grace Kelly, and Jane Fonda cannot embody, while also reflecting a resolutely different moment in American social history than that of Gish and Pickford. Significantly Taylor's white contemporaries promote an explicitly Anglo beauty ideal even as the fight for African American civil rights helps promote greater acceptance of other models of beauty best signaled by Pam Grier's ascendance as a new icon of Black feminine allure and sexuality in 1970s Blaxploitation cinema.[41] Elizabeth Taylor, on the other hand, uses her beauty to perform a racial masquerade as an oriental in whiteface that, while disavowing Blackness, is engaged in a performance about race and white subjectivity's formation through race nonetheless.

There is an extensive history of white American male stars citing Black masculine style and performance as well as white actors who have performed in blackface, notably Elvis Presley, Marlon Brando, James Dean, Warren Beatty, and even George Clooney in the former category and Al Jolson, Buster Keaton, Mickey Rooney, and Bing Crosby, in the latter as white men have always found tropes of Black masculinity to be inspirational if not aspirational in their affective labor. But because feminine beauty is always located to its proximity to whiteness and even more so because of the global-ization of white beauty standards, it should not be surprising that as a global beauty, Elizabeth Taylor does not cite Black femininity as a reference.

Elizabeth Taylor's performance of the Oriental in whiteface, whose self-exoticization makes her actually whiteness seem like the façade, is unique in that it does veer from blondeness and paleness and is possibly fur-ther obscured by the longer and more expansive discourses surrounding her male counterparts' Black-infused performances of the racial "Black" Other. It is harder to read the actual racial dimensions of her masquerade for two more reasons. It does not reference Black femininity or Black women's style, as Blackness by default stands in for race in American discourse. And it is based on white fantasies of the Oriental—a figure of luxuriating exuberant excessive sexual decadence that is an anathema to WASP conservatism—so her performance is doubly inflected as a construction of a construction.

Elizabeth Taylor's on-screen and off-screen projections as the Oriental in whiteface during the 1960s to 1970s are her explicit projection of a global non-Western glamour which began with her off screen adoption of a more regal style of dress inspired by the costumes she loved in *Cleopatra* designed by multiple Academy and Tony Award winner Irene Sharaff, who incidentally also made Taylor's yellow chiffon cocktail dress for her nuptials to Richard Burton in 1964.[42] Along with tanning, she grows out her dark hair and wears it in a more loose, breezy bohemian style instead of the short middy bob that she sported in the 1950s. As always she uses eye makeup including dark eyeliner and cool-toned eyeshadows to emphasize the violet color of her eyes. Even as she is darker-complected in the 1960s and 1970s, she is not using phenotypical Blackness as her beauty inspiration as her longer hair does not reference African American hair in its texture or style while her use of makeup explicitly highlights the blueness of her eyes, the most blatant marker of visual whiteness. While Elizabeth Taylor is directly shifting away from traditional visual whiteness through her swarthy glamour set off by her dark hair, hirsuteness, and large breasts, hers is an Orientalist vision of a kind of exotic beauty that is still a pointed evasion of visual Blackness. The most striking example of her off-screen Oriental in whiteface look is the gold clo-qué silk one-shoulder Balenciaga gold sari that she wears with golden ribbons in her hair fashioned to resemble a turban during a premiere at the Lido in Paris 1964.

In fact, Elizabeth Taylor's Oriental beauty is put into greater relief against the hyper-anglicization of other white stars as whiteness is a visual continuum of both slight and pointed gradations as Taylor's beauty and style can be imagined as examples of both. For example, many know, Marilyn Monroe's blondeness and well as her name are inventions. As Elizabeth Taylor's greatest rival as a fellow cinematic phenomenon in the late 1950s, the star's anointing as an icon of femininity after her untimely death in 1962 highlights the significance of sexuality as an index of identity in the mid-twentieth century. The exuberant celebration of her manufactured chromatics of blinding blondness and white pallor shines a glaring light on the cultural privileging of white female heteronormative sexuality over other formations.[43] Richard Dyer writes that "blondeness is the ultimate sign of whiteness," that it is not only "racially unambiguous," but that through the blonde woman, race and sexuality are conflated in at least two ways. Firstly, she is the most prized possession of the white man and the envy of all the other races as evidenced by imperialist narratives and popular imagery of the US South which is also pervasive in all of the racial imagery of the twentieth century. Secondly, not only is the white woman the most highly prized in white patriarchy, she stands as one half of the paradigm of sexuality itself.

Since Christianity links darkness and sin with sexuality and lightness with virtue and chastity, the rapist Black stud and the victimized white maiden become the stereotypes in this conflation of gender and sexuality. Marilyn Monroe's extreme blondness—achieved through the careful application of peroxide since 1947 paired with her screen image of vulnerability and availability to men—means she embodies the ideals of fifties American sexuality in its very narrow limitations.[44] Any danger that Monroe's sexuality can pose to the male gazer is systematically diffused in the film's end at her expense, often through her mockery or, worse, her death. Her mockery or death is the denouement that becomes the narrative resolution in films across genres including *Gentlemen Prefer Blondes* (musical, 1953), *Niagara* (thriller, 1953), *Bus Stop* (drama, 1956), and *Some Like It Hot* (comedy, 1959).

Marilyn Monroe's predecessor, Rita Hayworth, famously undergoes numerous painful electrolysis treatments to raise her hairline and dyes her dark brown hair to become America's red-haired "Love Goddess" of the 1940s. Columbia Studio head Harry Cohn insists on anglicizing her look and changing her name from Margarita Carmen Cansino to Rita Hayworth in order to obscure her Spanish ethnicity and to assure her mainstream stardom.[45] But Hayworth only becomes wholly Anglo-American after surviving her tumultuous marriage to Prince Aly Khan whom she divorces in 1953. Describing him as a "lazy, spoiled Oriental prince" whose religious views as a Muslim means he never treats Hayworth as "an equal," during their marriage, *Screen Guide* gleefully reports that the prince did not offer a settlement in their divorce for the upbringing of their daughter Yasmin equal to his two sons from a previous marriage, noting that, "by Moslem law" the "female child is entitled to half" of whatever amount is settled for the male heir in a divorce.

Rita Hayworth is reported to have declared, "Yasmin is just as valuable as a son," after spurning Aly Khan's offer. Using her unhappy marriage as a cautionary tale because everything that happened to Hayworth "happened to an American girl, a girl in many respects exactly like you," *Movieland* asserts that Rita returned "home" to continue her career, to work as "an American girl." The star is quoted saying, "Perhaps I did not realize how completely American I am until I was brought face to face with the differences in our way of life with almost *everything*." Condemning Aly Khan's lifestyle as an international playboy only interested in gambling, racehorses, and philandering with women, *Movieland* claims that Hayworth believes "working for one's living is a normal way of life and that there's a human obligation to be useful."[46] Through racist claims of Oriental misogyny attributed to her husband and her joyous repatriation to the United States and willingness to return to work in Hollywood, Rita Hayworth's new image as a world-weary professional actress is used to project ideals of American women's liberation through her participation in work and her re-entry into the proper circuits of capitalism and finally fully Americanizes the star. It is striking that while Elizabeth Taylor's Orientalism is celebrated, Aly Khan's perceived Oriental tendencies best characterized by his misogyny is decried—affirming that the only beloved Oriental is one played by a white body for white pleasure as "orientals"—like Aly Khan named as such by whites are hated and considered barbarous.

Decades after Rita Hayworth physically repatriates to the United States to great fanfare, the formerly politically controversial Jane Fonda is symbolically welcomed back within the good graces of middle-class white America by defeating her hungry body and becoming a fitness guru. The star has admitted to a fraught history with bulimia, a disorder that is characterized by bouts of uncontrollable overeating and purging throughout her film career.[47] But by dramatically displaying the censuring of her body in a series of blockbuster aerobics videos, by openly fighting the fat anxiety that has been a particular and ongoing obsession with white women and in increasing numbers white men, Fonda manages to revitalize her image in the 1980s as an ideal Hollywood body, and is welcomed back into millions of American homes through video and book sales.

While fat anxiety and its imperatives of slenderness have a formidable hold on medical discourses of proper health and white beauty norms, according to

Andrea Elizabeth Shaw, the African diaspora have often read and continue to read the fat body differently, as both an erotic object and as a form of resistance which Black women have used to protest "against the erasure of both fatness and Blackness as a means to gain aesthetic acceptability."[48] By working out, Fonda symbolically repatriates herself to the white American citizenry after having been investigated by the Internal Security Council of the House of Representatives—which succeeds the House Un-American Activities Committee—and placed on the Nixon administration's "secret enemies" list in 1972.[49]

Jane Fonda is condemned for her participation in FTA (Free The Army) shows, a touring antiwar vaudeville review that she, Fred Gardner, and Donald Sutherland conceive as a counteroffensive to Bob Hope's USO Tour, which the trio takes to military towns on the West Coast of the United States hoping to halt troop escalation in Vietnam. She famously visits Hanoi, Vietnam, in 1972 where she denounces the US government and its military leaders as war criminals and is photographed atop an antiaircraft carrier. For her actions the US government believes Fonda gave "aid and comfort to the enemy" and accuses her of treason.[50] But her success as a fitness mogul who fully embodies an image of white bodily desirability significantly defangs and distances the star from her past political history as a vocal anti–Vietnam War activist through her foregrounding of the national obsession for the thin body, a fixation with specific racialized dimensions that privileges proper whiteness. Her body work in the 1980s affirms her proper American identity and whiteness obscuring her past controversial political beliefs which were anticapitalist and favored the liberation of Third World peoples as the circulation of her fit white body helps further deny the acceptability of the fat Black body.

Other Hollywood beauties, Audrey Hepburn and Grace Kelly, both Elizabeth Taylor's contemporaries, embody visions of white beauty that veer more toward women's fashion, a delimited and constricting system that attempts to assuage both racial and class anxieties through bodily comportment. Audrey Hepburn projects a continental European couture style made possible by her gamine comportment, ultra-thin body, and European aristocratic origins through her Dutch mother, Ella Baroness van Heemstra. She cements her image as a fashion star through her symbiotic relationship with the French couturier Hubert de Givenchy, who designs the costumes for many of her Hollywood films including the caper comedy *How to Steal a Million* (1966) where the designer is even mentioned by name. In an amusing scene in which the two are planning their heist of an art museum, costar Peter O'Toole hands Hepburn a dreary cleaning lady's costume and tells her, "Givenchy has the night off. "[51, 52]

Audrey Hepburn's very thin body makes it an ideal "hanger" for couture clothing, a form she attains through extensive ballet training and starvation during World War II when food was often scarce and she tells of being forced to eat tulip bulbs to survive.[53] Hepburn maintains this almost impossibly low weight her entire life and looks extremely thin while working as a UNICEF Goodwill Ambassador for famine relief in 1988.[54] She visits an orphanage in Mek'ele, Ethiopia, to feed its hundreds of starving children, spectacularizing her off-screen desire to help Africans which she first expresses in *A Nun's Story* (1959) playing a young Belgian woman who enters a convent in order to become a surgical nurse in the Belgian Congo. While Hepburn's thin body is used to promote European high style, when read alongside her work in *The Nun's Story* she also becomes legible as a postcolonial white body whose gestures of noblesse oblige perform a series of hypermediated and symbolic reparations for European colonialism.

A Belgian by birth, Hepburn makes several fraught transnational crossings during World War II, moving from Belgium to England and finally to the Netherlands where she adopts a new name, Edda van Heemstra, during German occupation believing that a Dutch name would be advantageous and keep her safe from Nazi suspicion. As Hepburn arrives in Africa in the 1980s two decades after decolonization, she is a known war survivor. Her very thin high-fashion body ties her experiences of the war in Europe to the ravages of the Ethiopian famine and the African destruction brought about by European colonization in uncanny ways, particularly when she is seen holding, embracing, or carrying African children on her back during her time in Ethiopia. The presence of her emaciated body should not equate the horrors of the Second War World War to the atrocities brought about by the European colonization of Africa. But Hepburn's body does provide viewers through its acts of empathy and charity a set of staggering images to consider the destructive impulses of European power on its own continent, as well as its annihilation of Africa through colonial occupation.

In the case of Grace Kelly, her blonde hair, slender lanky body, and insistence on demure clothing, including her staple of simple shift dresses and white gloves, make her an unparalleled patrician beauty. When photographed with a large leather Hermès handbag purportedly covering her pregnant belly, the French luxury fashion house renames the bag after the star.[55] It along with the Birkin bag, an homage to the English actress Jane Birkin, are still coveted by well-dressed and very wealthy women the world over as the ultimate status symbols of high style, good taste, and European allure. Kelly's marriage to the Prince of Monaco in 1956 assures that she is the imprimatur of not only upper-class style but also royal glamour. Kelly's meteoric rise as the lovely daughter of a nouveau riche Irish American Philadelphia family to American movie star and finally European princess consort provides a romantic teleos of white ethnic gentrification that to many feels like a fairy tale come to life and is fully legitimated through the celebration of Kelly's style as the greatest model of good taste.

It bears mentioning that while Rita Hayworth's union to the Muslim Prince Aly Khan is thought to be a nightmarish clash of insoluble cultures, Grace Kelly's marriage to her Monégasque prince is considered a dream come true when she takes her rightful place among white European royalty, as the celebration of Kelly's royal wedding is further proof of the Irish having come into full-fledged whiteness. The best example of this is Princess Grace's state visit to the Kennedy White House in 1961. But Rita Hayworth's famous matrimonial debacle by comparison should be read as more than a melodramatic narrative of love gone wrong but as evidence of the larger cultural anxieties mainstream Americans felt toward interracial and interfaith marriage in the 1950s.

John Kelly, Grace's father, anchors this fantastic tale of class mobility and the Irish coming into proper whiteness almost as much as the star herself. He is the son of Irish immigrants, a three-time Olympic gold medalist in sculling (rowing) and a self-made millionaire whose fortune is based in his lucrative construction business who manages to stay rich because of his skepticism of the stock market. Having never invested his money, his avoids the crash in 1929 and remains solvent for the rest of his life, a proud outsider of the old-moneyed class and its multigenerational members living on accrued credit and inherited wealth. He is the ultimate victor in the game of capitalism because his savvy and his masculinity seem to precede his financial success while being affirmed by it.[56] Audrey Hepburn and Grace Kelly vet white beauty through the legibility of their class statuses as cultural capital which prove to be continuous feedback loops of white exceptionality. Their transnational mobility and iconicity are only possible because they are upper-class proper white beauties while their comportment, European geography, size, and sartorial choices all code as markers of elite whiteness.

ABERRANT WHITENESS AS IMPERIAL BEAUTY

Unlike her contemporaries whose bodily and geographical anglicization have made them exemplars of proper white beauty and fashion, it is Elizabeth Taylor's dark beauty which is far better suited for the cinema and its representations of new white subjectivities in the immediate postcolonial period. Taylor's ocular peculiarity makes her ideal for the genre for which she is most famous, the plantation film, a signifying system that works to solve the white queries tied to decolonization by romanticizing mobility as a new form of liberation and an amiable solution to the loss of empire. Her physical allure is framed by and paired with the sumptuous naturalness of the colonial environs on screen to mark hers as a peculiar presence in the wilderness, that is while she is white, she more closely resembles the nonwhite Other than do her blonde counterparts. This includes the previously mentioned Grace Kelly who stars as the unhappy, unsettled, and straying Mrs. Nordley in *Mogombo* (1953) whose time as a "fish out of water" on African safari almost destroys her marriage. Her estrangement from her husband ends only when she leaves Africa.

Elizabeth Taylor's looks hint at the suitability of the plantation mistress's presence in the bush and conversely serve as an argument against it—she visually compliments and stands in as a signifier of the colonial site in which she finds herself, but as a white woman she is an outsider participating in an imperial project that oppresses people native to that space as seen in her film *Elephant Walk* discussed in chapter 2. Her dark beauty makes her the object of desire among multiple competitive men while also metaphorically reflecting the dark and repugnant lust for the colonial prize amongst enterprising nations.

What I call Elizabeth Taylor's phenotypical exceptionalism is the ocular strangeness that makes her so visually alluring on film. Her 1950s coloring, her combination of very black, very thick hair, white skin, and violet eyes tinge her whiteness and makes her visual presence both pleasurable and striking. Taylor's looks are an explicit paradigmatic shift away the white blondeness of past decades in which whites desired to disavow racial Others completely and interpolates desires for both white domination over the racial Other and for the colonial space in which the Native resides through the desires of white men for Taylor's body.

In *Elephant Walk* and *Giant,* Elizabeth Taylor plays the ravishing colonial bride who ensures the continuation of white dynasties in the wilderness as her husbands strive to tame the land and envelope her within proper white domesticity. Still her ravishing mixture of light and dark, her "colored" ocularity, while gorgeous on film, also invites the consistent production of off-screen discourses that have made her whiteness aberrant and reveals how her body is a source of anxiety and disgust at critical moments when whites believe the stability of their identity is in danger specifically in the first decade of globalization in the 1970s. Taylor's off-screen body evokes the white fears of Blackness and the racial other that fuel both imperial desires for civilization and the cinematic taming of the star herself.

The paradox of Elizabeth Taylor's looks is a juncture in which racial fears can be expressed off screen while alleviated on screen, particularly in the imperial melodramas of the plantation film and its imperative of white domination over racial Others that solidifies her stardom as an adult actress throughout the 1950s. As the plantation mistress in numerous films, her face and body are bathed in soft light, photographed outdoors, and framed beautifully by the verdant splendor of the jungle, or the expansive miles of the Southwest and the golden sands of North Africa whose vastness is equaled and symmetrical to her great beauty. The strangeness of Taylor's particular beauty allows her to signify the strange beauty of savage lands that must be civilized. As white yearnings for the colonial space are sublimated onto Taylor, her filmic domestication makes safe the imperial landscape as an object of desire.

Noting how bizarre the star's body was even at the time of her birth, her mother, Sara Sothern, when writing in *McCall's* magazine in 1954, describes her newborn daughter in much less auspicious terms than as the most beautiful woman in the world as Taylor would come to be known:

> The child was the funniest baby I had ever seen! Her hair was long and black. Her ears were covered with thick black fuzz and inlaid into the side of her head; her nose looked like a tip-tilted button, and her tiny face was so tightly closed it looked as if it would never unfold. [57]

Sothern's fear of her daughter's overabundance of untamed hair—notice too her frequent use of the word "black" in the excerpt—is only assuaged after Taylor's face unfolds a few days later and she opens her eyes to reveal their violet color. Violet eyes are the rarest form of blue eyes and occur when the paleness of the blue is reflected through the red of the eye's blood vessels. Sothern's anxiety seems only abated when she learns that her baby has blue eyes, the overly prized, mythical markers of visual whiteness.[58] Her apprehension about her daughter's hirsuteness, her *darkness,* cannot be read outside an uneasiness about race, notably Blackness. Neither can the racist overtones of famed British portrait photographer Cecil Beaton's assessment of Taylor's physical body be ignored. After taking her photo at the Proust Ball (1971) in Paris he wrote in his diary,

> I felt I must be professional to the last ounce of energy and continued, but not without anything but disgust and loathing for this monster. Her breasts, hanging and huge, were like those of a peasant woman suckling her young in Peru. They were seen in their full shape, blotched and mauve and plum. [59]

Beaton's abhorrence at the appearance of Taylor voices his loathing for what he actually finds abject: a poverty-stricken woman of color from the emerging Third World. This encounter between Cecil Beaton as the colonizer and Elizabeth Taylor as she stands in visually for the colonized Other in this instance brings into relief the white panic that ensues when white identities are forced in flux as a result of postcoloniality that began in 1950s and continued well into the early 1970s as Beaton's interpellation of the "peasant woman in Peru" may allude to fears of political instability in South America and tied to Peru's ineffectual government toppled in a military coup led by General Juan Velasco Alvarado in 1968.[60] Beaton's disgust at Taylor speaks to his confrontation with feelings toward the abject body of color. Taylor's anomalous white looks elicit hatred and fear as some whites feel threatened by any association, real or imagined, with the Third World. Julia Kristeva suggests that the abject is repellent because it violates categorical boundaries and claims that it is essential to the formation of subjectivity. Kelly Oliver notes that Kristeva's notion of abjection is based on the work of anthropologist Mary Douglas and her concept of defilement. Douglas describes defilement as the threat to identity enacted through filth, which is always defined in relation to that very identity. The subject's identity is bound to the sanctity of the borders of the body, which are threatened by bodily secretions such as urine, feces, blood, spittle, and milk (2004, 47)

Cecil Beaton's horrified description of Elizabeth Taylor as a breastfeeding peasant woman in Peru marks her as the abject maternal body that forces him to question the very borders of his self-hood as a white man of the First World. Psychoanalysis links the imaginary father to law and culture and the bodily mother to nature and antisocialism, as the child must reject the mother to come fully into being. Taylor's looks inspire loathing because her body presents this binary. While previous examples of the blonde, white ideal are not obsolete, the movements of empire produce and contextualize the value of new models of visual whiteness. Her discursive racialization and her demonization through her looks expose the permeability of the border between whiteness and what is not white. Beaton rejects her through language to symbolically secure his whiteness and his First World status.

What makes Elizabeth Taylor dangerous to some is that she moves across the borderlands of desire and its fulfillment at will, while spectacularizing the precariousness of whiteness as a stable category. She operates through a perpetually self-sustaining system that guarantees that she can have anything. After all, Beaton does finish photographing her. Postcolonial whiteness at its crux is a category of identity that presents the possibilities of whiteness existing anywhere in the world affirmed by representations in various media and often conveyed by Taylor as a celebrity of white transnational mobility. Postcolonial whiteness is also a historical reality constructed through the forced coexistence of races and cultures and white domination within an designated space made possible by imperialism. Elizabeth Taylor's management of postcoloniality through her performance of an improper whiteness in this case, her unconscious projection as a "peasant woman in Peru," hints at the great extent to which white subjectivity at this particular moment is not closed, nor hermetic, but that it is inevitably shaped, formed, and remade from its encounters with the nonwhite Other. Elizabeth Taylor secures her stardom by being an exemplar of a fantasy of postcolonial whiteness as a malleable adaptability which actually reveals white identity as a source of unabated privilege, of always wanting and always getting everything.

Elizabeth Taylor's genius for getting everything she ever wanted which she expresses through conspicuous consumption makes her a figure of both envy and disdain for Cold War spectators and her detractors are motivated to discipline her through bodily discourses that disparage her looks. While as an American movie princess in the 1950s, her beauty becomes short hand for the dark-haired feminine ideal, by the early 1970s, as an international jet-setting star who travels on a British passport, her body is described as monstrous when it is still lovely. Cecil Beaton whose own unimpressive middle-class origins in his mind do not prevent him from becoming a professional arbiter of "good" taste chastises Taylor also on those grounds, his racist criticism of her being a narrow-minded repudiation of what he considers nouveau-riche taste.[61] He is wrong about Elizabeth Taylor. Beaton makes his stinging critique of Taylor's looks when she is sitting for him at the Proust Ball looking excessive and magnificent, with emeralds sewed into her long raven-colored hair, her waist corseted to accentuate its slenderness, her buxomness ever present, and her face demure and fine-boned. She is lady-like but comely and clearly beautiful.

THE EXPANSIVE BODY

A few years after the Proust Ball and her tense encounter with Cecil Beaton, Elizabeth Taylor divorces Richard Burton for the second time and ends their life together as international globetrotters. She returns to the United States and marries former Secretary of the Navy John Warner. By 1976, Elizabeth Taylor is middle-aged, well into her forties, and has gained weight. The change in her physical appearance is dramatized in popular media to punish her for relinquishing control of her expanding body. She is no longer the lissome teenage starlet who is the visual index of the American Dream Girl from *A Place in the Sun*. She is not only older, she is fat. She is mercilessly ridiculed by comedian Joan Rivers who makes Taylor's weight gain a part of her stand-up act and by avant-garde queer filmmaker and alternate Hollywood historiographer Kenneth Anger who uses a photograph of a heavy Taylor taken by paparazzo Ron Galella as the front cover of his book *Hollywood Babylon II* (1984). But by the book's publication, Elizabeth Taylor is svelte again.

In the book itself, Kenneth Anger composes a photo spread featuring a heavy-set Elizabeth Taylor eating and in another still, with a wine glass in her hand in his series dedicated to her which he titles "The Purple Princess."[62]

Beside the unflattering photo of Taylor placing a portion of food into her mouth with a fork, Anger has printed a caption that reads, "Eat it, eat it, open your mouth and feed it," referencing "Weird" Al Yankovic's parody hit "Eat It" which is given the 1984 Grammy Award in the Best Comedy Recording category. The success of the parody song is directly tied to its accompanying video which airs frequently on MTV. In the video, Yankovic stands in for Michael Jackson. He is dressed in a black jumpsuit with Jackson's iconic zippers and wears his hair in a Jheri curl, a processed and uniquely Black style briefly popular in the 1980s. The song he sings, "Eat It" is set to the music of Michael Jackson's "Beat It." The Jackson song is a hit from his *Thriller* (1982) album whose own success is propelled by its now legendary video where a very slender Jackson dances and inspires a climatic and fantastical dance battle between New York gang members.[63]

Not only does the Yankovic parody video frame its humor through blackface minstrelsy, a codified and inescapable entertainment form in American popular culture that celebrates white domination over Black bodies for at least a century by the time "Eat It" is produced, the viewer is supposed to derive pleasure from the impossible visual realization of a very fat Michael Jackson. As a brilliant and obsessive dancer and committed vegetarian, Michael Jackson never allows himself to be heavy. At five feet seven inches tall and weighing merely one hundred pounds, he like Fred Astaire and David Bowie is a men's size thirty-six regular in the early 1980s. The viewer finally sees Jackson lose control of the dimensions of his perfectly conditioned body expressing once again what Michael Rogin calls the surplus symbolic value of the Black body in the US imaginary. For centuries, whites have not only benefited from the surplus value of enslaved Black labor but have exploited the surplus symbolic value of the Black body in American entertainment.[64] Through the humiliation of Michael Jackson through a white body by proxy, his Black body becomes a source of white pleasure outside his control, a form of racial domination that is entrenched in American visual culture from its very beginnings as it is also reflective of the primary racist objective of white superiority that forms American Empire.

When the reader turns the page of *Hollywood Babylon II*, there is a still photo from an unnamed Hollywood film set in a circus, with hay, caged lions, and painted signs reading that shows occur twice daily. The scene takes up two pages. In the second page, a very heavy-set woman, who is much bigger than Elizabeth Taylor, with the photo that started Anger's series is there, with her back turned to the viewer. She is a faceless and anonymous corporeal mass with dark hair like Taylor's, meant to stand in for her in the author's explosive "big reveal" of the star. The author presents the physically larger Elizabeth Taylor stand-in as a circus "freak," a grotesque form to be mocked and gawked at. A newspaper clipping dated February 29, 1984, from the *San*

Francisco Examiner is inset next to the previous image of the actual Taylor holding a wine glass. It features a headline that reads, "Taking Out Garbage Helped Cure Liz" and describes Elizabeth Taylor's stay at the Betty Ford Clinic and the star confessing that she is an "addictive kind of person."[65] The article presents her weight gain as the logical consequence for her years of personal excess that finally spun her life and body so out of control that she has descended to the level of garbage.

ELIZABETH TAYLOR'S BODY AND AMERICAN EMPIRE

While Elizabeth Taylor is ridiculed when her body operates outside the cultural strictures which insist that she must remain beautiful or suffer humiliation, her body even when it is no longer an object of erotic beauty still signifies American imperial desire and power. As her fat body can be paradoxically used to tell a predictable personal narrative of lost control it also concurrently and uniquely connotes a premodern notion of power and prestige because of its frequent circulation in media culture as an indulgent body. While the fat woman's body is considered to bear no positive value as an open contradiction of the morally good, slender, beautiful body, Taylor moves capably through the world in her enlarged form to help elect her pro-US military husband John Warner to national power as the Senator of Virginia, even as philosopher Susan Bordo writes that thinness signals a "triumph over the body" and that fat is associated with "wantonness," "mental stupor," and "moral decay."[66]

While it is true that the fat body is a powerful iteration of an abject form because it signifies the loss of control, when Elizabeth Taylor assumes the enlarged body in the late 1970s, it is also metaphorical of the formidable expansiveness of American Empire whose territorial vastness initiates a "lost" sense of geography within the American imaginary. This is best explained by President William McKinley's declaration that he "could not have told where those darned islands were within two thousand miles" after being informed that Commodore George Dewey had sailed into Manila Bay, routed the Spanish navy, and claimed the Philippines for the United States in 1898.[67] The 1970s American constituents who see the fatter Taylor at rallies for John Warner vote him into office during the first decade of globalization in which the rise of multiple transnational corporations usurp the power of nation states through the increasing malleability of national borders and the devaluation of national currencies that leads to the unencumbered free flow of global capital. With the election of John Warner whose primary platform is the strengthening of the American military and its authority in the world, the

US government has a legislator committed to reinstating the United States to its traditional place of global prominence through deliberate violent acts of American nationalism around the world.

According to Neil Smith, soon after US imperial ambitions overtake European colonialism and new American dictates of global geography and economic imperatives reorder the world, the American Century of Theodore Roosevelt and Woodrow Wilson is initiated by the efforts of visionary geographer Isaiah Bowman who sits at the center of the State Department to construct and secure an expansive American Empire. He not only organizes the United Nations to fulfill the president's wish to see the world run by "four policemen" with the United States possessing the most power, he also spearheads the country's international excursions into Latin America including Cuba and Panama and post–World War I Germany to access former European colonies for American use.[68] These expansive maneuvers result in a general loss of geographic sensibility in the United States, and the actual value of geographical knowledge is questioned even during Bowman's four decades of national service.

The concurrent cultural disavowal of the fat body and Elizabeth Taylor's spectacularization of it during her re-emergence in American public life and active participation in US political culture are very much akin to the logics of "lost" American imperial geography as a system which functions to always accumulate power while its very workings and dimensions remain opaque.[69] Elizabeth Taylor's fat body signifies more than her resistance against punitive bodily disciplines that carry a moralizing stigma. Her fat body is also an empowering body whose size and indulgences connote an American imperiality in the actual the process of amassing wealth and power when globalism and globalization has lost track of the territorial borders of American Empire itself. Her fat body is a metaphor for imperialism that actually begets more power through John Warner's election and his leadership of the House's Arms Services Committee from 1999–2001 and 2003–2007 which guarantees lucrative military contracts for his home state of Virginia and fortifies the US military and its continuous expansive maneuvers in the wars in the Balkans and the Middle East.[70]

As an unapologetic icon of empire, Elizabeth Taylor is asked by insiders of the Republican party not to wear purple on the campaign trail because it denotes passion and is associated with monarchy (as opposed to democracy), the very conflation which comprises the imperiality that she clearly emblemizes. The request almost makes her laugh because it is her signature color, to her, seemingly from birth.[71] She stops wearing her purple Halston pantsuits for two months, only to wear one during a Republican luncheon held to thank her for her fundraising efforts, declaring, "Ladies, I wore this outfit today in your honor."

CONCLUSION

Elizabeth Taylor's exceptional beauty is at the service of both American Empire and capitalism in Hollywood films. It is an ideologically rich set of discourses and a phenomenological experience anchored in pleasure that make her an even more extraordinary star, in turn directly routing her projections of an exceptional postcolonial whiteness in narratives romanticizing imperialism that are designed to elicit still more viewer pleasure. While adapting beautification practices in the 1960s to project a darker, more exotic glamour than her blonder and lighter-complected counterparts, Elizabeth Taylor's exotic beauty of the 1960s and 1970s allows her to play out her racial masquerade as an Oriental in whiteface, a self-racialized global white sexual libertine, asserting that whiteness as a visual category is not a static formulation but adaptive and reflective of the times it is celebrated.

In Elizabeth Taylor's case, her beauty and unusual chromatics signify whiteness as a transnational, infinitely mobile identity, as those imperatives are being tested and affirmed during postcolonialism while whites traverse and continue to exercise authority over sites outside of the Western hemisphere. Most importantly, her beauty allows her to be turned into a racial fantasy of singular whiteness which is mobilized in visual media to justify both white domination and to naturalize the global citizenship bestowed upon white subjects by American Empire, which in its sum total makes Elizabeth Taylor a star without equal.

NOTES

1. Kitty Kelley, *The Last Star,* p. 30.

2. William J. Mann, *How to Be a Movie Star,* p. 89.

3. Kitty Kelley, *The Last Star*, p. 30.

4. C. Michael Hall and Hazel Tucker, *Tourism and Postcolonialism: Contested Discourses, Identities and Representations,* pp. 3–18

5. Helping maintain the twentieth-century hegemonic stronghold of the blonde as the beauty ideal of which Hollywood cinema is a major contributing factor, according to Clairol, one out of twenty women are born blonde, but one out of three is living as one. See Richard O. Jones, *Natural (The Beautiful "N" Word: Breaking the Psychological Bondage of the American Beauty Standard,* p. 97. Clairol's most brazen campaign asserted that, "If I've only one life, let me live it as a blonde, following its phenomenally successful "Is it true, blondes have more fun?" ads. Joanna Pitman, *On Blondes,* p. 235.

6. "George Masters, Magician of Styling and Makeup Dies 62" *New York Times* obituary. Masters was credited for taking her hair from yellow blonde to "pillowcase white." Retrieved 7.31.21.

7. Monroe shoots the spread on the condition that Schiller negotiates to publish the pictures in magazines that do not feature Taylor. Lawrence Schiller, "A Splash of Marilyn," pp. 137–138.

8. Neil Smith, *American Empire: Roosevelt's Geographer and the Prelude to Globalization,* pp. xix–2.

9. Kitty Kelley, *Elizabeth Taylor the Last Star,* p. 135. Thanks to Akira Mizuta Lippit for his astute theory of Taylor's conversion.

10. Immanuel Kant, *Critique of Judgment,* pp. 114–16.

11. Jean Epstein, "Magnification," p. 236.

12. Quoted from MGM producer Sam Marx who is recasting the main girl part in *Lassie Come Home.* He recalls his reaction to seeing Taylor in a 1983 interview. See *Time Magazine's* obituary of the star, Richard Corliss, "Elizabeth Taylor Dies at 79: Actress Defined Modern Fame."

13. See Jerry Vermilye and Mark Ricci, *The Films of Elizabeth Taylor.*

14. According to Taylor, the studio wanted to change her hair color because it photographed blue black, pluck her thick eyebrows in emulation of Joan Crawford, and suggested changing her name to Virginia. Quoted in Jonathan Cott's "Elizabeth Taylor: The Lost Interview" in *Rolling Stone* (1987) reprinted in the April 14, 2011, issue.

15. "Elizabeth Taylor's Distichiasis: Actress' Double Eyelash Genetic Mutation Revealed" retrieved 5.22.11 from http://www.huffingtonpost.com/2011/03/30elizabeth-taylor-distichiasis-extra-eyelashes_n_842539.html.

16. See Nancy Etcoff's *Survival of the Prettiest,* p. 43 and the origins of the European facial canon and the beauty ideal.

17. Ki Mae Heussner, "Elizabeth Taylor the Science Behind Her Great Beauty." Retrieved 7.29.11 from http://abcnews.go.com/Technology/elizabeth-taylor-science-great-beauty/story?id=13203775.

18. George Lockhart Rives, *The United States and Mexico, 1821–1848,* pp. 634–36.

19. Robert D. Sampson, *John L. O'Sullivan and His Times,* pp. 195–97.

20. Ibid., pp. 75, 201.

21. Robert H. Ruby and John Arthur Brown, *The Cayuse Indians: Imperial Tribesmen of Old Oregon.* p. ix.

22. Shawn Levy, *Paul Newman, A Life:* pp. 129–30.

23. See Hugo Münsterberg, *Hugo Munsterberg on Film: The Photoplay: a Psychological Study and Other Writings,* p. 38.

24. Roland Barthes, *Mythologies,* pp. 56, 57.

25. Paul Alexander, *Boulevard of Broken Dreams: The Life, Times and Legend of James Dean,* p. 83.

26. Stefan Kanfer, *Somebody: The Reckless Life and Remarkable Career of Marlon Brando,* p. 313.

27. Patricia Bosworth, *Montgomery Clift: A Biography,* p. 314.

28. Quoted from Jeanine Basinger in her interview for PBS's *Great Performances* Series "Elizabeth Taylor: England's Other Elizabeth" (2001).

29. Famed film critic Andrew Sarris notes that Taylor and Clift were the most beautiful couple in the history of cinema and that watching them in closeups "kissing was

sybaritic—like gorging on chocolate sundaes." See Ellis Amburn, *The Most Beautiful Woman in the World*, pg. 30.

30. Quoted in Newman's *New York Times* obituary published September 27, 2009.

31. Shawn Levy, *Paul Newman, A Life,* pp. 62–77.

32. Paul Newman signs his first film contract with Warner Bros. Studios in 1954, age twenty-nine, and stars in the peplum film *The Silver Chalice,* dressed in the requisite short toga, bearing his muscular arms and legs. Newman always hated this film. See Marian Edelmen Borden, *Paul Newman: A Biography,* p. xx.

33. Quoted in Newman's *New York Times* obituary published September 27, 2009.

34. Lois W. Banner, *American Beauty: A Social History . . . Through Two Centuries of the American Idea, Ideal and Image of the Beautiful Woman,* p.14.

35. Lois W. Banner, *American Beauty: A Social History . . . Through Two Centuries of the American Idea, Ideal and Image of the Beautiful Woman,* p.3.

36. Laura Mulvey, "Visual Pleasure and Narrative Cinema," pp. 837–38.

37. From *The New York Times,* "Marilyn Monroe Dead, Pills Near," published August 6, 1962. Retrieved 5.21.11, http://www.nytimes.com/books/98/11/22/specials/monroe-obit1.html.

38. Taylor's home studio was MGM, particularly well known for grooming and training beautiful actresses to become stars.

39. Pia Lindstrom interviews Hayworth's daughter, Yasmin Aly Khan, who speaks about her mother's illness and alcoholism to the *New York Times.* "Alzheimer's Fight in Her Mother's Name," February 23, 1997.

40. John Hallowell, "Don't Put the Blame on Me Boys," *New York Times,* October 25, 1970. Retrieved 8.8.11. https://www.nytimes.com/1970/10/25/archives/rita-hayworth-dont-put-the-blame-on-me-boys-dont-put-the-blame-on.html.

41. Mia Mask, *Divas on Screen: Black Women in American Film,* p. 62.

42. Donald Spoto: *A Passion for Life: The Biography of Elizabeth Taylor,* p. 197.

43. Richard Dyer, *Heavenly Bodies,* pp. 52–58.

44. Ibid., pp. 40–43.

45. Adrienne L. McLean, *Becoming Rita Hayworth,* pp. 43–44.

46. Ibid., pp. 93–93.

47. Bill Davidson, *Jane Fonda: An Intimate Biography,* p. 31.

48. Andrea Elizabeth Shaw, *The Embodiment of Disobedience: Fat Black Women's Unruly Political Bodies,* pp. 1–2.

49. Steven J. Ross, *Hollywood Left and Right: How Movie Stars Shaped American Politics,* pp. 241–42

50. Thomas Kiernan, *Jane Fonda: Heroine for Our Time,* p. 284.

51. Ian Woodward, *Audrey Hepburn: Fair Lady of the Screen,* p. 184.

52. Elizabeth Taylor's costumes for *The V.I.P.s* (1963) were also designed by Givenchy and she looks smashing.

53. Donald Spoto, *Enchantment: The Life of Audrey Hepburn,* p. 30.

54. Ibid., pp. 294–98.

55. Tessa Paul, *Handbags: The Ultimate Accessory,* p. 122.

56. Donald Spoto, *High Society: The Life of Grace Kelly, p.13.*

57. Ellis Amburn, *The Most Beautiful Woman in the World,* 14.

58. See Paul C. Taylor, "Malcolm's Conk and Danto's Colors," p. 57, and his notion of *anti-racist aestheticism,* which describes a deep-seated African American fixation with white standards of physical beauty. Using a passage from Toni Morrison's *The Bluest Eye* that details Pecola's poignant petition for (white) beauty, Taylor reflects on the "existential, social and psychological conditions" that motivate her preoccupation.

59. Cecil Beaton and Hugo Vickers, *The Expurgated Beaton: The Cecil Beaton Diaries as He Wrote Them, 1970–1980,* pp. 270–71.

60. David L. Bayer, "Urban Peru: Political Action as Sellout," p. 226.

61. Cecil Beaton wins the Academy Award for Best Art Direction and Best Art Design for *My Fair Lady* (1964).

62. Kenneth Anger, *Hollywood Babylon II,* pp. 299–300.

63. Michael Jackson's stylist Deborah Nandoolman, wife of the director, John Landis, who dressed him for his "Thriller" video says the star is a size 36. From Nancy Griffin, "The 'Thriller' Diaries," *Vanity Fair* p. 66.

64. Michael Rogin, *Blackface White Noise,* p. 80.

65. Ibid., 300.

66. Ibid., p. 153.

67. Neil Smith, *American Empire: Roosevelt's Geographer and the Prelude to Globalization,* p. 3.

68. Neil Smith, *American Empire: Roosevelt's Geographer and the Prelude to Globalization"* pp. xii–37.

69. Ibid., pp. 9–10.

70. John Warner chairs the House's powerful Armed Services Committee which he uses to put billions of dollars into the Virginia economy through naval installments and shipbuilding contracts. The 2011 budget request for the committee is $533 billion with an Overseas Contingency Operation request of $117.8 billion. Retrieved 8.8.11 from the US Department of Defense website, http://www.defense.gov/speeches/speech.aspx?speechid=1536.

71. Elizabeth Taylor, *Elizabeth Takes Off,* p. 39.

Chapter 2

Taylor Made

Race, Gender, and Discipline in the Plantation Films of Elizabeth Taylor

During the 1950s and 1960s, Elizabeth Taylor is the most famous and successful movie star in the world. She is both celebrated for her beauty and demonized for her off-screen excesses that prompt representations of her as a wanton seductress with an insatiable sexual appetite. When filming the epic *Cleopatra* in 1962, the Vatican denounces her as an erotic vagrant and the US Congress considers revoking her passport.[1] Her twice and future husband Richard Burton describes her as "walking pornography" in his diary and once mused, "Who knew she was more famous than Khrushchev?" while he was participating in an extramarital public affair with her that catapulted him from stage actor to movie star. In early 1963, when Kirk Douglas visits the White House, then First Lady Jacqueline Kennedy reportedly asks Douglas's and Taylor's publicist, Warren Cowan, "Do you think Elizabeth Taylor will marry Richard Burton?"[2]

Elizabeth Taylor has been a source of fascination for a ravenous public since the early 1950s as her numerous marriages, beauty, and films sold countless magazines and movie tickets and turned her into, in her own words, "a public utility." More than any other star, she is the object of desire that dared to desire. She is an explicit figuration of imperial excess who has spent her public life accumulating husbands, jewels, and fine art and who as an incarnation of Paul Bowles's traveler, dreams of encountering magic and ecstasy everywhere. She moves across the world onto numerous film sets with her menagerie of children, men, and animals and has confirmed that this time of wandering was the happiest in her life.

At the zenith of her Hollywood career, Elizabeth Taylor performs in a series of "plantation films" including *Elephant Walk* (1954), *Giant* (1956), and *Raintree County* (1957). These films are nostalgic reimaginings of past

49

colonial sites, including Southeast Asia and the US South for audiences during the era of global decolonization. In this chapter I theorize that the iconicity of Elizabeth Taylor, the amalgam of her official onscreen performances,
and her off-screen adventures form the social and textual body in which the
viewer can negotiate a Hollywood educative on postcoloniality as a political,
social, and cultural relation between whites and the newly decolonized peoples of the globe that reestablishes white domination over this liberated multitude. Postcoloniality as I use it here is meant to connote more than the next
stage after the end of colonialism. It denotes the emergence of the various
imperial perspectives, fantasies, and phenomena associated with the white
colonizer witnessing the new national movements that gave independence to
countries of the Third World after World War II.[3]Antonio Gramsci has noted
that educatives are meant to "raise the great mass of the population to a particular cultural and moral level" (1971, 258). I posit that Hollywood as the
national cinema of the United States produced these ideologically rich films
to reflect American imperial and racial interests concerning decolonization.[4]
They reference postcoloniality as a spatial and temporal plane that privileges
whiteness as the cultural imperative while geopolitical movements force the
readjustment of whiteness and the relocation of white bodies in relation to
and against its encounters with the nonwhite non-Western Other.

I have named these imperial melodramas plantation films with the understanding that the tools from genre studies can best be used in their relational
and collective analysis.[5] In the spirit of Andrew Tudor's assessment of genres
as cultural consensus, that "genre is what we collectively believe it to be"
(1976, 118) and in agreement with Thomas Schatz, I read genres as representational systems that promise viewers the filmic means to encounter, navigate
and solve the problems brought about by specific sociohistorical phenomena
in the social world.[6] Like other genres, such as the western, plantation films
as a group share the same iconography, formal tendencies, and ideological underpinnings. Alan Lovell writes that the western came into cinematic
prominence during the early twentieth century because it was an expression
of American consciousness during the time when waves of immigration to
the United States demanded the construction of an American identity that was
preoccupied by the making of civilization and the establishment of law and
order (1976, 168–69). As a result, the western is narratively fixated on the
lawman's policing of the white settlement, cajoling it to civilization.

Postcolonial plantation films reaffirm white identity and assuage white
anxieties about race, home, and the nation as these concepts are redefined
through the realignment of the globe in the 1950s and 1960s. This genre
demands the spectacularization of the plantation mistress striving to build a
home in the world outside the imperial metropole within the heart of the colonial settlement. Amy Kaplan reveals how fantasies of the American Republic

are limbed to dreams of American Empire and argues, "the idea of the nation as home is . . . inextricable from the political, economic, and cultural movements of empire"; likewise, these films show how the process of empire conjoins the concepts of home and abroad and blurs the boundaries between the domestic and the foreign to persuade viewers that whites can have a home in the world anywhere.[7]

The Taylor cycle of plantation films highlight postcolonial white fantasies and anxieties of the 1950s and 1960s and are separate or an evolution of the previous Southern plantation cycle that includes the films *Dixiana* (1930), *Mississippi* (1935), and *Jezebel* (1938) and culminates with *Gone with the Wind* (1939). According to Hernan Vera and Andrew Gordon, *Gone with the Wind* in particular was an apology for the failures of capitalism after its revival at the end of the Depression.[8] Through narratives of heterosexual romance, postcolonial plantation films have turned various decolonizing territories into the sumptuous environs in which white love and the white family hope to flourish. While romanticizing colonial sites by locating them as spaces of white liberation and modernity, they mobilize familiar racial tropes to idealize decolonization for white viewers off screen who may be distressed over the loss of white power and anxious about change. Particularly through the fetishization of master/servant relations, these films naturalize white domination over nonwhite subjectivities through the recuperation of the plantation, an economic, domestic, and racialized site of formidable significance in the United States. At the earliest beginnings of the British colonial era, the United States was built by a plantation-based economy fueled by Native American and Black slave labor.[9] The plantation has always existed as an extension of both race-based colonialism and capitalism in the Americas, and its imperatives of surplus production and racialized labor have configured white authority and nonwhite subjugation, respectively. As the plantation is germinal to American capitalism, it is no wonder that the plantation film reemerges in the 1950s to work to assure the continuation of these labor and social relations as the United States rises as the world's most formidable imperial power, even while large-scale decolonization movements begin to take hold in Africa and Asia, and conflicts between capitalism and communism most significantly the Korean War, test US ideological and military authority in the world. On US soil, the turn to the plantation film during the decade would buffer white viewers uneasy about communism, the looming battles for African American civil rights, and racial integration.

Through these films, Hollywood has constructed what Henri Lefebvre describes as "abstract spaces." He theorizes that capitalism is contingent on the turning of differentiated places into abstract space.[10] Grace Kyungwon Hong recalling Michel Foucault's work on this subject notes that the concept "refers more to a way of imagining space than in any particular space or even kind of space." She asserts that it is an imaginative notion of space in which all spaces are devoid of historical meaning and material value but that "contradictions of abstract spaces allow alternate epistemes of space to exist."[11] The plantation film produces abstract spaces through the refiguring of social relations that allow the shoring up of traditional gender roles and proper whiteness through the subordination of its plantation mistress. Therefore, traditional femininity, masculinity, and white hegemony remain intact on screen even as masses of nonwhite and non-Western subjects achieve postcolonial liberation in the profilmic world.

Because of the loss of white colonial power in the social world, a sense of imperialist nostalgia is displaced onto these films. Renato Rosaldo defines imperialist nostalgia as " a curious phenomenon of people's longing for what they themselves have destroyed" through a domination that disavows responsibility for the very destruction it has inflicted on the peoples and cultures it has collected.[12] For postcolonial viewers, plantation films narrate the colonial process as a mobilization of imperial domesticity by which whites can secure lasting fulfillment through a regimentation that insures proper whiteness achieved by the stabilization of traditional masculinity and femininity.

According to Amy Kaplan, imperial domesticity is the broadening of female influence that helps the separate gendered spheres coalesce in the imperial extension of the nation by redrawing the domestic borders against the foreign (1998, 47–48). It is the entry point through which white women labor in the service of empire to claim an agency that is simultaneously liberating and punitive: white women access power through the broadening of their feminine influence that subjugates the colonial Other and forces their femininity to comport to and exist under the dictates of the masculine imperial subject. Through the deployment of new forms of imperial domesticity, postcoloniality for whites becomes a continuation of the white colonial project: the work that allows the collection of still other spaces where new pleasures could unfold after the relinquishment of earlier white settlements.

The plantation mistress is a figure of Kaplan's notion of manifest domesticity, her theory of the imperial underpinnings of white American femininity that partly accounts for Anglo Saxon women's participation in imperialism, a fundamentally racist project. Mapping how the ideology of separate spheres contributed to the making of American Empire, she asserts that imperial expansion depended upon the outward expansion of maternal influence beyond the nation. She theorizes that domesticity is

> a mobile and often unstable discourse that can expand or contract the boundaries of the home and the nation, and that their interdependency relies on racialized concepts of the foreign.[13]

Therefore, the presence of the plantation mistress guarantees the establishing and protection of the white home in the world against racial Others, even if that (perceived) racial other, in the case of *Raintree County*, is herself.

These three plantation films starring Elizabeth Taylor mobilize race to guide whites through a trio of specifically desired outcomes of decolonization. These include the efficient management of the imminent white exodus and global mobility after the loss of colonies in *Elephant Walk*. Secondly, there is the acceptance of the making of new enclosures, meaning the privatization of public resources for profit that brings about modernity and is fundamentally beneficial to the white power elite. This also forcibly remakes white relationships with people of color (who are not Black) through various vectors, including labor, domesticity, and marriage as seen in *Giant*. And finally, there is the forced heeding of warnings that accompanies the imagined dangers of racial desegregation to whites which spurs their disavowal of race, racism, and Black subjectivities in *Raintree County*.

ELEPHANT WALK

Elephant Walk is a pedantic text that represents the making of proper whiteness and traditional gender roles through the utilization of a Frederick Winslow Taylorist version of imperial domesticity that idealizes master and servant relations and the filial conduct between husband and wife. Having just arrived from England as Elephant Walk's newly named mistress, Ruth Wiley (Elizabeth Taylor) learns the price of making tea for the white imperial subject. Upon her arrival, she claims she "thought tea came from tins." She quickly learns that tea starts its life as leaves growing in aerial bushes. Tamil workers then pluck the leaves for processing in the adjacent factory. The manufacturing of tea becomes a metaphor for the making of Ruth into Elephant Walk's mistress, who after the completion of this process comes fully into her imperial power and accepts her place in the plantation's racial and gender hierarchy.

Spectacularizing the modes of Fordist production and Taylorist labor management onto the fictive plantation space at a moment when these very methods were becoming obsolete in the making of Hollywood films, *Elephant Walk*'s celebratory representation of their use in the manufacturing of colonial goods and imperial identities interpolates the studio system's nostalgia for its methods of surplus production and its global hegemony in the market place.[14] The plantation film is the genre through which the studio system's own imperial mode of representational domination can be expressed moments before that domination is undermined by forces that lead to industrial reorganization. Through the continuous presentation of colonial efficiency onscreen and the film's visual excess replete with Elizabeth Taylor's resplendent beauty, lush forests, and an elephant stampede, *Elephant Walk* is a Hollywood melodrama that fetishizes the Fordist mode of production to produce visual pleasure and highlights what Thomas Schatz refers to as the "genius of the system" that once assured Hollywood absolute film market domination.

At Elephant Walk, proper white femininity and the colonial home are manufactured to the rhythms of Taylorism because of the significance of time management to the Western imperial imaginary. As the white mistress must build a sanctuary against foreignness on the plantation, her domesticity is intimately linked to efficiency. The notion of time being a commodity that can be saved, wasted, or spent is an after effect of the Industrial Revolution which gave rise to and spread the factory system in the West. These theories about time became fundamental to the West's perceptions of its modernity and its sense of superiority over all other people on earth, particularly the colonized whose management of time was considered deficient in comparison.[15] Frederick Winslow Taylor's ideas of scientific management that strove for technological and organizational advancements geared toward efficiency in labor were then exported onto colonial sites including the plantation, a space where the production of surplus was of the utmost importance.

As an embodiment of white civilization who is sent into the colonial wilderness as incentive for whites to protect themselves against racial Others, the plantation mistress executes the Western Taylorist methods of efficiency upon her arrival. Newlywed Ruth exerts herself in her efforts to run her home more efficiently and begins to feel overwhelmed by her task. Her husband, John (Peter Finch), quickly rebuffs her attempts. In one scene, Ruth, who had lived through the second World War by rationing in Britain, busies herself with the task of preventing food waste by ordering an inventory of the kitchen. Although her husband ignores her efforts, Ruth continues to export Western methods of efficiency as she continues to try to get her bearings at Elephant Walk and interject herself in the daily operation of the domestic quarters of the plantation. Ruth and John's marriage becomes a site of struggle for what is to be dictated as proper management. Ruth keenly desires to extend her influence on Elephant Walk through her domesticity, hoping to run the household of the Bungalow leaving John to run the daily operations of tea making on the grounds.

But the viewer is made to understand what Ruth quickly comes to learn: her negotiation of Elephant Walk is dictated by what Iris Marion Young describes as a series of delimitations, which are

A set of structures and conditions that delimit the typical situation of being a woman in a particular society, as well as the typical way in which this situation is lived by the women themselves.[16]

Ruth's life on the plantation and her imperial identity as a white planter's wife are made possible at the behest of her husband who sets the terms and conditions of her experience there. Furthermore, her embodied experience of space exemplifies Iris Marion Young's reading of female spatiality. She writes:

> Feminine existence appears to posit an existential enclosure between herself and the space surrounding her, in such a way that the space that belongs to her and is available to her grasp and manipulation is constricted and the space beyond is not available to her movement.[17]

The enclosure that Ruth must navigate is at times literal—as she is confined within the walls of the plantation's Bungalow left in the care of her husband's manservant, Appuhamy. Furthermore, Ruth yearns to be more than a spectacle deployed for the pleasure of the white men of the surrounding area. Her presentation to the other planters at a Wiley party brings to light her discomfort in objectification. Dressed in a form-fitting white gown and purple lace bodice that he purchased for her, John puts Ruth on display as a model of perfect white femininity to impress his colleagues, a bachelor collective that regards white women as rare commodities. The gown both visually illuminates Ruth's whiteness and reveals the constricting nature of her delimited existence as John's bride as she sits silently by his side.

Ruth's presence at Elephant Walk also wards off fears of foreignness for both John and Dick Carver, the lonely plantation overseer. Not desiring to marry a Native, John travels to England to find a white woman to make into Elephant Walk's mistress. Ruth's striking appearance compels Carver to note in admiration that the white men have not seen a white woman (like her) in a number of years. This scene foregrounds both her isolation and exceptionalness while arguing that the actual labor of the plantation mistress is to construct a white home in which the Natives are categorized as foreigners and kept away from or made docile within this white sanctuary. Her body also protects the white men against the threat of unwanted or unacknowledged sexual entanglements with Sinhalese and Tamil women. John alludes to this when he tells Ruth about how his father had commissioned the building of the wooden canopy bed for the bridal chamber even before he had gone to England to marry John's mother. Elephant Walk's previous mistress, who found plantation life disagreeable and master Wiley's plans for dynastic expansion untenable, subsequently fled back to England.

Ruth's physical entrapment and her proximity to enslavement through her encounters with Appuhamy spur her to secure her own power. When Ruth admires the comb in Appuhamy's hair, he tells her matter-of-factly that it is "mark of caste to signify that those who wear it are not bearers." Ruth shudders slightly realizing the extent of Appuhamy's subjugation. The laws of caste and imperiality intersect to extend their power over his access to social and sexual relations that relegate him solely to a life of service to the Wileys. As it turns out, his excessive devotion to his masters brings about his actual death. An elephant tramples him as he tries to save Ruth's life during a stampede. His sacrifice proves that the Native worker willingly accepts and is complicit in the system of servitude that holds him in bondage, sustaining and reaffirming white imperialist fantasy.

Ruth is desperate to circumvent the logic of enclosure that surrounds her, and accesses her power through the expansion of her feminine influence, vis-à-vis her domesticity that soon exceeds its original mission of maintaining an efficient home. Feminizing a vector of imperiality Ruth stridently oversees Appuhmany's work, venturing into spaces that were once cordoned off and forbidden to her in the Bungalow, including the old Master's study that John keeps locked. Ruth recomports her body in accordance to her role as Mistress through her literal elevation as she physically raises herself above the Native workers, intently looking over them as they labor and peering down upon them from her perch above the kitchen. Clothed in a series of white and beige dresses that visually mark her whiteness and her racial domination, she rules the Bungalow by implicit force, overriding the authority of a disapproving Appuhamy who has misgivings about her ability to run things.

Appuhamy as the film's fetishized Native is the one Sinhalese worker meant to stand in for the collective group of Elephant Walk's Native laborers. He embodies the exemplary qualities of the plantation worker whose loyalty and industriousness have no bounds. He is the perfect servant with a slave-like devotion to his dead master, John's father, whose shadowy presence even impels Appuhamy to pray to him by his tomb. Ruth's identity as the Mistress is formed through her relationship with Appuhamy, for all intended purposes a slave, who is interposed between the object she desires, the domestic efficiency manufactured through his labor, and herself.[18] He mediates her relationship to her imperial domesticity by executing her orders and works directly with the workers whose labor allows the Bungalow to function properly. Furthermore, within imperialism, proper white womanhood is predicated on the mastering of the devoted racialized servant. She must overcome his resistance to her control and he must accept her authority.

Ruth's processing into proper femininity is also secured through John's privileging of her domesticity over the masculine sphere of homosociality made up of the male planters of the Ceylonese plantation complex. In the early stages of his marriage, he was actively present in and engaged with the world of men that he had constructed with the other planters. John was an insensitive emotionally withdrawn and absent husband, more interested in entertaining his friends than doting on his wife. In one telling incident during the night of their weekly meetings, a tired Ruth retires early and explodes in

tears when John ignores her and refuses to accompany her to bed. His yearning for male bonding overtakes his filial obligations to Ruth and keeps any of
his emotional yearnings toward her in arrested development.

John had imagined the Bungalow primarily as a homosocial space rather
than a home, peopled with men who gathered in the evenings to smoke cigars
and drink liquor with Ruth by his side. Eve Sedgwick's formulation of homosociality states that they are intensive forms of same-sex male bonding that
are so engrossing that they eclipse the emotional connections in the heteronormative coupling of marriage that are oppressive to both men and women.[19]
In Western cultures, they exist on a continuum alongside heterosexuality and
homosexuality and are formed to secure the exchange of patriarchal power
between men.

The ritualistic gatherings of John and the other planters in the Bungalow
are examples of the transactions of male power from which Ruth is excluded.
Their origins are explained as a tradition that was started by John's father in
which the white men of the vicinity can participate in traditional masculine
activities such as smoking and drinking in luxurious accommodations in
comfort and relative isolation from women and Natives. Amongst themselves
they have established a network of wealthy white men that is designed to
sustain the plantation complex of Ceylon. But homosociality is revealed to be
useless in the protection of white interests as the end of colonialism nears for
the island. During dire times, such as the cholera outbreak and elephant stampede (the film's signals for the start of end of the British regime), the other
planters are too occupied with securing their own plantations to help John.

The deep male bonding that was a burden on the Wiley marriage then
becomes the portal through which Ruth fully comes into her power.
Previously Ruth found her husband's male friendships antagonizing because
they were unwelcomed obstacles in her project of the reorganization of her
home. But she ably broadens her power by expanding her feminine influence
outside the domestic labor of the Bungalow to the business of planting. After
a disastrous night of drunken frivolity during which John breaks a leg playing
bicycle polo with his friends, Ruth nurses him back to health and enlists the
help of Dick Carver to oversee the upcoming harvest. John's overinvestment
in homosocial bonding infantilizes him and physically incapacitates him to
the extent that he no longer manages Elephant Walk.

Ruth relinquishes her feelings of isolation and alienation from John during
his recuperation by seizing the opportunity to learn the day-to-day operations
of the plantation through Carver's guidance. Her entrance into the masculine
sphere of imperialism comes at a price. She fights sexual temptation, fully
submits to John by rejecting Carver's romantic advances, and suppresses all
residual desires to leave her husband whose patterns of stubbornness and
neglect had hurt her in the past. She displays her loyalty to him through a

series of domestic acts that include setting up and working in the plantation triage during the cholera outbreak even as John had assumed she will leave Elephant Walk with Carver. Ruth shows what Kaplan describes as a "capacity for domesticity" which is a "defining characteristic of the Anglo Saxon race" that refers to the domestic nationalism of colonial whites. Rather that becoming an object of exchange between the two men, Ruth chooses to align herself with the dominant masculine imperial subject, her husband. She claims her subjectivity, meaning her whiteness and femininity, that guarantee her survival at John's side even after the seat of their power, the plantation, is destroyed.

Ruth's imperial domesticity triumphs over the homosocial bonds of the colonial masculine sphere and nothing can distract the couple as they come together to travel the world. After Ruth props up John's heterosexuality and well as her whiteness, she and her husband form a dyad that represents the invincibility of white heteronormativity. The material practices tied to their imperial whiteness are secured through the cultural, political, and legal normalization of their heterosexuality which enables them to move united across the world unencumbered.[20] She is now truly free from the enclosure of Elephant Walk. The end of empire frees Ruth from enclosure to cosmopolitanism.[21]

The film metaphorically marks the end of Ceylon's colonial era through the destruction of Elephant Walk and the Wileys' exodus from the island. The film argues that its white settlers can still dream of building a home somewhere else, since this present territory is lost. Ruth even suggests that she and John can rebuild Elephant Walk elsewhere. In fact, after the end of their plantation the Wileys can now conduct their exalted quests for wisdom and magic and begin to look for the intoxicating qualities that were lacking in their life at Elephant Walk, a space of their strict marital regimentation. As they have connected through their recommitment to their marriage, they can pursue their dreams of a new adventure. And they can always journey to the next location.

At the film's end, Ruth and John will become what Paul Bowles described as travelers. A white subjectivity that he himself embodied and relished, as a traveler he perceived the decolonizing world as spaces of white leisure, self-discovery, and transformation. Writing in 1963, just seven years after Moroccan independence, Bowles proceeded to distinguish the differences between travelers, tourists, and Natives. As a traveler he describes his enthrallment as he witnesses a *moussem,* a pilgrimage conducted by Berbers in Morocco which delights him particularly because "the city Moslems (sic) complain that they [the Berbers] do not observe Ramadan properly":

The traveler who has been present at one of these indescribable gatherings will never forget it. To me these spectacles are filled with great beauty, because their obvious purpose is to prove the power of the spirit over the flesh. The sight of ten or twenty thousand people actively declaring their faith, demonstrating *en masse* the power of that faith, can scarcely be anything but inspiring.[22]

Organizing his taxonomy of untainted ethnic culture through his writing, choosing to view the cultural practices of the Berbers as beautiful and inspiring he tries to expose what he judges as the hypocrisy of city Muslims who denounce such practices as unacceptable even as they were participating in the same activities a generation ago. Bowles expresses his disdain for the tourist and the destruction of what he deems as Native culture by malevolent Western influences and asserts:

The North African knows that when it comes to appreciating his culture, the average tourist cannot go much closer toward understanding it than a certain condescending curiosity. He realizes that, at best to the European he is merely picturesque.[23]

He wails against "this total indifference to cultural heritage [which] appears to be a necessary adjunct to the early stages of nationalism." But his heart sickness for the loss of what he designates as authentic culture at the hands of ignorant Westerners and the changes brought about by nationalization such as urbanization do not obscure the asymmetrical power he enjoys as a nonobjective documentarian. His own condescending attitude toward nascent nationalism and his condemnation of the cultural adaptations that would follow after independence is an example of the imperialist nostalgia that bell hooks critiques. She writes:

Whereas mournful imperialist nostalgia constitutes the betrayed and abandoned world of the Other as an accumulation of lack and loss, contemporary longing for the "primitive" is expressed by the projection onto the Other of a sense of plenty, bounty, a field of dreams.[24]

Bowles's personal sense of betrayal as his perception of ethnic authenticity becoming compromised by Westernization through nationalism can only be assuaged through his collecting of new adventures, his replenishing "bounty" in sites yet untouched by the modernization brought about by decolonization.

Like Bowles, Ruth and John anticipate with great hope their future journeys across the globe to end their interminable loneliness. As travelers they consider themselves to be world citizens entitled to adventures that bring them joy, enlightenment, and healing and cinematically signal as much when they ardently embrace as their plantation burns in the background.[25] When

Ruth assures John that they can "build Elephant Walk somewhere else," she is stipulating that they will join the growing number of whites who will wander the earth after decolonization. The Wileys' forced exodus from the island is their new beginning, as the establishing of a global white hegemony becomes an after affect of the decolonization that coincides with white mobility after empire.

Here we see a key difference between the imperial domesticity that Amy Kaplan describes which is structured through and sutured within the physical dimensions of the plantation site and its transformation in the twentieth century. If *Gone with the Wind* ends with Scarlett needing her ancestral plantation in order to secure whiteness, the postcolonial plantation film anchors whiteness through unhampered mobility and cosmopolitanism that symbolically extends white purviews tied to the formerly static borders of previous colonial holdings. While reacquainting whites with the intimate racial contours of the plantation in its previous iteration, they help white subjects to disavow the emergence of contemporary racial liberation struggles of the 1950s and 1960s as they continuously wander the boundless and borderless new postcolonial world.

As mobile whites after nationalization, the Wileys are precursors of the Afrikaners that make up sociologist Melissa Steyn's work on white South Africans after Apartheid. Steyn's research unpacks the strategies of white relocation and helps glean meaning from such movement as it pertains to an emerging postcolonial white identity. Steyn notes that Afrikaners who left South Africa after the end of Apartheid attempted to embrace a general sentiment of a white global family as they resettled into Europe, Australia, and North America, positing that whiteness thrives across borders adapting to national and ethnic and cultural differences to ensure survival. They fled the country while grieving its loss to those whom they have considered uncivilized Natives incapable of rule.[26] Will the Wileys go to Britain, where Ruth was raised, from whence John's family once left to pursue its dreams of great fortune through the plantation economy of Ceylon? Or will the Wileys be on permanent global safari in Africa? Asia? South America? Only they know where their lust for adventure will lead them. They will settle still elsewhere as their white counterparts have done.

The Wileys' Ceylonese exodus provides images of the white transnational traveler, a fitting metaphor for US imperialism taking the place of formal European colonialization during the decade of the film's release. US authority in the globe is supported by its unparalleled military power in the 1950s, which allows it to bypass the sovereignty of other weaker states. The formation of NATO in 1949, a transnational military alliance established to fight the Cold War, in which the United States takes a primary leadership role only heightens American power.[27] The United States fights a brutal proxy war to ensure capitalism on the Korean peninsula that American administrators divide along the thirty-eighth parallel upon the surrender of Japan in 1945, notably without Korean consultation. It uses its considerable military power to the support the South in its war against the communist Soviet–supported North in the early 1950s. Seeking greater control in East Asia during the Cold War, after the end of formal military conflict in the Koreas, the United States helps establish the Demilitarized Zone along the thirty-eighth parallel in 1953 with American troops permanently occupying South Korea to guard it.[28] While the Wileys become rootless sojourners whose borderless travels are romanticized in *Elephant Walk*, the US military's global movements are considerably more violent. Its actions both remake the globe and allow Western access to distant foreign lands to mobile subjects in the social world who are much like the filmic Wileys.

ELEPHANT WALK: ALTERNATE EMBEDDED NARRATIVES AND NEW MEANINGS

Richard Dyer argues that stars are units of meaning constituted through inter-textual narratives of filmic and extrafilmic discourses. These include live pro-fessional performances in audio and visual media and their "natural" off-hand moments as they manage their private or "actual" lives in which "personal" information about them concerning relationships, lifestyle, and personality are circulated through ancillary products such as fan magazines and historio-graphical biographies. The melding of performers with their characters and their significations as stars produce multiple meanings that facilitate reading strategies for viewers based in part on their own levels of identification with the stars on screen.[29] I posit that the biographies of *Elephant Walk*'s stars, particularly its original plantation mistress, Vivien Leigh, are embedded into the text through the proper functioning of the star system that insists on the continuous circulation of discourse about them. This information exists to be read by the viewer often simultaneously, even if it is, as it so often is, con-tradictory to the film's intended code. For scholars, for fans, and for casual viewers it provides the continuous possibility to mobilize an alternate reading that brings new meanings to the official film text. Stars and the films in which they perform when read together hold a polysemy of meaning and remain always as open texts, if varyingly so.

Andrew Britton in his well-measured critique of Dyer's reading of star vehicles asserts "every Hollywood film of whatever genre must at least allow for a conservative reading" and that the contradictions enacted by stars in *their films* are always latent in a particular genre" (1976, 201–202). He understands that genres have particular limits and parameters in which the star vehicle is embedded. He asserts that while in one sense the star cannot affect the narrative that is predetermined, in another sense her effect is crucial. This is precisely because her films, whether or not they are star vehicles, designed specifically to promote her directly, are still embedded within the genre itself so that viewers can specify what that effect is.[30] As such, I posit that star discourse is the spectral body that accompanies all "official" (i.e., filmic) star performances in respect to the Hollywood discursive complex and its utilization of a star system and its ceaseless production of genre films. I argue that Hollywood films are always both genre films and star vehicles and as such should be read alongside the discourse of the star that is always conjoined to them.

VIVIEN LEIGH

The production history of the original iteration of *Elephant Walk* is a narrative that is centered through the regimentation of its plantation mistress, not unlike the film itself. The specter of a disturbed Vivien Leigh literally haunts the film as her figure can be seen in some long shots included in the official release. Paramount Studios first cast Leigh who was then replaced by Elizabeth Taylor after an especially volatile episode of her manic depression manifested itself on set, signaling her nervous breakdown. Leigh had confessed that she had fallen in love with her costar Peter Finch and threatened to run away with him. Her husband, Laurence Olivier, was then called to Ceylon in an attempt to help her.[31] She can be seen in some long shots since salvaging footage featuring her image proved to be more cost effective for the studio. Elizabeth Taylor was primarily cast in her place because she fit the costumes made for her predecessor and the actresses resembled each other enough, at least in (very) wide shots, to make the old footage usable. Because of the studio system's assembly-line method of production compartmentalizes all work, arguably mimicking the plantation mode, it makes workers at least partially interchangeable and takes away differentiation.[32]

Elizabeth Taylor took the role of Ruth Wiley in 1953, soon after the birth of her son Michael Wilding, Jr. and the restructuring of her MGM contract. Profits were $3 million below the preceding year due to an all-time low in the number of ticket sales in 1952 and the panic ensued at the studio's parent company, Loew's Inc., lead to the corporate reorganization of MGM. The studio replaced the head of production famed mogul Louis B. Mayer with Dore Schary and unconditionally released many of its stars including Clark Gable, Spencer Tracy, Mickey Rooney, Jane Powell, Greer Garson, and Esther Williams. But MGM wanted to keep Taylor, whose agent, Jules Goldstone advised her to also leave the studio to start her own production company. He explained that as a free agent she could negotiate for better scripts, choose the parts she wanted to play, control the production, and make more money which would be taxed at a lower rate due to capital gains. But Taylor stayed with MGM, according to biographer Kitty Kelley, because she needed the security of the studio and also refused to give up its perks, including access to the MGM wardrobe department.[33]

As the studio system's domination was nearing its end, due mainly to its forced divestiture in its distribution and exhibition companies by the federal government and the competition from television, Taylor invests her body and her labor in this dying empire. Enticed by a new five-year contract for $5,000 dollars a week, forty weeks guaranteed, a new four-year contract for her husband Michael Wilding, a former British matinee idol whose career was waning in Hollywood, and $300 a week for her mother, Sara, Elizabeth Taylor had tied herself to the studio because it had guaranteed her wages and the wages of her family. After losing the thirty-eight pounds she had gained during her pregnancy, she presented herself for inspection to Benny Thau, the head of casting, who had to gauge if she was ready to resume filming at full contract compensation. She was then "loaned" to Paramount for *Elephant Walk*.[34] I read Taylor's participation in this production as a form of imperial domesticity that parallels Ruth's labors onscreen in which the feminine influence of Taylor/Ruth is extended through imperial labor, in the name of the heterosexual family and secured through the comportment of her body. It may be no wonder that her performance in *Elephant Walk* is assessed by *New York Times* film critic Bosley Crowther as "petulant" and "smug"[35] when she must gracefully meet the various demands of studio and family at critical junctures, as she saves a troubled production and sustains her household as the film makes its budget back at the box office and her husband is allowed to continue to work in the United States at her behest and features as the pharaoh Akhenaten in *The Egyptian* in 1954.

Furthermore, a case in point is a publicity still featuring a twelve-year-old Elizabeth Taylor as Velvet Brown that marks her as always already an industrial worker. By the early 1950s, she was a responsible wage earner who has navigated the Fordist Hollywood factory since the age of nine.[36] Her years of entrenchment in part can account for her willingness to work (during this particular moment as a young mother and primary breadwinner saddled with a husband who conversely did not like to work) within the studio system and the constancy of her quest for capital. Dressed in a woolen coat and headscarf, she is wearing an English schoolgirl costume for a test during the production of *National Velvet* (1944). Standing beside a chalked slate that reads, "#11 Change Red Dress of #10 For School and Go Home——Pie Sick," Taylor holds what can be considered her preternaturally large hands at her side. Her huge hands remind me of the "Hands" from Charles Dickens's

Hard Times (1854), a name given to the masses of industrial workers who are dehumanized and anonymous and become reduced to their hands, their most practical and therefore most valuable parts by the factory system that demands their labor. The conditions surrounding Taylor's work life were not actually Dickensian, although the notion of a child earning a wage through regimented labor is certainly untoward. I do not minimize the differences between Elizabeth Taylor and actual factory workers whose wages and working conditions vary significantly. But "Elizabeth Taylor" the social actor, historical figure, and postcolonial white subject must always be considered through her identity as an industrial worker since her film work enables her to enter and participate in the making of the postwar and postcolonial cultural imaginary.

Elizabeth Taylor's work in the making of plantation films is one avenue of possibility for the white subject as she negotiates postcoloniality through a pursuit of capitalism while Vivien Leigh's fraught experience with the film marks still another outcome for the postcolonial white subject whose performative work is interpolated in the claiming of an imperial identity. Vivien Leigh's major psychic break occurred when she was acting with Laurence Olivier and hints at the severity of the strain that her work had caused her. Her psychosis then followed her, years later, to the set of *Elephant Walk*. After Olivier became a member of the Board of Directors of Britain's hallowed Old Vic Theatre in 1948, the couple soon after embarked on an acting tour of Australia and New Zealand to raise funds. Olivier had ambitious hopes for this tour: he wanted to raise money for the Old Vic which would then be used toward the building of a national British theater company under the subsidy of the government. Equally important in his estimation was his desire to help quell some of the anti-imperialist British sentiment in Australia after the Second World War. [37]

The Oliviers' presence in Australia foregrounds the significance of the institution of the Commonwealth to imperial whiteness as a feedback loop in the shoring up of British identity. [38] The Commonwealth is a voluntary association of nations comprised of former British colonies of which Australia's membership is indexical. As Prime Minister of Britain, Lord Rosebery first uses the term "Commonwealth of Nations" to assure Australia's stable familial relationship to the Empire during his state visit in 1884. [39] This union of independent states has taken the place of the British Empire after its dismantling in World War II. While its power is more symbolic than political it is a lasting after effect of Britain's imperial legacy to its former colonies through the transmission of English language, culture, and political systems such as parliamentary rule. [40] Olivier relished his work because it was a way through which British culture was shared between the two nations. As a cultural emissary who was Britain's national actor in renown as well as through his capacity as the head of the Old Vic, he was permitted to give pro-imperial speeches and even review Australian troops in Melbourne. His duties in Australia both on and off stage with his wife, Vivien, at his side, were giving him his bearings as he navigated the new horizon after the sun has set on the British Empire.

The couple reenacted key pieces of canonical British literature to their adoring Commonwealth audience, but the continuous delivery of repetitive performances in which her husband controlled all aspects of the three productions, *Richard III, The School for Scandal*, and *The Skin of our Teeth,* broke down Vivien Leigh. Before a performance of *The School for Scandal* in Christchurch, New Zealand, Leigh refused to go on stage. She had become furious when she could not find the red shoes to complete her costume and refused to perform without being properly attired. This prompted Olivier to slap her face, insult her, and goad her to go on stage. She swore at him and smacked him in return. After the diffusion of the initial explosion Leigh was able to perform that night and according to Olivier remained charming to the press publicizing their tour. I read her break as a violent reaction to the conditions she was facing under the strain of her husband's discipline. He even later claims that he lost his wife's affections in Australia.[41]

In Olivier's overeagerness to demonstrate the superiority of the English theater and by extension English culture to the impudent colony, he had overworked his cast and regimented how everyone should and would do their work. He began to conduct rehearsals aboard ship while sailing to the continent, breaking his promise to give the actors ample time to relax and adapt to their new surroundings. He dictated every part of production from overseeing rehearsals and character development to directing the actors on stage. By denying them the freedom to do their work as they saw fit, these actors were no longer artists crafting performances unique to themselves but workers producing a set of gestures and dialogue under the strictest management of a watchful supervisor directly invested in generating an efficient company capable of securing a profit.

Since a workplace organized in the imperial endeavor was the site of Vivien Leigh's initial trauma, it should not be surprising that she could not work on the set of *Elephant Walk*, itself produced by and producing the overarching themes of the securing of imperial identity. The film's narrative of disciplining a woman and processing her traditional femininity through constricting domesticity in which she is complicit must have been too much for her to bear. Her affair with Peter Finch could be read as her protest against filial duty as it was remade through Taylorist management. Her confession of love for Finch was an expression of a desire that falls outside the narrow perimeters of what is sanctioned by marriage and her imperial duty. It was a poignant gesture precisely because it was a desperate counterpoint to proper filial and imperial conduct. Olivier, after all, discovered Finch, a working stage actor, during their Australian tour.

French Marxist philosophers Gilles Deleuze and Félix Guattari read schizophrenia, characterized by mismemory and the break from cohesive narrative as an acute mental state that is synchronous with capitalism, a system that continuously incites neuroses to maintain normalcy. They assert that the schizophrenic's delirium is

> First of all an investment in a field that is social, economic, political, cultural, racial and racist and pedagogical, and religious: the delirious person applies a delirium to [her] family . . . that overreaches them at all sides.[42]

Vivien Leigh was hallucinating on the set of *Elephant Walk* and because of her delirium had no recollection of Olivier's coming to the set. Nor did she recall her attacking him in New Zealand some years prior to her break in Ceylon. In her off-screen life adjacent to *Elephant Walk*, she defies Taylorism and imperial work, which Ruth cannot do in the film. Vivien Leigh expresses her experience of an imperial postcolonial whiteness as one of trauma while Elizabeth Taylor on and off screen performs the circumnavigation of that very trauma. Leigh's psychic fissures when read alongside *Elephant Walk* makes visible these Oedipal ellipses. The explicit metaphor of incest through her entanglements with Finch, the remnants of the actual extramarital affair that Ruth cannot conduct, coupled with the palimpsest of Elizabeth Taylor's performance breaks open the official text of *Elephant Walk,* a film which previously elicited no critical interest. But now Vivien Leigh's discordant voice can be heard.

GIANT

While *Elephant Walk* speculates how postcoloniality will produce a mobile imperial white identity after a colonial site is lost to burgeoning nationalism, *Giant* is an earnest reclamation of a colonial site through its incorporation within a greater narrative of US nationalism. *Giant* provides a sympathetic, even loving glimpse into twenty-five years of the lives of the Benedicts, a Texas dynasty, as they come into modernity when Texas transitions from a cattle economy to petrol-capitalism. Texas is filmically recuperated through a narrative account of its racial intolerance and its resolution through the Benedicts' relationships with Mexican laborers. Because Texas is oil rich and integral to the postwar national economy, its cultural uniqueness is examined, admired, and celebrated and discursively reincorporated as part of the symbolic fabric of the nation through an amendment on race. *Giant* ably represents the traditional aspects of white patriarchy as racist, sexist, and exploitative to explain that modernity brought about by the Texas oil boom is the remedy to ignorance and hatred.

The film's valorized ideals of petro-modernity are recirculated through the film's multiple re-releases in 1963 and 1970 when during ensuing years it becomes clearer that the continued American dependence on oil is not only stifling to the United States but used to expose its oppressive control of the Middle East.[43] The film's romantic vision of petrol-capitalism precedes the 1973 oil crisis in which the Arab members of OPEC and Egypt, Syria, and Tunisia proclaimed an oil embargo as a response to US interventions in the Yom Kippur War.[44] Although the inflation of oil prices and shortages during the embargo spur various other nations to contain their dependency, the United States faces the second oil crisis of the decade in 1979 when the Iranian Revolution fought to depose the American-supported Shah disrupts oil production and suspends oil exportation.[45] The US need for foreign oil from international suppliers resentful of American Middle Eastern policies gives new uses for representations of a healthy national oil industry on American soil which *Giant* well provides. Its visions of US oil independence through the depiction of Texas as the formerly isolated Lone Star State now fully integrated into the service of the nation promotes images of American unity and invincibility. Perhaps most importantly, its celebratory representation of white Texas culture as familial and loving is also circulated through re-release in 1963 as the national reclamation of the state is necessary after the assassination of John F. Kennedy in Dallas that year. *Giant* presents a picture of Texas as a space capable of racial tolerance and social progress that can counter general perceptions of the state as a hub of violent right-wing political extremism.[46]

Still, the film tries to work through Mikhail Bakhtin's notion of heteroglossia, the idea of the existence of a plurality of voices within a novel that he asserts accounts for the disunity of discourses within a culture. It reflects his theory of centripetal and centrifugal forces. The centripetal forces of a novel work toward ideological centralization and unification while the centrifugal forces display and redistribute diversity and stratification—producing the heteroglossia inherent in all discursive constructions.[47] Producer George Stevens, Jr., the son of the film's director, notes that his father wanted to explore racial intolerance and depict the independent woman, a sentiment that represents the film's centripetal forces. *Giant* provides a rather simplistic and teleological solution to racism through white paternalism and an intriguing formulation of a noblesse oblige toward Mexican Americans through the actions of "Bick"/Jordan (Rock Hudson) and Leslie (Elizabeth Taylor). The centrifugal forces of the film are expressed through the presence of Hudson and Taylor as extraordinary performers whose embodiment of sexual and gender aberration off screen always potentially rupture the film's codification of white dynastic power and Texas greatness as pure, closed, and whole.

Giant is a film deeply invested in the making of white imperial identity and modeling proper race and gender roles much like *Elephant Walk* even if it also deploys different narrative strategies. Through the mobilization of a proto-feminist imperial domesticity, its plantation mistress compliments and cultivates the paternal noblesse of the film's male protagonist. Its fixation on proper whiteness is first expressed through the use of the crude metaphor of animal husbandry. The opening scene of the film shows Bick traveling to lush Maryland to Dr. Lynnton's horse farm to buy a breeding stallion. His train goes from screen left to right, moving Westward, signifying westward expansion—a disorienting gesture since geographical logic dictates that Bick should be heading East or right to left. Nevertheless, the mise-en-scène implies that he is searching for more than a horse. Bick is also looking for a consort and learns that Dr. Lynnton's gorgeous daughter, Leslie, is a legitimate member of the East Coast American-landed aristocracy. Mesmerized by her majestic presence atop War Winds, the stallion he travels to Maryland to purchase, he refers to Leslie as a "beautiful animal" upon first glance and sets new sights on marrying her. Because of her racial and class status, she has the literal "breeding" to be deemed worthy of an imperial marriage. Bick is a Texas feudal lord dreaming of greater Western expansion and building a white dynasty on his "parcel" of land named Reata, with its 595,000 acres.

During their marriage, while Bick as its patriarch heads the Benedicts nominally, it is Leslie who is its moral center. It is significant that she is presented as an Easterner whose feminist and racially progressive views are the result of a life in Maryland where she claims to have cultivated her interest in national politics. Leslie's origins as a politically sophisticated and socially progressive Eastern blueblood links those progressive discourses to the nation's capital in order to symbolize the United States's modernity.[48] As the voice of moral and social enlightenment within the Benedict household Leslie is allowed to momentarily question Texas history, at least during the beginning of her courtship to Bick. Voraciously studying Texas history through her reading of *Texas the Marvelous* and *The Alamo,* she asks her future husband, "Well, Jordan, we really did steal Texas from Mexico, didn't we? It's right there in all of the history books." Angry and flustered, all Bick can do is retort, "You think all the glory was in the East with Valley Forge and Bunker Hill, but have you heard of the Alamo?" While he chooses to read the hostile US annexation of Texas as a glorious chapter in American history, akin to its very founding, Leslie simply declares it as out right theft.

According to Charles Ramirez Berg, as the Louisiana Purchase accelerated the US Westward expansion, it initiated the country's dispute over Texas ownership which many felt was included in the purchase. While the United States ceded claims over Texas to gain leverage to bargain over Florida in the Transcontinental Treaty of 1819, this only delayed American demands for Texas, for which two wars were fought: the Texas War (1835–1836) and the Mexican American War (1846–1848).[49] The first was an Anglo revolt against the Mexican state lead by Stephen F. Austin and his retinue of 35,000 settlers (ten times the size of the Mexican population in the region) who urged that the best interests of the United States required that Texas become Americanized.[50]

There were many reasons for the war, including the desire of Texians (North American immigrants to Texas) to maintain their slaves after Mexico abolished slavery in 1829 and the rage of Anglo settlers who were protesting the Mexican government's prohibition of immigration to Texas in 1830. Many of these settlers who fought in the Alamo were actually illegal immigrants. The Republic of Texas was created after the defeat of General Antonio López de Santa Anna at San Jacinto on April 21, 1836. The latter Mexican American War was the ensuing armed conflict between the United States and the Mexican state over the annexation of Texas. Arnold De León argues that racism was certainly a prominent reason for the war as well. He writes that the unique psycho-historical experience of Texians was tinged with racist attitudes that negatively affected their perception of Mexicans particularly because many white Texas settlers shared an aversion to colonial Spain, Spaniards, Catholics, Native Americans, and Blacks. For them, Mexicanos, who were mostly mestizos, were "doubly suspect" because of their Catholicism and their mixed Spanish, Indian, and African heritage.[51]

Giant does not narrativize the creation of the American Texas as the result of a race war but produces a speculative fiction of the making of a new Texas through racial reconciliation that incorporates the Mexican body into a greater schema of the remade, racialized but non-Black American body, which is both a social and moral victory. In verbal jousting, Leslie defeats Bick in a series of political arguments through her deployment of logic and feminine charm, suggesting that there is power albeit temporary and symbolic in moral victory. The narrative motif of the moral victory is repeated used in the film, an indulgent and reflexive gesture, as the film's producers strive to present what they consider to be compassionate and realistic portrayals of Mexicans as part of a more progressive view on racial acceptance.

Archival materials from the film's production included script changes and casting choices that generally point to the producers' desire to present more realistic portrayals of Texas and Mexican culture. They were especially interested in casting actual Mexicans for the Mexican roles as noted in the publicity that recorded the hiring of Spanish language translators and Mexican actors. Even so, producers gave Sal Mineo, a noted Italian American actor, the film's most prominent Mexican part. Besides *Giant,* he has played against his ethnic identity in numerous films including his role as the "Sioux" (Lakota) Native, White Bull, in *Tonka* (1958) and the young prince Chulalongkorn opposite Yul Brynner in the stage musical *The King and I* (1952).[52,53] The film also mobilizes a process called Warnercolor, patented through Warner Bros. Studios using Eastman film stock developed in Warner's lab, which was meant to compete with Technicolor's 3 Tone process to capture colors realistically. The discourses of verisimilitude associated with Warnercolor were used to promote the film as many cast members were playing their actual ethnicity and not in brownface.

Agreeing with Christine Gledhill about the cultural work of melodrama, Linda Williams declares that

> Melodrama is structured upon the "dual recognition" of how things are and how they should be. In melodrama there is a moral, wish fulfilling impulse towards the achievement of justice that gives American popular culture its strength and appeal as the powerless yet virtuous seek to return to the "innocence" of their origins.[54]

Within the logic of melodrama that Williams lays out, the Mexican characters of *Giant* occupy the space of victim-heroes as the film draws attention to their virtues as hard working, industrious, and self-sacrificing Americans. This is so specifically in the case of Angel Obregón II (Sal Mineo), once the sick Mexican baby Leslie saves through her intervention at the "Village" and who grows up healthy and strong to serve in World War II as a private in the US army, only to die in battle. He is buried in Reata under the flag of Texas, with all the Benedicts present as military officials ceremoniously give his mother a folded American flag. While Mineo's casting may have perhaps made this representation of the Mexican as American more palatable for resistant white audiences accustomed to seeing him play men of color, his inclusion in this film as a (relatively) openly gay actor who lost parts at various studios due to his sexuality, along with both Hudson and Dean's participation, gives the film a queer subtext that can complicate its trajectory of traditional masculine valor.

The US annexation of Texas qualifies as an example of what historian Matthew Frye Jacobson terms "barbarian virtues." Taking cues from the letters of Theodore Roosevelt whose image is represented in various media in the form of the colonial white hunter, Jacobson has constructed a historiography of US international policy in which the superior, "civilized" West was justified in carrying out whatever policy it considered fit over the "primitive," meaning the parts of the pre-industrialized world that Roosevelt named "waste spaces."[55] As the dynastic lord of Reata, Bick believes he has inherited the right and been bestowed the duty to continue to perform acts of "barbarian virtue" that consolidate his power over his land and the Mexicans who toil on it. Clinging to a sense of a gallant white masculinity and a notion of rugged American individualism, he owns 595,000 acres and 50,000 head of cattle and the indentured servitude of generations of Mexicans. The actions tied to his investiture bring the destruction of the natural environment and the exploitation of its people and natural resources. The desolate mustard land-scape, cracked under the hot sun symbolizes both the vastness and the emptiness of Texas and is proof that those ways of living and producing capital through ranching are backward, isolating, and ultimately unsustainable. The discovery of oil in the region and the economic boom it accompanies brings technology and modernity and therefore reinstates the state into the greater US nation.

Rock Hudson as Bick Benedict physically embodies both the mythic size of Texas, the promise of wealth connected to a land that is oil rich and the fallacies of that fantasy.[56] Standing 6'5" at full height, the film capitalizes on his size, symbolic of phallic power, and emphasizes this through close-ups of his feet and in long shots of his body as he disembarks the train in the film's opening sequence. To borrow from AIDS scholar Simon Watney and his apt sketch of the star, Hudson was a "sensitive" postwar male figure. His performance of masculinity both on and off screen is comforting, safe, and malleable. Watney writes that while Hudson had come to embody the traditional patriarchal values tied to the 1950s, his own film persona is often removed from the mainstream macho masculinity of that era as represented by the stars Victor Mature and Clarke Gable.[57] His image is often linked to scenes from nature rather than men's culture and his role as an unassuming gardener in love with a rich, older woman in Douglas Sirk's *All that Heaven Allows* (1955) is a well-known example.

In *Giant,* Rock Hudson's masculinity hinges on the visible evidence of his good health and youth (he was thirty-one during production). His intricately constructed on-screen and off-screen images as a nonthreatening sex symbol for heterosexual women is made possible according to Richard Meyer by his good looks and a "sanitized" sexuality that makes his projection as a "gentle giant" possible despite his formidable size.[58] As he towers over Leslie/Elizabeth Taylor, who is more than a foot shorter than he, his Bick is still vulnerable to her charms, criticisms, and her sexual appetite. He is embarrassed and hurt when she compares him to a caveman for excluding her in a conversation about local politics and at first is too angry to sleep with her that night. Leslie seduces him back to bed by looking at him mischievously and telling him to "kick off his spurs." The screen fades to black, signifying sexual intercourse. The next morning she is ebullient and he is exhausted. Bick's sexual passivity mimics Hudson's image as a "safe-sex object" for straight women.

Richard Meyer queers Rock Hudson's 1950s-era image through his mapping of the moments in which his body, contained, closeted, and "sanitized" within dominant culture interpolates the very queer desire it tries to destroy. He writes,

> Rock Hudson's homosexuality—however disavowed by Hollywood, by the film viewer, or by Hudson himself—registered in his star image, in the sexual immobility of his masculinity, in the way that women really *could* count on him to maintain his erotic distance. Many of those who orchestrated Hudson's stardom were aware of his homosexuality—certainly his agent, probably his directors, photographers, and fanzine journalists and of course, Hudson himself. It seems likely that the framing of Hudson's hunky but deheterosexualized masculinity worked off this knowledge, responded to it, *used* it as a source and a building block.[59]

Its "building block" of knowledge, the "open" secret of Hudson's homosexuality must be taken into account when reading this film and Bick/Hudson's presentation of heteronomative masculine values. As these values are meant to stand in for Texas itself, the contradictions endemic to Hudson as a closeted gay actor playing this particular role serves as an example of the star as open archive of ongoing performances meant to be read and reread. Stars are often contradictory symbols that open spaces for new textual interpretations. Reading strategies hinge on anticipating that the star as a discursive object often invites disparate readings, not a finite linear or teleological set of texts but a series of narratives that are continuously discovered and amassed and read which can disrupt and fissure the intended code of various official performances such as film work. The viewer can read the images of Hudson's shocking physical deterioration, what Meyer calls the "anti-body" that was added to his archive as the public learned he was dying of AIDS.[60] This image of an ailing Hudson must be read against his performance as the vigorous, oversized Bick, since the image of Hudson's withered body often overrides all other images of him. For contemporary viewers of the film if not for spectators then, this in turn forces open the space to reconsider the potency of Texas myth produced by the film and the myth itself as a nationalist construction incongruous to reality.

Elizabeth Taylor's on screen imperial labor should also be read against her extra-cinematic signification of domestic chaos as her frequent remarriages made her home a site of seemingly infinite permutability, a destabilized and open network of husbands and children that feed on her unruly femininity, unlike the dynastic and imperial homes of her filmic counterparts. She must also be considered as a body whose main engagement with the world was through the public and not the private sphere. She extends her global influence precisely by embodying a fantasy of undisciplined domesticity that spectators undoubtedly found fascinating. Taylor was a driven career woman who was rocketing through the Hollywood stratosphere (three Academy Award nominations for Best Actress in 1957, 1958, 1959 and a win for *Butterfield 8* in 1960) with little time left for housekeeping or intensive childrearing. Her exquisite onscreen performances of the subordinated and regimented plantation mistress play out these contradictions and the asymmetry between the on-screen and off-screen Taylors sustains her stardom and enthralls viewers worldwide.[61] Like her filmic counterparts, Elizabeth Taylor attains personal agency, financial freedom, and physical mobility through performances of perfected white femininity through the production of imperial fantasy that romanticizes white women's active participation in colonial endeavors of the past.

Nicholas Dirks realizes as women "were used as a measure of civility," they also became the fundamental symbol of tradition. Using India as a case study, he notes the colonial collision of tradition and modernity took place in

Figure 2.1. Elizabeth Taylor takes home first Best Actress Oscar for *Butterfield 8* **in 1961. Source: Bettmann/Getty Images.**

a succession of contests over women's bodies (2001, 55). This is also the case in the Texas of the film. Over time, Leslie's imperial domesticity becomes reorganized through concessions much as the characters learn to concede to social changes such as the acceptance of Anglo-Mexican marriage and urbanized Mexican professional labor that supersede her feminism: Leslie has become rather weary, her hair gray at the end of the film, allowing the viewer to forget that she had once symbolized the postsuffragette feminist woman unafraid to question her husband's staid values and political regression. Ironically, as Texas comes into modernity through oil, she is now firmly traditionally feminine, conceding to her husband and dutifully attending galas at Bick's side when he must begrudgingly acknowledge the success of their former ranch hand, Jett Rink.

As oil fuels the progression of *Giant's* narrative, the viewer learns that it feeds Jett Rink's (James Dean) racial malice and has turned him into an imperial monster. It is his profound racism that is used as a foil to redeem Bick's past racial ignorance. It is somewhat stunning to witness Dean's portrayal of the avowedly racist Jett as he still cuts a dashing figure in his costumes, all icons of American sportswear that eroticize his body and makes his working-class aesthetic desirable. Wearing a series of jeans and button-down shirts that make him look for lack of a better word, "timeless," as the changes in menswear vary little between decades, Dean's image of white American cool becomes further complicated and racialized through his association with Marlon Brando who has notably influenced Dean since before his time at the Actor's Studio. Dean's acting style is in dialogue with Brando's, which Brando derived partly from his love of jazz and admiration of Black masculinity that has compelled scholars to name it as a "white Negro aesthetic."[62]

In *Giant's* most shocking scene, Jett strikes oil on the plot of land bequeathed to him by Bick's racist sister Luz (Mercedes McCambridge). She dies when she is thrown from Leslie's wild stallion War Winds in a stubborn attempt to overrule her authority as the new mistress of Reata. This is a convenient ending for a figure too backward to stand in as an example of modern Texas as Leslie has already replaced her as the primary domestic manager of the ranch. Drenched in black grease, Jett is newly baptized and symbolically reborn. With a maniacal gleam in his eyes the whites blazing in stark contrast to his blackened body, he dances.[63] He taunts Bick by making an open sexual pass at Leslie. At this moment, he is rich beyond his wildest dreams, emboldened, and masked in black oil and adopts a parodic masquerade of hypersexualized Blackness that affirms his whiteness.[64] Marking his white rebirth he embraces the original white American fantasy of the "Other" as an embodied displacement of hatred, fear, and desire. This sequence presents Jett Rink/ James Dean in blackface, as he fully becomes the figuration of a whiteness not modified by caveats or qualifiers.[65] Rink is diametrically opposed to the Benedicts whose aristocratic bearing enables them to extend a largesse, particularly through Leslie's domesticity, her nurturing of her children and her willingness to help improve living conditions for Reata's Mexican workers. Jett is nouveau rich and gauche, and his exclusionary racial politics is divergent from the idealized formulation of Texas modernity. Ironically, it is Dean himself who embodies a modernity through Method acting precisely by adopting and adapting a liberated, emotionally raw filmic performance style that is produced partially through a white appropriation of Blackness.

Jett Rink/James Dean's frenzied blackface dance recalls the Jewish vaudeville performers in Michael Rogin's *Blackface, White Noise.* Rogin notes that by engaging in blackface minstrelsy, those Jewish performers came into generic American, nonethnic, and nondescript white identity and modernity. By mocking Blackness through grotesque caricatures for the pleasure of white audiences their mastery of this foundational, intertexual, and pervasive American form brought them not only fame and fortune but cultural and racial acceptance. Rogin explores this phenomenon through the indelible example of *The Jazz Singer* (1927) starring Al Jolson. This film is entrenched in the canon of early American cinema and depicts the Jewish Jackie Rabinowitz's defiance of his cantor father. Relinquishing Jewish musical traditions to become Jack Robin, a mainstream American jazz singer, he performs blackface to great renown and comes into a nonethnic, secular, white identity. He not only narratively comes into American modernity by letting go of Old World Jewish cultural forms but his entrance into mainstream American popular culture is marked sonically as the film, primarily a silent feature comes into sync sound precisely when Jack's plays a permutation of "jazz" music that is an example of American mass culture (1996, 118–120).

Jett too comes fully into his white power when he can express his disdain for the nonwhite Other through his performance of a mad, darkened figure. Through his body, postcolonial whiteness is an identity structured through imperial desire as an expression of embodied affect. It assures his new imperial identity by helping him to ceremoniously abandon his liminality, which borrowing from Matthew Frye Jacobson could be called his "probationary whiteness." In the past, his poverty that made him, to his horror, closer in status to the Mexican workers of Reata than to the Benedicts. His windfall only exacerbates his longstanding resentment of Mexicans, which is already apparent when he was working at Reata. There he referred to them as "wetbacks" and was indifferent to their plight when a potentially fatal illness infected the residents of the "Village"—the slum settlement adjacent to Reata proper, where the Mexican laborers are forced to live.

The "Village," or Biendecito Village, is a space that film uses to connote the injustice of racial segregation and the impossibility of the notion of "separate but equal." A muffled articulation of contemporary 1950s US racial discourse that implicitly critiques Jim Crow laws, Leslie's protest against the miserable, unsanitary living conditions in the Village speaks to her intrinsic sense of noblesse oblige that ennobles her imperial domesticity and maternalizes her while inculcating Bick and demonizing Jett. When Leslie informs Bick that she must help Mrs. Obregón's baby, he tells her, "You can't do that! You can't go there . . . He's our doctor." She pointedly asks, "You mean the Benedicts' only?" Befuddled, he replies, "They have their own way of doing things by themselves." Leslie tells him, "Jordan, darling, I don't think you quite understand, there is a child who is very sick. I must take Dr. Walker." She then escorts Dr. Walker to the ailing Mrs. Obregón and her ill baby. When she returns, Bick tells her, "I feel much better, honey." She responds by saying, "That's a good boy." Her reply infantilizes him and again reinforces her symbolic maternity, a position she uses to educate and nurture Bick to help him navigate his reformed masculinity while taking his place in the new Texas.

Jett assesses his poverty to be the result of the Benedicts swindling land from some "ignorant Mexicans," whom he considers fundamentally unfit for landownership. He asserts that his "folks was in Texas long enough to get rich too, except they weren't as foxy." He believes his whiteness still entitles him to owning the land that his meek forbearers had taken by the ruthless "sons of Benedicts." The Mexicans with whom he has worked alongside at Reata do not warrant his sympathy or care. The sociopolitical reasons for their poverty, disenfranchisement, and oppression are not his concern.

Figure 2.2. Elizabeth Taylor and Rock Hudson squaring off as Leslie and Bick in *Giant* **(1956). Source: Bettmann/Getty Images.**

Jett's arrogance and animosity toward Mexicans compel him to ban them from his hotel. His segregationist policy directly affects Jordan II's wife Juana (Elsa Cárdenas) and by association the rest of the Benedicts during the night of Jett's gala.[66] After she is refused service in the hotel's beauty salon, Jordan II (Dennis Hopper) is forced to publicly, physically challenge Jett. After Jett humiliates his son, Bick's antipathy for his former employee and his compulsion to restore his familial pride makes him take action. He tries to best Jett through violence but decides not to hit him because he realizes Jett Rink is an empty vessel, a dehumanized apparatus through which petrol capital flows and nothing else. From this moment forward, Rink is contained off screen, his racial intolerance having been foregrounded as an unacceptable mode of operation for imperial whites renegotiating their relationships to people of color. Still, Bick has another opportunity to express his racial "progressiveness" through ritualized masculine violence. His paternalism has been developing steadily throughout the film. His staunch disappointment that his son chose to become a doctor and not succeed him as the head of Reata follows his acceptance of his career choices and his son's marriage to a Mexican nurse and finally his acceptance of his mixed-race grandson. As a somewhat condescending but doting grandfather during the film's climatic final scene, Bick defends his Mexican grandson's honor by fighting the racist short order cook who refuses to serve another Mexican family.

The last shot of *Giant* is a close up Bick's grandson with a perplexed look on his face that gestures to the film's major erasures. I posit that the baby's face holds a look of bewilderment that could stand in for the viewer's own sense of dismay as this violent act is supposed to provide narrative resolution and textual closure. In a classical Hollywood sense, this codes as the film's happy ending that delineates Bick's (comparatively) progressive racial politics through a machismo that reaffirms his and (Hudson's) masculinity after the loss of the ranching culture from which he derived great pride. But the baby's face, with its look of absolute wonderment simply disrupts the seamlessness of the film's ending.

Scholar Rafael Pérez-Torres supports my reading of the ending stating that, "In *Giant* mestizaje does not offer an empowered subjectivity" nor does it "offer agency in the epic battle over racial/national redefinition." José E. Limón agrees, noting that Bick still refers to his grandson as a "wetback" and the toddler is sometimes not even fully acknowledged while he is on screen. The film frames him as unequal and an outsider.[67] Racial difference, according to Pérez-Torres "marks alterity and inferiority." While Bick Benedict's paternalism is presented as a form of practical liberal humanism, the mestizaje, used here as a politicizing term that describes the enabling formation of subjects claiming mixed-race and mixed-cultural identity of the Americas often specified as people of mixed Indigenous, Latin, and European, and/

or Mexican and European heritage, including the young Benedict heir, are acceptable only when they serve a greater US authoritative discourse, the teleological narrative of postwar American equality. But ultimately, the baby's explicit racial difference makes him a source of repugnance.[68]

RAINTREE COUNTY

Giant recuperates Texas and apologizes for its racist past through its discourse of begrudging acceptance primarily because its petrol-capitalism supports the national economy and therefore saves it from becoming a part of the demonized South. But *Raintree County* symbolically annihilates the South after making it the designated site of national racial trauma. While it represents the destructive effects of the internalized (self) hatred of the nonwhite subject on the white psyche through the white body, it asserts that reconciliation with the South is impossible. In the film, Susanna Drake (Elizabeth Taylor) is a troubled Southern belle who has no cohesive narrative of her biography. Because of her attachment to her father's Black Caribbean mistress, Henrietta, whom she refers to as a "great lady," she thinks that Henrietta is her mother, and believes she herself is Black.

Susanna's racial confusion and her family history of racial secrets drive her to madness. Her mentally ill mother killed her father and Henrietta when she found them in bed together and then set fire to the plantation. Only Susanna, the child, survived. She feels guilt-stricken about telling her mother about the affair, which sets off the series of tragic events. She mistakenly assumes Henrietta, whom she loves to be her mother while hating herself for being Black. This is evident during an extraordinary moment when Susana played deftly by Taylor who was Oscar-nominated for her performance expresses her incredulity at the de facto blood quantum rule organizing American race which dictates that having one drop of Black blood makes her Black. For most of the film she is waging a war within herself, trying to reconcile her perceived mixed-race identity against the racism of the Antebellum social world in which she lives. Not only this, Susanna's body represents the possibilities of the impurity of whiteness itself as her psychic break from reality displaces the very real violence whites inflict on Black bodies through her mental anguish. She signifies the bisected subjectivity of Southern whiteness, a formation that defines against and alongside the Blackness it fears and suppresses.

Therefore, the South, which Susana symbolizes as a belle, becomes a space of horror for herself and for viewers. Ultimately the South is contained through Susanna's institutionalization in a mental hospital and eventually, inevitably and symbolically destroyed through her suicide. Tara McPherson argues that if the Southern lady is

> a key image around which the South constructed (and still constructs) its Postbellum identity, this lady was (and is) most often situated within a particular Southern landscape.

Using the work of literary critic Diane Roberts, McPherson also asserts that Southerners have carried the symbolism of the white "sacrosanct" Southern lady onto the Southern landscape itself.[69] The presentation of the deranged and racially liminal Southern belle in this case imbues the South that she represents as a site of racial crisis. This is meaningful not only as the South at the time of production is the center of the necessary American racial reckoning of the civil rights movement but because it also aligns the region with the postcolonial revolutions in Africa. Ghana, historically the starting point of the trans-Atlantic slave trade where Black captives are held in its forts to be transported as human cargo including to the United States, becomes the second sub-Saharan African nation to break free from European colonialism in the year of the film's release as twenty-three other nations win independence by 1962.[70]

Raintree County reflects national anxieties about racial integration through the metaphor of Susanna's troubled marriage with the Hoosier John Shawnessey (Montgomery Clift). While arguing that the incorporation of the South into the national body is not possible, it elevates John's efforts as an abolitionist and his attempts to investigate her personal history to heal her psychic wounds. Tricked into marriage, he still loves his wife and joins the Union Army during the Civil War to find her after she has run away to Louisiana with their son. According to Hernan Vera and Andrew Gordon, the film depicts John as "the ideal white American subject as a natural-born leader" and uses a debased Black image, an image constructed through the racialized and gendered trauma of Taylor's Susanna to glorify him while the Civil War is used to dramatize a split in the white subject. This split is not based on white versus Black but white versus white subjectivity. The narrative then works towards a reconciliation with the white masculine self (1991, 64–266).

Even with John's help, Susanna's sense of shame toward her self-assumed mixed-race identity overcomes her. I read Elizabeth Taylor's Susanna as a civil rights era reimagining of the tragic mulatto who is mobilized here to explain why racial integration in the South and elsewhere in the United States is beyond the bounds of possibility. One of the five tropes of Black representation in American film that Donald Bogle discusses in his work, the tragic mulatto's earliest appearance in US cinema is in a two-reeler titled

The Debt (1912). Bogle speculates that audiences were positioned to like the tragic mulatto, often female, because of her "white blood." Films present her as "a victim of her divided racial inheritance" who passes in the white world because of her visual whiteness. But her Blackness is revealed during a crucial moment, often during the making of a heterosexual romance.[71]

The film positions the viewer to identify with John and sympathize with Susanna and presents racial integration through a white perspective. As the issue of desegregation is represented through the troubled Shawnessy marriage, it then becomes a social-historical dilemma that is detrimental to the white psyche while Black subjects are relegated to the background to passively receive white compassion or to aid whites, especially John in his futile quest to save his wife.

Susanna's psychic traumas make her performance of imperial domesticity for the Antebellum Southern belle impossible, since her "Blackness" makes any extension of white empire mostly outside her purview. For example, she gives into John's demands to free her slaves when he threatens to leave her. Unlike the other plantation mistresses of this genre, her domesticity does not manifest her power but becomes the conduit through which she unravels, as the racial trauma of slavery and race-mixing are linked to domestic upheaval and turmoil, of which she, her mother, and Henrietta are all victims. As Susanna's mental instability becomes more apparent, the film suggests she may be a danger to herself and her family. She feels distraught, alienated, and unloved by her son. Her inability to hide her instability makes her a bad mother by default. Believing that she is a burden to her husband and the ambitions others have placed upon him for national office, she drowns herself. Never properly white nor properly feminine, there is no place for Susanna in the South of Reconstruction. Her sacrifice signifies another baptism, a trope in the plantation film that washes away the sins of the racial past so that all who wish to move forward, can distance themselves from this old South.

The conservative racial politics of *Raintree County* reflect the mainstream public's reaction to the Little Rock Nine in Jackson, Mississippi, and undoubtedly elsewhere in the country that was resistant to desegregation. The film was released in 1957, the same year in which members of the "Little Rock Nine," a group of African American students were registered to attend Little Rock's Central High School by the NAACP. Ernest Green, Elizabeth Eckford, Jefferson Thomas, Terrence Roberts, Carlotta Wells, Minnijean Brown, Gloria Ray, Thelma Mothershed, and Melba Pattillo were blocked from entering campus by the state National Guard who was deployed by segregationist Arkansas governor, Orval Faubus.[72] The ensuing struggle between the students and the state had prompted the airing of the one-sided program, *The Little Rock Crisis* by WLBT-TV in Jackson, Mississippi, in October

1957. It featured a panel of prominent segregationist politicians including Mississippi senator James Eastland that forced NAACP field secretary Medgar Evers to request that WLBT give airtime to a "group of Mississippi Negroes . . . to accurately and pointedly express the feelings of the Negro on this very vital issue." Evers's request was denied.[73]

According to Steven D. Classen, the WLBT airing of *The Little Rock Crisis* as well as the replacing of the national anthem with an advertisement for the Citizens' Council that warned, "Don't let this happen in Mississippi, join the Citizens' Council today," after President Eisenhower's appearance on national television explaining his actions supporting school integration in Little Rock were pointed gestures that coincided with segregationist Mississippian views insisting that the government outside their own state was against them, seeking to break apart their notion of a cherished and distinctive way of life (2004, 43). Even as the cherished way of life that Jackson's citizens are so desperate to save has ended in the South represented in *Raintree County,* it is done so to preserve the cherished ways of life in the North, where slavery is illegal but the contamination of race, or more precisely the mixing of Blacks and whites is forcibly contained within the South, to remain a Southern *white* problem.

Elizabeth Taylor's remarkable embodiment of aberrant whiteness through her destabilized body centers her portrayal of the symbolic tragic mulatto. Her casting is particularly fascinating since her example can illuminate that whiteness is a disciplinary masquerade, as Susanna must "act" white and "pass" to maintain her social status and freedom. Fears of losing white privilege or a formulation of a whiteness that is unanchored and precarious is undoubtedly dangerous and must be resolved, especially during a historical moment in which whiteness itself is being redefined against the image of the Black subject seeking liberation. These cultural anxieties are refigured through Taylor's body, a site that spectators understand to be in constant crisis, through medical catastrophe or the emotional chaos tied to her frequent changing of husbands, a body that is in danger of unraveling but at this juncture is still white.

Elizabeth Taylor's ensuing racial instability signaled by her widely publicized 1959 Jewish conversion and aberrant femininity make her an ideal plantation mistress whose proper white femininity then becomes secured through her management of the plantation and her subordination of racial Others. More importantly, her performance as Susanna Drake reveals the dark secret of the very precariousness of white American identity, a secret shame that kills the belle she plays. Within the detective story of *Raintree County*, in which Montgomery Clift investigates the truth of Susanna Drake's racial identity, Taylor ably performs the white subject's overidentification with Blackness and presents a tragic scenario of the dangers of Blackness to white identity precisely because it is so intimately tied to it even while Black and white racial reconciliation seems impossible. This is reiterated through the film's audio register with the use of Nat King Cole's singing of "The Song of Raintree County" during the opening credits. While the singer is never featured on screen, his distinctive velvet baritone provides the musical metaphor for Susanna's life as a Southern tragedy. Cole mournfully sings of two lovers whose pure hearts enabled them to see the mythical raintree alluding to the heartfelt but untenable love between Susanna and John.

Just one year before *Raintree County's* release, Nat King Cole, a virtuoso jazz pianist who parlayed his multiple musical talents into a very successful touring and recording career by singing beautiful and sad romantic ballads became the first Black performer to have his own show on US network television.[74] In production for just thirteen months, *The Nat King Cole Show* was critically successful and featured musical luminaries such as Ella Fitzgerald, Sammy Davis, Jr., Harry Belafonte, Pearl Bailey, and Tony Bennett as guest stars but was never able to secure a national sponsor because Cole surmised, "Madison Avenue is afraid of the dark." While mainstream audiences loved Cole as a singer, buying hundreds of thousands of his hit records in the 1950s which in turn helped finance the building of the famed Capitol Records building on Sunset and Vine in Los Angeles, corporate sponsors afraid of offending white viewers never supported Cole's television efforts. That same year, in 1956, while on tour in Birmingham, Alabama, the singer was badly hurt during a botched kidnapping attempt while on stage by three members of the White Citizens' Council. Understandably shaken, Cole cancelled the rest of his shows in Alabama, the state of his birth, quickly retreated to his adopted hometown of Chicago and never performed in the South again. [75]

Hearing Cole's disembodied voice during opening titles lays out the film's racial politics straightaway. As a Black subject who was a victim of racial violence and racial discrimination, Cole voice holds unquestionable authority that testifies to listeners the pain of American racism for Blacks while relaying just how the South is avowedly racist, the site that forced the mass migration of Black families from the region to the North including Cole's. The Coles were amongst the millions to move North not only hoping for better jobs but often for fear of their safety during the 1920s. Cole's disembodied voice is a form of Michel Chion's notion of the "acousmêtre," a haunting sonic presence in film not bound to a body but appropriating all the powers of sound—including invisibility, omnipresence, and omniscience—made possible through its association to the eye of the camera.[76] Nat King Cole as the film's acousmêtre highlights to viewers the unresolved white American fears toward the abject Black male figure, even one characterized by the performative excellence and masculine elegance of Nat King Cole through his very pointed visual erasures from both the big and small screens.

Along with its refusal to consider racial integration as a political and cultural possibility, *Raintree County's* narrative conceit of racial mismemory became sublimated onto the rearticulation of its production history. In the summer of 2007, the people of Danville, Kentucky, commemorated the fiftieth anniversary of the filming of *Raintree County* in their town with a celebratory festival. Its production history as "remembered" by the townsfolk of Danville makes no mention of race or the Civil Rights Movement even when the film was produced during the era for the struggle for African American rights and the film is set in the Antebellum South, during the Civil War and Reconstruction.

The festival was funded partly by the state of Kentucky and organized around an erasure of race. This included no discussion of how the film could be in dialogue with the major event of 1957, the forced integration of Central High School, a historical moment of both national and regional significance. Nor was the film's narrative about Susanna's psychic trauma discussed as an extension of her/national racial anxieties in any of the planned discussions during the festival. That this epic film could actually be about race, racial trauma, or racial inequality was not evident in the paraphernalia sold during the festival that included a DVD in which the townspeople provided their recollections of the production. Produced by the organizers and featuring folks who were present during filming, participants regaled the audience with tales of meeting the film's stars and befriending the crew or expressed their excitement that a major Hollywood production had taken over Danville. They chose to remember Montgomery Clift's public drunkenness and Elizabeth Taylor's affair with future husband producer Mike Todd whose voice was heard over the telephone by Danville's nosy operators. Their historiographical account of the production contains stunning critical blind spots regarding race while turning those various accounts into items that helps us imagine a raceless South that is collectible.[77] Danville's and Kentucky's erasure of race from the production and reception of *Raintree County* suggest that the South is not only the national designated site of racial trauma but also a geographical space and temporality in which the wounds of racial injustice are made invisible.

CONCLUSION

Elephant Walk, Giant, and *Raintree County* utilize the filmic plantation to orient the spectator toward an understanding of the intersections of the making of whiteness through the sublimation of imperial desire onto various sites after the death of empire. Through the labor, discipline, and sacrifice of the plantation mistress, proper whiteness, and traditional gender roles are secured and white subjectivity is inculcated with the knowledge to adeptly navigate postcoloniality, through white mobility, paternalism, and racial mismemory.

Filmic genres and film stars present and solve imaginative problems. The plantation films of the postcolonial era of the 1950s featuring Elizabeth Taylor provide narrative solutions to the problems tied to race for white subjects that strive to diffuse the racial panics tied to the emergence of postwar multiculturalism and Black power movements tied to decolonization. Elizabeth Taylor's extrafilmic instability during this period requires the cinematic plantation to allow for her racial discipline that teaches viewers the strictures of proper whiteness as not only empowering, but fulfilling and necessary.

NOTES

1. See Melvyn Bragg, *Richard Burton: A Life,* 163. Georgia Representative Iris Blitch introduced a bill to ban Taylor and Burton from re-entering the United States.
2. Ellis Amburn, *The Most Beautiful Woman in the World: The Obsessions, Passions, and Courage of Elizabeth Taylor*, 152.
3. See Ella Shohat and Robert Stam, *Multiculturalism, Postcoloniality, and Transnational Media,* 14. They discuss the limitations of previous formulations of postcoloniality as just the step after the demise of colonialism.
4. See Ella Shohat and Robert Stam, *Unthinking Eurocentrism,* 100–101. They discuss the birth of cinema coinciding with the emergence of high imperialism in the late nineteenth century. The most prolific film producing states during the silent era were Britain, France, the United States, and Germany, all nations engaged in an imperial race against each other as their film-viewing working-class audiences were also becoming enthralled with the notion of imperial conquest. Films were codifying their sense of national identity through a desire for imperial dominance.
5. Thanks to Curtis Marez for his careful reading of this chapter in its earliest and most rudimentary form and for suggesting the genre be named "hacienda films."
6. See "Film Genre and the Genre Film," 650.
7. Amy Kaplan, *The Anarchy of Empire in the Making of U.S. Culture,* 1.
8. Hernan Vera and Andrew Gordon, "Sincere Fictions of the White Self in American Cinema, 271.
9. See John J. McCusker and Russell R. Menard, *The Economy of British America, 1607–1789 with Supplementary Bibliography*, 137, 173.
10. Henri Lefebvre, *The Production of Space, 57.*
11. Grace Kyungwon Hong, *The Ruptures of American Capital,* 70.
12. Renato Rosaldo, *Culture and Truth: The Making of Social Analysis,* 87.
13. Ibid., 26.
14. See Thomas Schatz, *The Genius of the System,* 19, and his discussion of *United States v. Paramount Pictures* (1948) and its decree that the distribution and exhibition schemes of the Hollywood studios were monopolistic and illegal, forcing the studios'

divestiture. This in turn gave rise to independent studios and producers that helped end the studio system mode of production.

15. See Michael Adas, *Machines as the Measures of Men,* 242–243.

16. Iris Marion Young, *Throwing Like a Girl and Other Essays in Feminist Theory and Social Philosophy,* 143–44.

17. Ibid., 152.

18. See Eugene D. Genovese, *The Political Economy of Slavery,* 32, and his reading of the Black Southern slave's role in making of the slaveholder's identity.

19. Eve Sedgwick, *Between Men: English Literature and Homosocial Desire,* 1–5.

20. Lauren Berlant and Michael Warner, "Sex in Public," 365.

21. See Amy Kaplan, *Anarchy and the Making of U.S. Culture,* 39, and her reading of nonwhites being excluded from domestic nationalisms in the writings of Sarah Josepha Hale.

22. Paul Bowles, *Their Heads Are Green and Their Hands Are Blue,* p. 24.

23. Ibid., 30.

24. bell hooks, *Black Looks Race and Representation,* 25.

25. See Christopher Ondaatje's *A Woolf in Ceylon: An Imperial Journal in the Shadow of Leonard Woolf* as he traces Woolf's adventures as a British civil servant in Ceylon. It maps the formative effects of Ceylon, a place which Woolf described as the site of his rebirth at the age of twenty-four and his exodus from the island after the end of British rule, 24.

26. Melissa Steyn, "White Talk: White South Africans and the Management of Diasporic Whiteness," 125.

27. Lawrence S. Kaplan, *NATO Divided, NATO United: The Evolution of an Alliance,* 5.

28. Bruce Cumings, *The Korean War: A History,* 35.

29. Richard Dyer, *Heavenly Bodies,* 1–16.

30. See "Stars and Genre," 199–202, Britton still asserts that Dyer is conflating "a set of star vehicles" with genres and claims star vehicles are not "like" genres because genres are prior conditions of the vehicle while the vehicle is a distinct highly individuated subset of conventions that accompany the star.

31. Anthony Holden, *Olivier,* 257.

32. See James Rinehart, "Transcending Taylorism and Fordism? Three Decades of Work Restructuring," 180.

33. Kitty Kelley, *The Last Star,* 97.

34. Ibid., 96–98.

35. See "Screen in Review 'Elephant Walk' Opens at Astor Theater" retrieved https://www.nytimes.com/1954/04/22/archives/the-screen-in-review-elephant-walk-opens-at-astor-theatre.html

36. J. Randy Taraborrelli, *Elizabeth,* 38. Universal signs nine-year Taylor to a five-month contract, at one hundred dollars a week.

37. Anthony Holden, *Olivier,* p. 250.

38. See also Christopher Kelen, "Hymns for and from White Australia" and his reading of the Australian national anthem, "Advance Australia Fair" that presents

Australian nationhood as an investment in whiteness and its familial ties to Britain, meaning Australian-ness is also shored up through its sense of British-ness, p. 207.

39. W. David McIntyre, *The Commonwealth of Nations: Origins and Impact, 1869–1971,* 4.

40. See Timothy M. Shaw, *Commonwealth: Inter- and Non-State Contributions to Global Governance,"* x.

41. Anthony Holden, *Olivier,* 295.

42. Gilles Deleuze and Felix Guattari, *Anti-Oedipus,* 272.

43. Warner Bros. Archives contains re-release books for *Giant.* The film makes an additional $12 million for the studio in re-release.

44. Benjamin Schwadran, *Middle East Oil: Issues and Problems,* 72.

45. Franklin Tugwell, *The Energy Crisis and the American Political Economy: Politics and Markets and the Management of Natural Resources,* 118–22.

46. See Dennis Hevesi, "Warren Leslie Dies at 84; Wrote Book That Rankled Dallas "in *The New York Times,* published July 23, 2011. Warren Leslie a former executive at Neiman Marcus publishes *Dallas Public and Private: Aspects of a City* (Southern Methodist University Press) less than four months after the JFK assassination in which he examines the city's right-wing stridency and the dominance of its business elite positing that its sentiments against the US government made the city unable to receive a sitting president.

47. M.M. Bakhtin, *The Dialogic Imagination: Four Essays,* 271–72.

48. To make this point, the film's producers turn Leslie who was a Virginia Southern belle in Ferber's novel into a Maryland blueblood, circumventing the South's history of racism entirely. See Edna Ferber, *Giant,* 55.

49. Charles Ramirez Berg, "Manifest Myth-Making, Texas History in the Movies," 11–12.

50. David Montejano, *Anglos and Mexicans in the Making of Texas, 1836–1986,* 29.

51. Arnoldo De León, *Mexican Americans in Texas,* p. 4.

52. See Douglas Brode, *Multiculturalism and the Mouse: Race and Sex in Disney Entertainment,"* as he asserts that Mineo's casting in *Tonka* imbues the film with a homosexual subtext made explicit through Mineo's relatively open gay lifestyle of which casting directors were well aware, as well as the symbolic triangulation of himself, Rock Hudson and James Dean in *Giant* which further queered his image, 242.

53. Mineo made his first appearance as the Crown Prince in the spring of 1952, after being an understudy for the part of Chulalongkorn for months. He recalls how star Yul Brynner had taught him how to apply his "Oriental" makeup. This scene of making up was probably their first bonding experience. Not only was Brynner an early acting mentor for Mineo, but the younger performer considered the star as his second father. For more on this see Michael Gregg Michaud, *Sal Mineo,* 23–24.

54. Linda Williams, "Melodrama Revised," p.48.

55. Matthew Frye Jacobson, *Barbarian Virtues: The United States Encounters Foreign Peoples at Home and Abroad, 1876–1917,* 3.

56. The 2000 United States Census Bureau states that Texas is the second largest US state, with its "parcel" of 268,581 square miles.

57. *Policing Desire: Pornography, AIDS, and the Media,* 87.

58. Richard Meyer, "Rock Hudson's Body," 279–82.

59. Ibid., 259–60.

60. Meyer notes that he borrowed "anti-body" from Timothy Landers's "Bodies and Anti-bodies: A Crisis in Representation," 282.

61. *Giant* was not only box-office smash in US theaters but received the full backing of the Warner Bros. Studio as the film was exhibited worldwide including its markets in Europe, South America, and Asia. News clippings from the *Giant* international tour are part of its Warner Brothers Archives file and give details of the film's screenings in France, Paraguay, and Hong Kong amongst other locations.

62. I am aware of Norman Mailer's "The White Negro: Superficial Reflections on the Hipster" and that certain forms of coolness are cultural formations predicated on white male appropriations of Black masculinity and Black musical forms such as jazz that are not unproblematic. Dean's performance as Rink can be delineated through Brando as they are both trained in the "Method" of the Actor's Studio. Also, there is the off-screen image of a bongo-playing Dean playing homage to his idol Marlon Brando, whose own image scholars have examined through the white Negro aesthetic, notably Krin Gabbard in "Marlon Brando's Jazz Acting and the Obsolescence of Black Face in his book *Black Magic: White Hollywood and African American Culture.*

63. Production notes from the Warner Brothers Archive reveal the secret recipe for the "oil" used on screen concocted in order to achieve the color and consistency necessary for maximum effect: B.F. Goodrich Chemical Company had made "ersatzoil" for special effects man Ralph Webb from a combination of carbon black, water, and carbopol as a thickening agent.

64. See Matthew Frye Jacobson and his theories of "probationary whiteness" in his *Whiteness of a Different Color.* He discusses whiteness as a privilege bestowed to European immigrants in part to separate and distance them from Blacks. These immigrants in time become fully "white."

65. American Film scholar J.E. Smyth also makes note of Dean in blackface in her article "Jim Crow, Jett Rink, and James Dean: Reconstructing Edna Ferber's *Giant*," 6.

66. Dennis Hopper and Elsa Cárdenas were reportedly romantically involved during production. Their off-screen pairing was used to promote the film in no small part due to its filmic acceptance of interracial marriage between Anglos and Mexicans.

67. José E. Limón, *American Encounters: Greater Mexico, the United States and the Erotics of Culture,* 122.

68. Rafael Perez-Torres, *Mestizaje: Critical Uses of Race in Chicano Culture,* 59–60.

69. *Reconstructing Dixie: Race, Gender, and Nostalgia in the Imagined South,* 39.

70. See John D. Esseks's "Political Independence and Economic Decolonization: The Case of Ghana under Nkrumah," 59.

71. Donald Bogle, *Toms, Coons, Mulattoes, Mammies and Bucks,* 9.

72. Karen Anderson, *Little Rock: Race and Resistance at Central High School,* 2.

73. Steven D. Classen, *Watching Jim Crow,* 44.

74. Mary Ann Watson, *"The Nat 'King' Cole Show" from Encyclopedia of Television, Volume 1 Second Edition,* 1593–94.

75. Daniel Mark Epstein, *Nat King Cole,* 254–61.

76. Michel Chion, *The Voice in Cinema,* 24.

77. See Tara McPherson's *Reconstructing Dixie* and her reading of the collectible, commodified South that ties amongst other things, tourism and *Gone with the Wind,* 4, 39–65.

Chapter 3

"If It Be Love Indeed, Tell Me How Much"

Elizabeth Taylor, Richard Burton, and White Pleasure after Empire

Providing further insight into their romantic pairing, a topic of engrossing and escalating fascination for the global popular media in the early 1960s, Elizabeth Taylor has often delighted in saying that Richard Burton would call her "Ocean" even while admitting that their initial coming together during the filming of *Cleopatra* cost her "oceans of tears."[1] Taylor's nickname from Burton—one she on occasion would use to also describe him—reveals how the fusion of these two figures as an extracinematic duo operated within a logic of excessive desires that charted the vastness of their love but their term of endearment also explained how they were ultimately drowning in their endless compulsions, including their need to be incessant, constant performers.

This chapter explicitly presents postcolonial whiteness as a mutable performative formation to examine the iconicity of Elizabeth Taylor and Richard Burton the actors who reigned as perhaps the most famous movie stars in the world during the latter part of the era of decolonization in the 1960s. I argue that Taylor and Burton function as spectacularized amorous subjects who emote imperial desire as they are forced to renegotiate their relationship to labor and leisure during the last days of the Hollywood studio system. These performers transfix anxious viewers fearing the loss of white power after the end of colonialism through the making of their off screen heterosexual romance, conspicuous consumption, and, of course, their film work in which they play a number of imperial characters in various colonial spectacles. For white subjects encountering the burgeoning postcolonial world, the image of the two stars as lovers on and off the set of *Cleopatra* (1963) in particular allows for the modeling of a new white subjectivity produced through an imperative of unending pleasure and a distantiation from Blackness. In fact, the pairing of Taylor and Burton not only doubles, reflects, and accelerates their significations of imperiality but points to postcolonial whiteness as fundamentally performative.

Richard Burton's complex iconicity is not only bound up with Elizabeth Taylor's image of the 1960s but his filmic roles midcentury are deeply imbricated within the reconfigurations of white power which this larger examination of Taylor is also so concerned. Certainly Elizabeth Taylor's manipulations of femininity as a filmic plantation mistress reveals how American Empire's white subjects are reconfigured through a commitment to a disciplined heteronormativity that is cultivated within the plantation and thrives unbound by the new postcolonial logistics of space and national borders. Taylor's embrace of imperial roles alongside Burton on and off screen also maps the spectrum of the adaptability of postcolonial whiteness as a form of pleasurable performance that confirms and extends white power as expansive and mobile. As whites can easily traverse newly formed national borders, white imperial subjectivity in the 1960s is framed by evasions of Blackness which itself is being remade through global movements of Black liberation. In fact, imperial whiteness becomes a racial masquerade, in the case of Richard Burton a form of colonial mimicry, enacted for white pleasure that works to assuage white racial fears tied to the emergence of Black freedoms. Taylor and Burton perform as whites veering away from the traditional strictures of whiteness namely rationality and self-control even while depicting a coming to greater white power for enraptured audiences fearing its loss.

For Homi Bhabha colonial mimicry exists as an "ambivalence" and must continuously produce its "slippage" to be successful.[2] It is an open contradiction that reveals the configuring of identities through the projection of difference that also operates as a disavowal. He writes in "Of Mimicry and Man,"

> Mimicry is, thus the sign of a double articulation; a complex strategy of reform, regulation and discipline, which "appropriates" the Other as it visualizes power. It is also the sign of the inappropriate, however, a difference or recalcitrance which coheres the dominant strategic function of colonial power, intensifies surveillance, poses an immanent threat to "normalized" knowledges and disciplinary powers.[3]

Bhabha continues:

> Mimicry conceals no presence or identity behind its mask . . . The *menace* of mimicry is its *double* vision which in disclosing the ambivalence of colonial discourse also disrupts its authority.[4]

Of course, mimicry locates the breaks in colonial dominance, as the copy is "almost the same but not quite" and contains both a mockery and a certain "menace" (1994, 86).

Richard Burton's acting is a postcolonial form of colonial mimicry as his stardom hinges on the exposure of the contradictions that undergird his identity without the burden of race. Viewers have him under surveillance in his imperial roles in films and his expressions of imperial desire off screen while he simultaneously promotes working-class Welsh masculinity. This is read as emblematic of masterful performance because it is predicated on the acceptance by the actor and the audience of the mutability of his identity as both colonizer and colonized. Because of and through the use of his phenotypical white body, his acting as such is read as essentially performative.

Richard Burton is rewarded handsomely for his brilliant articulation of the English language in his stage and screen parts as his offscreen persona conjoins the heart of the British literary canon to the oral culture at the crux of his Welsh identity to the delight of audiences and critics. His iconicity as the rags-to-riches Welshman temporally disrupts British colonial power while at its service as he circuitously claims and disavows white imperiality through the delivery of his dual consanguine performances, while his ascendance to film stardom initiates his personal narrative of coming to full-fledged whiteness. His repeated births into imperial whiteness on screen and his close proximity to Elizabeth Taylor's own racial instability of the 1960s make up the compelling and extended duet of racial masquerade that is at times contradictory but always complementary to their respective offscreen performances. They ease apprehensive white subjects by providing a sense of white subjectivity's emerging new forms through performance during this crucial moment of global realignment and white authorial recalibration after the official death of empire. By doing so, they become arguably the biggest stars of the decade.

Richard Burton's mastery of colonial mimicry through his command of English elocution is especially meaningful precisely because the British monarch during his formative years until the very beginning of his rise as a professional actor is King George VI (1895–1952) a well-known stammerer who overcomes his difficulties with public speaking to ascend the throne and head off the constitutional crisis of his brother's abdication.[5] By ably addressing his millions of subjects in Britain and in the Commonwealth particularly through radio, George VI assures the stable continuity of the British Crown and nation to the globe through his able transmission of the English language. As the last Emperor of India and the first Head of the Commonwealth, George VI's articulation of English unites the dozens upon dozens of autonomous polities under British sovereignty that stand in for the Empire after its official demise. The continuing overarching policy of promoting English in the schools of the Commonwealth maintains the linguistic imperialism of the Crown and is one of its most formidable legacies. One pointed example is the extensive use of English as a part of its civilizing project during the British colonial era in India as the English language is viewed as a source for modernizing the country and used to educate a class of Indians to serve as intermediaries between British colonial power and the Natives it governs.[6]

Even while British rule is relatively brief in Africa, English becomes the dominant language as the lack of preparation for a post-colonial education system gives English proficiency an even higher value that it would have otherwise had, particularly in Tanzania. In West Africa, including Ghana and Kenya, education by definition means the ability to read and write English. English is used in entrance exams at the university level barring nonspeakers access to better jobs and livelihoods while members of the postcolonial elite rise to the top of Africa because of their English language abilities.[7] Robert Phillipson, charting the path of how English became a global language, defines English linguistic imperialism as part of the "ideologies, structures, and practices which are used to legitimate, effectuate, and reproduce an unequal division of power and resources (both material and immaterial) between groups which are defined on the basis of language."[8] Richard Burton's stardom is a symbolic extension of this power that moviegoers encounter in cinemas across the world at the height of the postcolonial era of the 1960s as his voice reassures and reminds them of the continuance of British cultural and bureaucratic authority in the world.

RICHARD BURTON BECOMES A STAR

Richard Burton was born Richard Walter Jenkins, Jr., the twelfth child of a Welsh miner named Dic, and Edith, a barmaid who dies of childbed fever, an infection that can be avoided through improved hygiene during childbirth.[9] Born into acute poverty, he is raised by his sister Cecilia in Port Talbot, a steel town where English is spoken. A charismatic young man, his precociousness manifests itself in a love of poetic recitation and a voracious appetite for reading. He becomes the ward of Philip Burton, a Welsh schoolteacher who manages to avoid a life in the coal mines by matriculating at the University of Cardiff. Philip Burton also helps a desperate young Richard to avoid mining through an intensive tutelage that gives him the cultural/linguistic capital to escape the Welsh valleys. While in his care, he not only cultivates Richard's passion for Shakespeare and Dylan Thomas but more importantly teaches him to speak English without a Welsh accent by guiding him through a series of breathing and projecting exercises.

Philip Burton insists that his young ward give full attention to details such as diction, interpretation and delivery and coaches him through long passages of Shakespeare, particularly the monologues. He asserts, "Shakespeare is the best way to learn English . . . and the best way to learn all about acting."[10] With Burton's support, Richard completes a brief stint as a cadet in the Port Talbot Squadron of the Air Training Corps in order to study at Exeter College in the University of Oxford for six months due to a special compensation for young men conscripted to later military service. After fulfilling his duties as a navigator for the Royal Air Force during the war, he quickly takes the name of his adoptive father out of gratitude and finds steady stage and film work in Britain.

Reviewers take notice of Richard Burton's acting talent early on. For his performance in *The Last Days of Dolwyn* (1949), one critic notes that

> Burton has all of the qualifications of a leading man that the British film industry so badly needs at this juncture: youth, good looks, a photogenic face, obviously alert intelligence, and a trick of getting the maximum of attention with a minimum of fuss.[11]

His critically acclaimed performance as Prince Hal in Shakespeare's *Henry IV, Part I* during the 1951 season at Stratford establishes his British stardom. Critic Kenneth Tynan exclaims,

> His playing of Prince Hal turned interested speculation to awe almost as soon as he started to speak; in the first intermission, local critics stood agape in the lobbies.[12]

At this time Burton is already famous for the off-stage persona most familiar to US film audiences: he is the heavy drinking, garrulous Welshman, alive with story-telling and excessive sexual exploits. Eager for financial security, he signs a three-picture deal with 20th Century Fox and stars in *My Cousin Rachel* (1952), *The Robe* (1953), and *Desert Rats* (1953) and is nominated for Academy Awards for his performances in his first two Hollywood films.

Besides Richard Burton's much celebrated tenure on Broadway in 1964 as Hamlet which ran for an unprecedented 136 performances, his famous roles include his Tony Award–winning performance as King Arthur in Lerner and Loewe's musical *Camelot* (1960), reportedly a favorite of John F. Kennedy's that becomes a metonym for his administration and its projects to expand American Empire and rally against Cold War antagonisms through the containment of Vietnam and the conquest of the moon.[13] According to Mary L. Dudziak, while Lyndon Johnson's embrace of Kennedy's civil rights legacy after his assassination secures the foundation for the myth of America's Camelot, US racial discrimination is only a concern for the Kennedy White House when it is perceived as a threat to national security, possibly affecting

US relations with a newly emerging bloc of countries in Asia and Africa who may align with the Soviet Union against the United States because of American racism.[14] In fact, John F. Kennedy is considered by aides to be unconcerned with civil rights when he is elected in 1960. His priorities in office according to Harris Wofford, his chief advisor on civil rights matters during his presidential campaign, continued to be foreign policy, peace, and relations with the Soviet Union.[15] The Kennedy administration's choosing to extend US authority in the world over the pursuit of racial justice on domestic soil coincides with Richard Burton's timely rise as a star of imperial dramas that celebrate the global expansion of white power.

Burton achieves international film fame for his portrayal of Roman general Mark Antony in Joseph L. Mankiewicz's *Cleopatra* (1963) and his performances as Alexander the Great (1956) and King Henry VIII (1969) are well-known. All of these imperial figures exist at a junction between the consolidation of power and its unraveling, and all are performed precisely at a historical moment when imperiality is being reconfigured in the postcolonial social world. Filmically, these flashpoints are represented as crises in masculinity that are resolved through the subordination of the unruly woman which then reestablishes imperial order.

For example, Alexander, the young king of Macedonia, conquers the Persians with the encouragement of his overbearing mother Queen Olympias (Danielle Darrieux) and only through his triumphs as a colonizer and a transmitter of Hellenistic culture in Asia does he finally meet her expectations, assuage her disquieting temper, and overshadow his father's royal legacy. Henry VIII breaks from the Catholic Church to wed and bed the ambitious social-climbing Anne Boleyn (Geneviève Bujold). Hoping to guarantee the survival of his dynasty through the birthing of a male heir, he ultimately beheads her when she fails him and feels only a semblance of domestic tranquility during his short subsequent romance with Jane Seymour (Lesley Paterson). In the case of Cleopatra, the Roman Republic girds itself against the dangerous queen, destroying her and forcibly subsuming Egypt, the site of her cultural transgressions, within the newly established greater Roman Empire.

Richard Burton's role as Mark Antony and his extramarital affair with Elizabeth Taylor on set of *Cleopatra* are of particular interest because their pairing becomes a performative site that shows how imperial desire after empire does not dissipate, but rather claims the white imagination and body as it configures white postcolonial identity through a fetishization of personal power and pleasure. When costar Martin Landau asks Burton about the origins of the affair, he tells him that Taylor's body is intoxicating. Their director Joseph Mankiewicz theorizes about the attraction saying

She was virtually brought up in Hollywood, and she knew how to get what she wanted, and people fell over themselves to give it to her. This is incredible power, and Richard loved that about her. She had a great contract because she had a great head for business, and he was mesmerized just by her contract. You put all that together as well as her staggering beauty and you have a very potent combination of sexual and economic power which Richard clearly found unable to resist.[16]

Burton's inability to resist Taylor and his delirium in her presence is partly a discourse of addiction, a subjectivity that is first socially constructed through British colonialism and the coming of modernity. According to Eve Sedgwick in her reading of Virginia Berridge and Griffith Edwards's work on opium eating, drug use shifts from being a set of acts to a practice that is tied to an identity that emerges from the changing of class and imperial relations and the pervasiveness of medical authority in nineteenth-century Britain.[17] Sedgwick writes that the taxonomic reframing of the drug user to the addict changes the basic terms about him from a subject who operates in relative stability and control to one who is propelled into a narrative of decline and fatality. Burton of course is an actual addict whose excessive drinking ravages his health. While undergoing surgery in February 1981, doctors discover that his entire spinal column is coated with crystallized alcohol.[18] Taylor also seeks treatment for alcohol abuse in 1983 at the Betty Ford Center where the former First Lady becomes her first sponsor.[19] In fact their addictions play no small part in their projections of postcolonial imperiality, perhaps fittingly so as the cultural phenomenon of addiction first emerges during the age of high imperialism and envelopes these two imperial icons in the throes of ecstatic and excessive encounters with postcoloniality a century later.

In particular, Richard Burton's drinking and love for and unwavering fascination with Elizabeth Taylor constitute a discursive body reliant on imperial metaphors to become a narrative of boundless colonizing desire. The couple embodies a compulsive postcolonial whiteness that reorganizes their labor and leisure under the rubric of the constant pursuit of pleasure that rivets audiences. They perform whiteness as a renewing and continuous site of personal power, erotic adventure, and seemingly infinite mobility through the glamorization of sex, outrageous consumption, and globe-trotting. When Richard Burton marries Elizabeth Taylor (the first time) in 1964, he presents her with a suite of emeralds from Rome's famed Bulgari jewelry store and continues to shower her with diamonds throughout their tempestuous eleven years of marriage. These sumptuous gems, including his most famous acquisitions, the Taylor–Burton and the Krupp Diamonds, are her trophies of romantic conquest.[20] But more importantly they are forms of commodity fetishism which according to anthropologist Michael Taussig are the almost magical objects that separate and alienate the worker from his labor and mark Richard Burton's bypassing of the coal mines of Wales to his path of real and imagined imperiality.[21]

An avid diarist, Richard Burton recalls his first encounter with his twice and future wife, Elizabeth Taylor in 1952 at his first Hollywood pool party, years before seeing her again on set in Rome. Burton has her under surveillance and his description is replete with imperial metaphors:

> It was my first time in California and my first visit to a swank house. Wet brown arms reached out of the pool and shook my hand. I affected to become social with the others but out of the corner of my mind—while I played for the others the part of a poor miner's son who was puzzled, but delighted by the attention these lovely people paid to him—I had her under close observation. . . . She was unquestionable gorgeous. . . . She was lavish. She was a dark unyielding largesse. She was, in short, too bloody much, and not only that, she was totally ignoring me . . . I became frustrated almost to screaming.

He continues to write about Taylor on another occasion exclaiming,

> She was famine, fire, destruction, plague, the only true begetter. Her breasts were apocalyptic, they would topple empires before they withered . . . her body was a miracle of construction.[22]

Richard Burton writes the quoted entry twelve years after this foundational encounter with Taylor. Even with hindsight or because of it, he is enthralled by her beauty, and exhilarated as an outsider by his entrance into this exotic and forbidden Hollywood world of "brown arms" and suntanned bodies. His hyperbolic description is akin to the words of the other Richard Burton, the prolific European translator of *The Kama Sutra* (1883) and *A Thousand and One Nights* (1885).

A soldier, explorer, and ethnographer, Captain Richard Francis Burton is a noted British Orientalist during the era of high imperialism and his most famous exploit is his hajj to Mecca in 1853 for which he disguises himself as a Muslim to record the rites prohibited to nonconverts. His observations fuel British imperial fantasies of the racial Other as he and his contemporaries actively participate in the production of discourses that categorize notions of Eastern difference on the basis of linguistics, biology, and culture that captivates the Victorian imaginary.[23] He enters Mecca on September 11 and he finds himself before the huge square catafalque, the Ka'aba, the most sacred site of Islam and exclaims,

There at last it lay, . . . realizing the plans and hopes of many and many a year. . . . Few Moslems contemplate for the first time the Ka'abah without fear and awe.[24]

Captain Burton tries to observe all rites including drinking from the sacred well of Zamzam and the ceremony of Tawaf, the circumambulation of the Ka'aba in imitation of the triumphant Prophet Muhammad when he returned to Mecca as a conqueror after his exile in Medina. The next day following midday prayers, while trying to take notes, Burton writes that he becomes distracted by

A tall girl, about eighteen years old, with regular features, a skin somewhat citrine-coloured, but soft and clear, symmetrical eyebrows, the most beautiful eyes, and a figure all grace. . . . The shape was what the Arabs love, soft, bending, and relaxed, as a woman's ought to be.[25]

He flirts with the girl and claims, "She smiled imperceptibly, and turned away. The pilgrim was in ecstasy." Arguably she is not the only pilgrim in ecstasy.

Historian James Clifford defines travel as a "range of practices, for situating a self in a space or spaces grown too large, a form of both exploration and discipline."[26] I use these two episodes separated in space and time to illustrate the tangibility of masculine imperial desire through the eroticization of the racialized feminine body. Furthermore, both Burtons highlight the role of performance as a form of discipline in the imperial endeavor. The Victorian Burton is a polyglot, purportedly with the ability to speak a dozen languages including Hindustani and Arabic and is taken into imperial service because of his aptitude for languages, his desire for fortune and renown and his eagerness to assimilate amongst nonwhites to gather forbidden (often sexual) knowledge. After all he has himself circumcised in order to pass as a Muslim in preparation for the hajj and to be able to visit Muslim prostitutes while in the Middle East.[27]

ELIZABETH TAYLOR AS AN ORIENTAL IN WHITEFACE

As he foreshadows in his diaries, the postcolonial Richard Burton falls in love with Elizabeth Taylor as Cleopatra when her staggering beauty is framed by her exotic turn. I posit that this gesture is initiated through her encounters with what Toni Morrison calls an "Africanist presence" on the set of *Cleopatra* (1963) itself. She describes Africanism as a term for the denotative and connotative Blackness that African peoples have come to signify as well as the entire range of views, assumptions, readings and misreadings that accompany Eurocentric learning about these people.[28]

It is most often a trope mobilized to help white Americans define modernity, individualism and freedom. Morrison in agreement with sociologist Orlando Patterson asserts that

the concept of freedom did not emerge in a vacuum. Nothing highlighted freedom—if it did not in fact create it—than slavery.[29]

Elizabeth Taylor's persona is reforged and permanently melds with that of the mythic Oriental queen and captivates the public imagination because of her expressions of ecstasy in her newfound freedoms. Her release from an iron-clad MGM studio contract and her ensuing affair with Burton are contrasted against her participation in the production of images of Black bondage, discursively and visually rearticulating white power through scenarios of Black enslavement as commercial entertainment. Her rebirth as a despotic and powerful international superstar follows the representations of her death in various media: on film, in tabloids, and in the set of memento mori portraits of her by Andy Warhol, the *Liz* series (1963) which he produces because he fears for her death.[30]

Elizabeth Taylor's emergence as a white Oriental in multiple media whose hypersexuality and explicitly non-Western glamour on- and off-screen beguiles the public and occurs at the eve of the death of the Hollywood studio system while coinciding with a historic cycle of African independence movements that initiates statehood for seventeen nations on the continent in 1960 alone.[31] This pivotal shift in Taylor's image cites a tradition of the white artist's transcendence into genius during moments of white uncertainty. Here it takes the form of melancholia that follows the loss of imperial power. Its primary effect of grief forms a new imperative of white pleasure and is then expressed within systems of visual representation through narratives of death and rebirth.

These expressions reset the limits of white liberation, best expressed by the celebration of the unhindered pursuit of white revelry most often through and against the presence of Black subjects struggling for freedom. And so often they become "breakthroughs" for white artists and seminal moments in Western art. During this film, Elizabeth Taylor becomes more than just the world's most famous movie star but turns into an extrafilmic iconic figure who orchestrates her break from the archaic modes of labor and image circulation tied to the dead studio system and paves her way to do different cultural work after her tenure as a film actor is over, primarily her AIDS activism, which she begins in the 1980s. This separation between star and studio echoes the nostalgic impulses of *Cleopatra* production discourse that mourns the end of the studios' former imperial dominance through a celebration of its produc- tion values that have then been revised as both highly artistic and artisanal. Not only are the stars of *Cleopatra* representing newly formed white affects and subjectivity at the reconstitution of empire, they are also representing shifting modes of labor and its management, from Fordist to post-Fordist modes of production that affect the extrafilmic discourse surrounding them- selves and their filmic projects.

The photos and the ancillary gossip that follow the onset Taylor–Burton affair as specters during production become objects of commercial exchange within a media landscape that is shifting in correspondence to both the changes in Taylor's image as a sexualized and racialized body—the spectacu- lar racially liminal seductress unencumbered by the bonds of marriage and thriving beyond the control of the studio—and the new trajectories of stardom and vectors of star power that Taylor's particular rise and divorce from the contract system of the studios make possible. The majority of the photos of the two stars together are glimpses into their life off-set, as lovers in and of leisure, often with Elizabeth Taylor still in full Cleopatra makeup.

The most famous photo of the pair which ushers in a seminal shift in the production of candid celebrity photography and its rabid consumption fea- tures a gorgeous Taylor in a frilly bikini with her face and considerable cleav- age facing Burton. He is wearing swim trunks with his back turned to the camera as the couple sun themselves on a yacht off the Italian coast of Ischia. Taken with a telephoto lens by noted photographer Bert Stern most famous for his gallery portraits of Marilyn Monroe, Elizabeth Taylor shows audi- ences that she is always Cleopatra, her face ornately decorated with exotic cosmetics and seducing men on her barge in the Mediterranean even when not filming. Her performance as the unapologetic white Oriental globally markets a fantasy of sexual liberation, at the core of the personal freedom desired by white subjects who do not find the pleasures that are supposedly guaranteed through marriage and work to be enough.

Elizabeth Taylor takes the image of the Oriental woman that has been an object of fantasy in the white Western imagination for centuries to adapt for her own use fully transforming into the exotic figure that Richard Burton fantasizes about in 1952, a formation the preceding Burton marvels about in Mecca in 1853. While the Oriental woman and her perceived uncontrollable licentiousness are tied to foreign spaces of lawless paradise and used to jus- tify their control, the star becomes the Oriental who cannot be controlled.[32] Taylor's inversion of the colonial fantasy of Oriental sexuality functions in ways to give her inordinate amounts of pleasure while tapping into her new- found power to experience the gains produced through her freelancing as a film actor including the astounding fee for *Cleopatra* which she negotiates herself. Photographed adrift on her love yacht, she spectacularizes her trans-national unstoppable sexuality and expands the purviews of white pleasure to be both boundless and borderless for postcolonial whites fearing the loss of power after decolonization.

While in this form, Elizabeth Taylor shoots *Cleopatra*'s most magnificent scene. Richard Burton becomes so hypnotized by her power to enthrall her audience that he speaks for weeks on end about her entrance into Rome sitting atop a fifty-foot tall onyx Sphinx. She is adorned in a gold gown and wears an impressive golden headdress as a throng of slaves pulls her through the Arch of Titus. As she passes through this monument of Western architectural achievement she signifies to viewers everywhere her cinematic rebirth as an Oriental in whiteface. She internalizes, claims, embodies, and projects an earnest yet fantastical image of the exotic Oriental for her own use, ultimately signaling that her whiteness, which marks her as an unruly aberration, is the mask. She ends her outmoded tenure as an American movie princess by crowning herself as a global superstar whose Oriental persona eclipses the power of Hollywood largely because of her mesmerizing extracinematic racial masquerade.[33]

Theorist Edward Said describes Orientalism in several ways, including as "a Western style of dominating, restructuring and having authority over the Orient," and as "a way of coming to terms with the Orient that is based on the Orient's special place in European Western Experience."[34] As is the case of *Cleopatra* and Elizabeth Taylor's remade image concurrent to the film's production, "authority over the Orient" does not only pertain to territorial and administrative jurisdiction but also to representative and discursive powers that reset the Occidental understanding of the Oriental, almost always as a site that provides Western pleasure through experiences of sexual adventure and control. After Taylor is lifted onto a royal sedan and is carried by a group of Nubian slaves she carefully walks down a set of stairs to first bow to Julius Caesar played by Rex Harrison and then to wink at him, showing viewers that she and Cleopatra are both masters of this exotic spectacle. Not only is her physical elevation made possible by the labor of Black bodies as she sits raised in foreground, the scene's visual economy puts the primary focus on her, orienting the viewer away from the black Sphinx statue, which is placed at a distance behind her.

While the blackened sphinx implicitly suggests that Egypt is a cradle of Black African culture, this sequence utilizes a spectacle of Black slavery as both an object of white pleasure and to assert that Blackness only signifies subservience and is purely ephemeral, as the slaves are mobilized mostly for show to highlight Cleopatra's and Elizabeth Taylor's surplus of power to her

Roman rivals and quickly disappear from screen. Even with the sequence's outrageous visual excess, what enraptures the viewer is Taylor dressed in gold in the guise of the Egyptian goddess Isis. In fact during shooting, the director tells the throng of Italian extras to rush to the Sphinx and yell out, "Cleopatra!" When the scene is finally shot, the Italians run to Taylor as ordered, but instead of screaming, "Cleopatra!" they shout, "Leez! Leez! Leez!" Afterward, a thrilled Taylor thanks them in Italian.

Having remade Elizabeth Taylor into a figuration of Isis, the deity who stands in for the Egyptian tributary state, the film which uses Cleopatra as a metonym for Egypt throughout also therefore conflates Taylor's image with that of a fictive Egypt not once but twice. Borrowing a method from simple reductive mathematics since Cleopatra is Isis, and Isis is Egypt, and Elizabeth Taylor is Cleopatra, Elizabeth Taylor is Egypt through a specific visual register that obscures an extensive history of contradictory and imbricated African American identifications with the ancient land as both its bonded slaves and as the proud descendants of the great Black emperors who oversaw the building of the pyramids. Scott Trafton asserts that African American intellectual and spiritual connections to this space as well as Black American transcontinental migrations to and from it, including Frederick Douglass's trek to Egypt in 1887, have spurred American Afrocentrism and helped shore up Black American masculinity as an enabling formation. Members of the mobile Black diaspora of the nineteenth century were ennobled in Egypt and returned from their Eastern sojourns crowned as African American men.[35]

Off-screen, Africa once again becomes a site that enables African Americans and the Black diaspora to access their political power through their work for African anticolonialism from the late 1930s to the late 1950s as they believe their struggles for US civil rights are inextricably linked to liberation struggles on the continent. According to Penny von Eschen, the efforts of global Black Americans including Ralph Bunche, W. E. B. Du Bois, and others during the inception of the United Nations in the 1940s and the ensuing work for the liberation of Ghana in 1957 particularly shape and contextualize the fight for African American civil rights and help reformulate models of global and American democracy.[36] But by the early 1960s, Hollywood's *Cleopatra* appropriates Africa to initiate a narrative of proper whiteness and white domination.

To this effect, Elizabeth Taylor's Cleopatra embodies the visual signs of the decadent, dark non-Western Other by adapting the iconography of ancient Egyptian art wearing countless body-conscious goddess gowns and wigs. Taylor as Cleopatra continues her reign as a '60s beauty ideal through her projection of hyperfeminine indulgences that makes over her face and body with intensely vibrant and hypercommodified cosmetics and resplendent jewelry. She was the American Dream Girl in the 1950s, the dark beautiful woman whose looks were commensurate with the highest echelon of capi-talist success, a feminine trophy worth killing and dying over in *A Place in the Sun* (1951). Here she is an Oriental queen in whiteface who graphically blots out the possibilities of expressing the decade's most powerful axiom of "Black is beautiful" that helps inspire and sustain the fight for US Black liberation and equality in the social world outside the screen.

Still, in this particular iteration of the mythic queen, Cleopatra's body is also a split white form. While composed of a partially Hellenistic subjectivity and a white phenotype it is also self-constructed to represent difference. The film represents Egyptian culture as strange, decadent and excessively femi-nine purposefully setting itself apart from the stable white masculinity of the Roman Republic. The Republic wary of the dangers of Cleopatra's unruly, racially-liminal body must make itself into the Empire precisely because it fears being vulnerable to or compromised by this notion of "Egypt" and its "associations with chaos, uncertainty and the uncanny."[37] The Romans con-sider Cleopatra's feminine Egyptian-ness, and particularly her sexual allure as explicitly dangerous to masculine Roman identity evoking the off-screen anxiety caused by the gradual freeing up of women's sexuality in the 1960s considered threatening because it potentially dilutes masculinity. For instance, after demonizing Cleopatra for being a sexy woman throughout the film, Octavian takes over her palace in Alexandria with his retinue of Roman soldiers. When he finds a dead Apollodorus, who has committed suicide by ingesting poison, he describes his discovery of the dead white slave by saying, "Strange people. Poisons that smell like perfume." Perfume is con-sidered an accouterment in the service of feminine seduction, a tool wielded by women in the craft of bewitching and befuddling men. In this instance, perfume is actually a poison and symbolizes the collapsing of pleasure and death onto a feminized enslaved white man and makes Egypt, where such a conflation is possible, all the more dangerous for men in which their once stable racial and gender superiority cannot protect them from enslavement. Because of this they must put it under Roman control.

Appollodorus's mistress, a self-described "almost all-Greek thing" and Elizabeth Taylor are both "white," but even as this Egypt conclusively splits from Blackness through the deployment of her body, I assert that the Egyptian queen and the star who portrays her are still "not as white" as scholars have previously assumed. She is more than simply the "white grotesque" that characterizes Francesca T. Royster's reading of Taylor's Cleopatra who argues that the star's bodily excesses are analogous with Hollywood decay. Nor is she just the white Cleopatra to be read oppositionally against Tamara Dobson's Black Cleopatra Jones as Ella Shohat has done.

Elizabeth Taylor's Cleopatra insists on political, economic, and cultural reciprocity with the masculine sphere of the Roman Republic, a new world order with Rome and Egypt as dual centers of the ancient geopolitical universe and, more significantly, a melding of Eastern and Western culture, characterized by the intermarriage of the Western Roman man (Antony) and the Eastern Egyptian woman (Cleopatra). Identity, including race, is represented as anchored through cultural practices rather than visual phenotypes since Cleopatra and the Romans look white, but to the Roman imagination Cleopatra signifies insoluble differences through her gender and culture that re-racializes her whiteness and her aggressiveness as improper. The space which Taylor inhabits on screen is a speculative site that refuses to suture the rupture between East and West and becomes a metaphor for the forced split between Black and white subjects in the social world contemporary to the film's production. In fact, *Cleopatra* reenacts a race war using white bodies, with the victors calibrating the meaning and strictures of proper whiteness.

The film directly references Cleopatra's Greek lineage as a Ptolemaic princess as her royal line directly descends from one of Alexander the Great's trusted Macedonian generals, Ptolemy, once a coded allusion to proper whiteness used now to devalue her liminal racial identity and argue against her suitability for power. When Cleopatra angrily berates Caesar after Roman troops accidently set fire to the Great Library of Alexandria, she forcefully delineates Egypt's linkage to Greece as cradles of Western culture and Egypt's role as a sanctuary of ancient learning. This conjoining of Egypt and Greece has long been a strategy taken up by scholars who use Egypt to present both a Eurocentric and Afrocentric view of history.[38] And in the film the Library is an archive of both Eastern and Western knowledge containing the manuscripts of Aristotle, the Platonic commentaries, histories, plays, and even the "Testament of the Hebrew God" according to her teacher Sosigenes (Hume Cronyn). It was meant to be the film's other emblem of the symbiotic fusion of Eastern and Western culture. But the loss of the Library, one of the film's signifiers of a new world order that incorporates the values of the Eastern and Western spheres represents the impossibility of such world-making.

Furthermore, the film makes continuous strategic emphases on Cleopatra's/ Elizabeth Taylor's violet eyes to argue that her visual whiteness even as a marker of her Hellenistic origins cannot override her hyperfemininity and racial instability. Cleopatra is seen applying expressive makeup, often blue or green eyeshadow contrasted against extended black kohl eyeliner encircling her eyes that put focus on their color. The color is referenced again in a scene in which she spies on Caesar through a peephole cut through an artistic rendering of her violet eyes on a palace wall. This doubly cites Cleopatra's visual whiteness as well as Taylor's off-screen chromatic iconicity precisely when she peers through an enormous graphic depiction of her eye in a closeup. She watches intently as Caesar and his men strategize ways to maneuver Egypt for further Roman use and discuss its queen's numerous aberrations including her intellectualism and rampant sexuality.

The foregrounding of Cleopatra's eyes also evoke the blue eyes of Faruq I (1920–1965), the extravagant penultimate king of Egypt who is deposed in the Egyptian Revolution of 1952 led in part by Egypt's future president Gamal Abdel Nasser. The king is infamous for his ostentatious lifestyle, including his vast collections of cars, rare coins, and pornography. While in power, his enormous appetite for food, womanizing, and political incompetence mortifies the Egyptian public.[39] The extrafilmic Oriental as played by Taylor aligns quite well with Faruq's iconic image of relentless indulgence. Her casting in the role while still speaking to the body of Cleopatra as a site of struggle for both Eurocentrists and Afrocentrists in their projects of racializing Egypt to suit their political needs also links it to an actual historical figure who intrigues the Western European imagination, not so much because he is partly European himself, with an Albanian ancestor as the founder of his dynasty, but because he is an Oriental unfit to rule his land. His conjuring through Elizabeth Taylor further allows the film's representation of Egypt as suitable for white colonization. [40]

For Ella Shohat, the film's use of blue eyes, whether they are a direct reference to Cleopatra's, Faruq's, or Elizabeth Taylor's actual eyes, unequivocally signal white authority, signified through Cleopatra's ability to see without being seen and best expressed through the film's power to erase the Blackness of Egypt itself.[41] Even so, for Shohat, the Black Cleopatra Jones (Tamara Dobson), while operating "through a subversion of Hollywood's racialized dream factory" that mythologizes whiteness as a signifier of beauty and goodness, and bearing the signs of the Black Power Movement with her "Afro hairstyle, clenched fist and dashiki clothing," still works within the film's overdetermined US nationalism that functions to maintain the existing social order, symbolized by the CIA headed by her white male boss.[42][43]

Elizabeth Taylor herself at this time is a public figure who embodies a notion of whiteness as a set of gradations, presenting it as an identity that must be secured through the performance of cultural acts exactly at a historical moment when white power and the subjectivities it anchors must be redefined after the official end of colonialism. Her precarious whiteness off screen is routed through the pursuit of pleasures that exist outside the strictures of normative white identity, notably self-control. She becomes the flesh for fantasy of whites who yearn for the gratification and bliss that they imagine non-white bodies must experience, including the Oriental and the liberated Black subject, possibly at their expense. While proper whiteness must be ensured through the following of cultural codes, both Taylor and Cleopatra refuse to do so. In fact, Taylor's off-screen life invites readings of her various adventures at this juncture as those of a race traitor.

Elizabeth Taylor's well-publicized conversion to Judaism in 1959 during her marriage to singer Eddie Fisher, much to the dismay of her disapproving mother, spurs the writing of anti-Semitic hate mail and posters for her hit film *Cat on a Hot Tin Roof* (1958) which bear her image are emblazoned with the word "Jewess."[44] Taylor herself is frequently quoted as saying, "As a kid I had a Walter Mitty dream about being Jewish and wished I was," an aspiration that precedes her actual conversion and unequivocally sets the affective values of the claiming of her new, historically minoritarian identity through a subjectivity now comprised partially through the notion of bell hooks's theory of "eating the other."[45] For dominant white subjects seeking pleasure, eating the other often functions to color the blanched landscape of dull whiteness through encounters with fantasies of the primitive and a return to innocence.[46] Perhaps more unsettling and (titillating) for some American audiences is Elizabeth Taylor's friendship with fellow star Sammy Davis, Jr. another famous Jewish convert whose romantic relationships with white women and adopted religion means that his image like Taylor's is formed in part through his racial and sexual transgressions, including what can be read at times as his distantiations from Blackness.

For Davis, as a Black performer whose cultural emergence precedes the civil rights movement by three decades and who was living under the constant threat of racial violence, his 1954 Jewish conversion can be read as the proactive claiming of an assimilationist identity that otherwise was historically and politically not available to him. For 1950s white Americans and filmgoers, Jewish identity had already been presented as a social formation of workable white assimilation in a cycle of films including the critically acclaimed *Gentleman's Agreement* and *Crossfire* (both 1947) coinciding with the founding of Israel. Elizabeth Taylor's film *Ivanhoe* in 1952 can be loosely considered the tail end of the cycle, in which anti-Semitism is criticized as not only detrimental to state unity but made visible as an unfortunate social and historically based reality through its foregrounding in Crusades-era Britain.

While Davis converts soon after losing his eye, which is officially narrated as the result of a near fatal automobile accident, there exists a compelling alternate Black historiographic discourse that claims Davis was blinded as punishment for his sexual relationships with white women including Jean Seberg and Kim Novak.[47] During his life, Davis often describes himself as a "one-eyed Negro Jew." He uses his reconfigured identity to his advantage, a twisted logic that is exploited for crass humor in the film *Ocean's 11* (1960) in which Davis as Josh Howard says he "knew this color would one day come in handy someday " as the white characters are blacking up before their heist. In real life he cultivates his stereo-blindness or mono-vision, his inability to see dimensions through his work as a roving photographer and uses it to aesthetically re-vision moments in Hollywood and Black America through the viewfinder of his camera. Not only does he shoot candid moments on and off stage and set with friends and luminaries such as fellow members of the Rat Pack, Marilyn Monroe, and Elizabeth Taylor, he becomes a social documentarian of significant and lost moments in Black American life, photographing Martin Luther King, Jr., actors Ossie Davis and Cicely Tyson, as well as his Black roadies and the anonymous Black fans he meets in his role as star and photographer that gives him access to spaces that white photographers in a segregated America did not traverse.[48] While it is uncertain if Davis's unique visioning of space was actually the result of outright racial violence, his choice to navigate pre-Civil Rights era America as a Jewish convert speaks to the overarching tendency of forced adaptability that characterizes his life. This is especially significant as he lives his life at an accelerated pace, a man who began his career performing in vaudeville as a child with his father and who must have been aware that Black men in America often do not live long lives. In fact contemporaries such as Nat King Cole and Jackie Robinson his fellow Black pioneers, work, suffer, and die appallingly young (Cole dies in 1965 age forty-five while Robinson dies in 1972, age fifty-three) having never lived long enough to fully enjoy the gains of legalized Black citizenship which is achieved in the mid 1960s after the passing of the Voting and Civil Rights Acts.

For Elizabeth Taylor, a self-taught Method actor who cannibalizes melodramatic affects from her personal life for her film work and vice versa, her conversion gives her open access to a trove of historical experiences of collective suffering and oppression that she otherwise could not have as an upper-middle-class Anglo-Saxon Christian (Scientist) woman. Her newfound Jewishness also helps shift perceptions of her as merely a beautiful film princess to one that producers of prestige projects can rely on to deliver rousing dramatic performances. As her roles in the first half of the 1950s can be largely characterized as one-dimensional pretty girl parts in forgettable romances such as *Love is Better Than Ever* (1952), *The Girl Who Had Everything*, and *Rhapsody* (both 1954), her claims and proximities to Jewishness through her marriages to Jewish men accompany her as she actively begins pursuing and successfully playing more serious dramatic roles including that of Leslie Benedict in *Giant* written by Jewish author Edna Ferber who creates the part of Leslie as a stand-in for herself as a perennial outsider, which Taylor ably plays as a fish out of Texas water. Correspondences between Ferber and director George Stevens indicate the author's deep interest in this film adaptation, unlike other Hollywood treatments of her novels as she was kept abreast of happenings on set. While Ferber's feelings about Taylor's casting in the part is unknown, which was originally designated for Grace Kelly, Taylor's successful performance of what can be read as a Jewish role begins a major transition in her career that leads to her first Academy Award in 1960.

According to Francesca T. Royster and her fascinating reading of an October 1964 article in *Photoplay Magazine* which features a cover story detailing Taylor's friendship with Davis and his white wife, May Britt, "The Friendship That Everyone [is] Talking About," the story and photos which accompany the article imply both miscegenation and wife-swapping. But while Taylor's relationship with Burton is under great media scrutiny, it is not fraught with the dangers the highly visible Davis and Britt face since interracial marriage is legally forbidden in a majority of states at the time the article is published. The socializing foursome who frequent each other's parties and appear in benefits together are linked through what Royster calls a "guilt by association." They in her estimation, are "phenotypic misfits," and Taylor in particular is a "white Negro."[49]

The actual racial identity of the historical Cleopatra not withstanding, the reimagining of Cleopatra's race through Taylor's racial and sexual transgressions assuage white fears of Blackness through a displacement onto her explicitly non-Black but racialized body. As an Oriental in whiteface rather than a white Negro, her performance of identity is an amalgamated whiteness contoured through discourses of the exotic and aberrant that sanctions her ebullient pursuit of pleasure.

THE GHOSTING OF CLEOPATRA

For Royster, Elizabeth Taylor as Cleopatra is a white grotesque who is "synonymous with the increasingly outdated excesses of the Hollywood epic" which she figures through the "deterioration of [Taylor's] body" (2003, 27). But Elizabeth Taylor's body could not be so grotesque. After all, Royster and her publishers Palgrave Macmillan decide to use an image of Taylor's Cleopatra for the front and back covers of her book both approving of and financially benefitting from an image that she argues as abject. While Taylor did fall into a brief coma during filming, her body certainly was not deteriorating. She is thirty-one years old at the time of the film's release and a global sex symbol who spurs a major beauty and fashion trend in the 1960s due her iconic turn as Cleopatra. Her physical recovery during this time cements her legend as an invincible body.[50] With many fans having forgiven her sexual dalliances and praying for her life, her surviving the health scare during the making of *Cleopatra* both renews audiences' affection for her and allows Hollywood to show its full acceptance of her star power as she is finally given the Academy Award for Best Actress after four consecutive nominations.[51] Elizabeth Taylor very much enjoys adding to her myth by telling listeners tales from her greatest near-death experience for many decades thereafter.

Royster goes to some lengths to commend Black Cleopatras such as Josephine Baker for "harnessing the Cleopatra legend" to signify what she calls "divahood," a trope from African American queer culture which she reads as the strategic use of a greater performative self to protect oneself from persecution (2003, 15). She praises Baker's management of the incessant battles with the racial delimitations of her life and the demands of constantly becoming "something" by reinventing herself through her embodiment of Cleopatra. While reading Taylor's work she bemoans it as a form of "ghosting," meaning the residue from Taylor's performance haunts future iterations of the role. Rightly, Royster is uneasy with Taylor's iconic turn as Cleopatra because of its erasure of Blackness and its potential power to eclipse all other versions of the queen, Black, white, or even Egyptian (2003, 115).

But Elizabeth Taylor's portrayal of Cleopatra is still more complex. While Elizabeth Taylor ascends to the top of the pop cultural stratosphere and survives the death of the studio system and the limitations of studio-sustained stardom, her status as Western culture's most famous Cleopatra can also be read as self-expressed desire for gender justice as a woman star. Her achievement in this fabled role is made possible by her onscreen performance as well as her masterful strategic navigations of the strictures of labor and gender dictated by Twentieth Century Fox, a bastion of mismanagement under the leadership of men who are wary of Taylor's burgeoning power. In defiance of the male-centered power structure of Hollywood, her insistence in accessing her own authority as a global star through director and photo approval and her enormous salary with its shrewdly negotiated extras are well earned and clearly deserved. Not only does a global audience wish to pay to see Taylor in movies and magazines, but like Cleopatra she stands unafraid of the cabal of men who want to control her and her image. She defies the heads of film firms which have made billions of dollars through their unyielding control of the representations of femininity often at the women performers' expense as a plethora of tragic female star narratives attest. While adopting a Cleopatra image becomes an enabling projection for Josephine Baker, it empowers Elizabeth Taylor to make the necessary strides to construct and secure her off-screen persona, to author her iconicity and continue to function and circulate as a performer and symbol even after the death of the studio system.

THE SELLING OF CLEOPATRA

The fact remains that the ocularity of Elizabeth Taylor's image as Cleopatra and the racial fantasy of sexualized white Orientalism that it represents is what makes the film engrossing for audiences, the top box-office earner in 1963.[52] White women in particular who wish to look like Taylor does in

Cleopatra trigger a major phase of Egyptomania in the United States and other Western nations. This craze interpolates her racial transgressions by commodifying her sexuality as an enticing site of previously unknown personal freedoms. Elizabeth Taylor as Cleopatra inspires trends in fashion and cosmetics that sell not only the queen as a signifier of an Oriental seducer of men, but Elizabeth Taylor's status as 1960s sexual icon, an unstoppable woman who intoxicates men and turns them into her successive husbands during the decade in which women first begin to experience the new sexual agencies tied to the commercialization of the birth control pill.[53]

Many of the objects inspired by Cleopatra evoke Taylor's image as a beautiful woman to argue that these products, which vary from the luxurious to the banal, are endowed with the same seductive powers of Cleopatra and Taylor to bend men to a woman's will. The film becomes the source of inspiration for evening gowns designed by Oleg Cassini, Virginia Wallace, and Samuel Robert. Modernist day dresses with graphic abstract prints and geometric haircuts by Vidal Sassoon also reference the looks from the film. Alexandre of Paris, a celebrity hair stylist and personal friend of Taylor's, invents a mini-Cleo half-up do. Millstein, a New York clothing manufacturer makes faux leopard and cheetah skin coats and Whiting & Davis puts out a collection inspired by the jewels of Cleopatra that of course includes a snake coil cuff.

US cosmetics giant Revlon produces Sphinx Pink lipstick claiming that "any other pink is positively pallid" along with Sphinx eye shadows and directions to ensure the proper application of the elaborate designs that Taylor wears in the film. The reference to "pallid" is striking here, since even as the film insists on deploying a phenotypically white Cleopatra, the notion of pale/pallid lips or a pallid Oriental seductress is framed as undesirable. There are Cleopatra inspired tunics and swimsuits for the Mexican market undoubtedly to ensure great tans, another safeguard against pallid Cleopatras. While an absolutely white Cleopatra remains unacceptable, as Taylor's casting in the role and the Revlon ad both assert, a Black Cleopatra is still impossible. In this moment of global Black liberation, the Black Cleopatra remains invisible and unrealized as Rouben Mamoulian's proposal of casting Dorothy Dandridge instead of Elizabeth Taylor is ignored.[54] And advertisements tied to this Cleopatra trend feature only white models, marking its designated demographic as white women.[55]

This early 1960s phase of selling Cleopatra is a postcolonial form of what Melani McAlister calls commodity Orientalism.[56] It is a phenomenon that was once associated with post-Victorian norms present in the early twentieth century that produced discourses linking the emancipated New Woman, companionate marriage, modernity, and consumerism. Orientalism in the previous form was a cultural logic that helped Americans symbolically break from the bleakness of nineteenth-century piety and come into modernity. The East spoke to what was missing within the American work ethic and what Americans longed for, elements the Orient with its sexual iconography provided. The purchasing power of consumerism provided opportunities for reverie and pleasure that were not produced through working hard.

Scott Trafton in his survey of American Egyptomania in the nineteenth century argues that images of ancient Egypt that proliferated through American culture were explicitly linked to the nation's anxieties about race and slavery, even as ancient Egypt was used as a signifier for American Empire and US aspirations. In fact, the making of an American identity was being actively manufactured in the nineteenth century through white and Black visions of ancient Egypt. Even while white Americans fiercely admired the power of the ancient land since it was a great empire built through the labor of slaves, both white and Black Americans closely identified with its captive victims.[57] Discourses about the end of ancient Egypt also narrate a grand scenario of the death of empire that results from race-mixing which annihilates Egyptian subjectivity, a cautionary tale for both Antebellum white Americans of the 1860s and postcolonial white subjects of the 1960s so fearful of race and newly liberated Black subjects.[58]

The Egyptomanic commodity fetishism initiated by Elizabeth Taylor as Cleopatra signals desires for greater white pleasure devoid of the anxieties tied to race, primarily that Black freedoms impede on white power. For white women a revaluation of their sexuality mobilizes racial masquerade as a safe and pleasurable form of women's style cast through a 1960s frame. But through the ensuing joys of sex and consumption, the process of Oriental commodification with its promises of feminine indulgences actually attempts to structure the further disciplining of the female body to enable or sustain white heterosexual marriage as one French magazine layout claims that Cleopatra makeup "will create eyes that captivate husbands." Still for white women seeking opportunities to openly express their sexuality with the men they desire to be with, items such as clothing, jewelry, and cosmetics and the advertising magic that is attached to them promises success and a reliable source of hope and pleasure. The image of Cleopatra as a rabid consumer, as a collector of beautiful objects on screen as well as Elizabeth Taylor's public life of outrageous accumulation are counterpoints to the staid discourse of anticommunist ideology at the time and alleviate some of the anxieties surrounding proper consumption produced during the Cold War. This must have been particularly true for a majority of women who are forced to have intimate relationships with responsible consumerism as the careful managers of household budgets. This new white Orientalism allows them a powerful space of fantasy, a way to escape the strictures of domesticity and gender and to imagine an exotic and luxurious life elsewhere.

ELIZABETH TAYLOR, RICHARD BURTON, AND THE MEANING OF CONSUMPTION

Elizabeth Taylor and Richard Burton's open pursuit of pleasure is best signified through spectacular sexualized consumption and organizes the public lives and codifies the personas of the duo as not only erotic legends but exemplars of postcolonial whiteness. They demonstrate that whiteness after the end of colonization can remain as a sanctuary against the imagined loss of white power and pleasure through the active restructuring of work and play and a symbolic marriage of the two that openly celebrates capitalism. Many speculate that the Taylor–Burton affair began in part because the shooting of *Cleopatra* was so mismanaged and overextended that the two actors became idle and bored enough to fall in love. Reportedly, the cost of bottled water for the cast and crew exceeded $100,000 a week.[59] Their relationship is in part a reaction to their dissatisfactions with their work, as they must find gratification elsewhere when their labor fails to provide them with satisfaction. Their life of conspicuous consumption is a rejoinder in a sense as well, a method of producing contentment for themselves and for their audience when filmmaking, the process through which they must deliver their official performances becomes less interesting, less rewarding, less challenging, and less exciting.

Elizabeth Taylor and Richard Burton's consumption is glaring even within the surplus logic of exchange value, which dictates that capitalism always manages to naturalize the notion of continuous work not through necessity but for the purpose of always producing capital.[60] Michael Taussig examining the experiences of South American copper miners newly initiated into capitalism details how these workers have used images of the devil in order to "exorcise" their subjugation under capitalism. Anthromorphizing their enslavement in the figure of the devil, a symbol of evil, their use of the devil reifies the logics of market exchange as unnatural especially when it insists on the undermining of social unity in favor of systems that produce profits.

Elizabeth Taylor and Richard Burton spectacularize rabid consumption to show capitalism as a system whose rate of escalation is unrelenting. Rather than being subsumed under capitalism's insistence on exploiting the worker, Taylor and Burton spend money and manage to make more, never escaping the system but staying it seems, one step ahead, which for spectators is exhilarating. Their combined film grosses in 1967 was $200 million, which one industry advisor estimates was half of the US film industry's income at the time. With some of their earnings they buy a ten-passenger twin-engine de

                        Chapter 3

Figure 3.1. Richard Burton and Elizabeth Taylor on the set of *Cleopatra* **celebrating her 31st birthday. Source: Gamma-Keystone/Keystone-France/Getty Images.**

Havilland jet for $1 million named *Elizabeth*; his and hers Rolls-Royces; 685 acres on Tenerife in the Canary Islands where they grow bananas; ten acres in County Wicklow, Ireland; where they breed horses; an estate in Puerto Vallarta, Mexico, dubbed Casa Kimberley; homes in Hampstead, England, and Céligny and Gstaad, Switzerland; and paintings by Utrillo, Monet, Picasso, van Gogh, Renoir, Rembrandt, Pissarro, Augustus John, Rouault, and Degas. Burton also reportedly supported forty-two people at one time, including his brothers and sisters.[61]

As Michael Taussig notably asserts, "the exchange ratios of commodities mediates and determines the activities of people. Hence social relations between persons become disguised as social relations between things."[62] The outrageous spending of Taylor and Burton while framed as expressions of romantic love also provides an accounting ledger for the management of their newly realized freedoms as non-contract actors. This renavigation of their labor through its fusion with leisure is the consequence of the transition from

Fordism to post-Fordism that follows the end of the assembly-line mode of industrial filmmaking after the divestiture of the studios.

Arguably, as a nine-year-old with a film contract, Elizabeth Taylor is an archetypal film studio professional, who while firmly entrenched within the system feels both the acute alienation from the end of that mode of labor even as she felt hostility towards its methods of labor management and discipline.[63] Taylor, a former prodigy, as an adult becomes an amiable and brilliant film professional of the highest degree who once astonishes a director by knowing how far away in yards the film camera was set from her by the intensity of the lights hitting her cheeks.[64] During the filming of an adaptation of Shakespeare's *The Taming of the Shrew* (1967), she works closely with the shorthanded makeup unit and applies cosmetics to her costars and extras at five o'clock in the morning. While filming a particularly emotional scene for *Virginia Woolf,* which requires for her to cry, understandably a source of anxiety for many actors, she patiently films the sequence twice for the infuriated Mike Nichols who realizes he cannot use the previous take because a crew member had fallen asleep. After hearing him snoring on the monitors and deciding to fire him, the director relents when Taylor asks to save the man's the job and summons her emotions to film the scene again.[65] In fact, Nichols was continuously awed by her virtuosity and professionalism saying, "Elizabeth can keep in her mind fourteen dialogue changes, twelve floor marks and ten pauses—so the cutter can get the shears in and still keep the reality." She also learned twenty-six pages of dialogue one weekend and showed up "very well-prepared" to set, according to screenwriter Ernest Lehman.[66]

Elizabeth Taylor's resentment toward film studio heads and executives is well-known, having stood up to MGM's Louis B. Mayer for bullying her mother when she was seventeen years old, and despising the studio for forcing her to film *Butterfield 8*, a film she hates even after winning an Oscar for her performance as Gloria Wandrous. Often referring to it as "Butterball 8" because she considers it a "turkey," her disdain for the film began because the studio had, in Taylor's understanding, unfairly voided its gentlemen's agreement with her husband the late Mike Todd, who verbally negotiates with MGM to end Taylor's contract after *Cat on a Hot Tin Roof.* She is forced to make the film because MGM threatens to prevent her from filming with any studio for two years and only relents because she is eager to shoot *Cleopatra.*[67] She also likely hates the film because she plays a high-class call girl, a clear reference to her off-screen expressions of unabashed sexuality during her coupling with Eddie Fisher (who has a small role in the film) that titillates audiences, invites their scorn, and is exploited by MGM in the film's advertising that featured the star naked wrapped only in a white sheet on a poster which read, "The most desirable woman in town and the easiest to find . . . Just call BUtterfield 8."[68]

Elizabeth Taylor's love of film sets, and affection and respect for and from film crews and her costars is somewhat less known perhaps since as a woman star, her scrums with studio executives can be used to better publicize her film projects as well as to construct her image as a difficult worker, like other powerful women performers who have preceded her. To quote Bette Davis whose legendary battle against Warner Bros. Studios sends her to court in England in 1936 to wrestle control of her career, "In this business, until you're known as a monster, you're not a star."[69] The woman star as monster is not only a canonical trope of stardom but deployed as a punitive measure by studios when women performers are perceived as unruly, thought to be acting up against their bosses when they are actually acting out to try to have greater control of their working conditions, often because they desire to make better movies as in the case of Davis, who wanted more agency in her choice of scripts and roles.

Just as daunting is the alienation that Richard Burton feels through his very singularity. His status as the first man in his family in multiple generations to escape the mines through his meteoric rise as an actor is both thrilling and isolating.[70] He counters his separation from the traditional trajectory of men's work through the repetitive valorization of his father's mining as the idealized formulation of Welsh masculinity, comparing his father's skill to that of a surgeon.

Burton is a guest on *The Dick Cavett Show* in 1981 when he speaks of mining in Wales. Not only does he elevate his father's mining as if it were a profession, he claims that his oldest brother who had gone down into the mines at age thirteen and retired at age sixty-five, loved coal mining his entire life even though he dies of black lung disease, Coal worker's pneumoconiosis. He also speaks admiringly of the Great Atlantic Fault which according to the actor produced a coal face that ran from northern Spain to Wales and Pennsylvania suggesting it united coal miners across borders before the age of mechanization. To Burton these figures were all brave, skilled, and pure masculine men who masterfully performed work that was tremendously difficult and dangerous without the aid of machines. For Richard Burton coalmining is significant because it imbues Welsh masculinity with its heartiness, traditions, and authenticity disavowing that it organizes and exploits the poor men of Britain and the Commonwealth to help the Crown come into industrialization and remain economically dominant in the world.

While the South American miners' inventive use of the devil in their dealings with capitalism prove invaluable to anthropologist Michael Taussig's work on commodity fetishism, Burton also deploys images of the devil in his own work multiple times, including in his only foray as a director, making a film version of Christopher Marlowe's *Doctor Faustus* (1966) that he stages with Nevill Coghill at the Oxford Dramatic Society. In the film, Burton plays the titular Faustus who sells his soul to the devil in exchange for knowledge and beauty, promising to join him in hell after twenty-four years of world renown as a brilliant scholar and the lover of Helen of Troy, played by Elizabeth Taylor.

A passion project that he undertakes with his beloved mentor, its narrative demonizes Burton's off-screen desire for fame and fortune, allowing him to conjure the devil in these instances as avowed acts which symbolically punish him for putting into practice what he famously tells Laurence Oliver, to the elder actor's dismay, that he would like to be *both* a "household name and a great artist." The story's punitive bent falls in line with the primary criticisms surrounding the latter half of Burton's career, mostly his collaborations with Taylor excepting *Who's Afraid of Virginia Woolf,* that have insisted that he foolishly pursued global fame at the expense of his art, squandering his stagecraft to act in bad films for big money.

Richard Burton's fixation on the notion of a damning compact with the devil suggests the strain of his separation from traditional modes of Welsh masculinity through his adoption of an imperial whiteness. The potential of any spiritual bankruptcy that results from the pursuit of power is briefly glimpsed through Burton's portrayal of Henry VIII who regrets his excommunication from the Catholic Church but accepts it as punishment for securing his dynasty. Certainly, many have chastised Richard Burton for his pursuit of fortune, but general disdain for his choice to become a member of the nouveau riche speaks more to the anxieties of the middle and upper classes of Burton's unique case of class mobility than the working poor's fears of newfound freedoms and great wealth, which Burton, before his employment as an actor, certainly was. Most likely, too, Richard Burton can only express the strangeness of the extraordinary change in his fortunes from film acting by his choice of magically devilish projects. With *Doctor Faustus* and *Hammersmith Is Out* (1972), yet another retelling of the Faust tale, it is quite possible that Richard Burton uses the devil to not only exorcize his guilt for becoming outrageously rich but to explain how very improbable both his rise as an international performer and the extended period for which he and his wife maintained global interest as the world's most fascinating stars would seem.

Elizabeth Taylor and Richard Burton manage to band together, as least for an extended period of time to travel extensively throughout Europe, making notable stops in Paris after befriending members of aristocratic Rothschild family and in Yugoslavia after Burton grows close to Josip Broz Tito and agrees to portray him in *The Battle of Sutjeska* (1973).[71] The couple also goes to Africa to shoot *The Comedians* (1967) in Dahomey (now Benin) and to remarry on the grounds of Chobe National Park in Botswana in 1975.[72] Through the adventures provided by transnational white mobility they travel to numerous newly established national spaces across the globe to participate in the various international coproductions that are made possible through the final voiding of their studio contracts. As they costar in eleven films together during their union, they mostly relish their experiences as members of the globetrotting jet-set for the decade that follows. Their sojourns speak to mobility as a part and parcel of postcolonial whiteness as a performative formation.

Elizabeth Taylor and Richard Burton are white postcolonial superstars because they spectacularly highlight the pursuit of pleasure as an organizing principle for white subjects through the deft management of their labor and leisure. By the melding of the two they raise their commercial value as performers and guarantee their fiscal freedom. For anxious white subjects concerned for the loss of power with the liberation of people of color, particularly Black subjects, Taylor and Burton during the 1960s through the spurring of capitalism perform postcolonial whiteness as site of continuous possibility. As their fantasies of imperiality and consumption seem to exist without the burden of race and function outside the struggle for civil rights, Elizabeth Taylor and Richard Burton model a new mode of subjectivity for nervous white subjects that manifest new forms of labor, leisure, and mobility through the performative, as their images reflect the pleasurable processes tied to new kinds of white self-racialization.

NOTES

1. Sam Kashner and Nancy Shoenberger, *Furious Love: Elizabeth Taylor, Richard Burton and the Marriage of the Century,* 29. David Kamp, "When Liz Met Dick," 368.
2. Homi K. Bhabha, *The Location of Culture,* 122.
3. Ibid., 122–23.
4. Ibid., 126.
5. The continuity of the British monarchy is well romanticized in the George VI biographical film *The King's Speech* (2010) which wins the Academy Award for Best Picture and Colin Firth's performance as the king wins him an Oscar for Best Actor.
6. Robert Phillipson, *Linguistic Imperialism,* 109.
7. Ibid., 129–30.
8. Ibid., 47.
9. Melvyn Bragg, *Richard Burton: A Life,* 7.
10. Michael Munn, *Richard Burton: Prince of Players,* 27.
11. Ibid., 56.
12. Ibid., 58.

13. Melvyn Bragg, *Richard Burton: A Life,* 123.

14. Mary L. Dudziak, *Cold War Civil Rights: Race and the Image of American Democracy,* 295, 103.

15. Ibid., 155.

16. Michael Munn, *Richard Burton: Prince of Players,* 117. Elizabeth Taylor was paid $7 million dollars for *Cleopatra.*

17. Eve Kosofsky Sedgwick, *Tendencies,* 131.

18. Michael Munn, *Richard Burton Prince of Players,* 232.

19. Ellis Amburn, *The Most Beautiful Woman in the World,* 248–49.

20. The Krupp Diamond was renamed the Elizabeth Taylor Diamond and sold at auction for $8.8 million in 2011.

21. Michael T. Taussig, *The Devil and Commodity Fetishism in South America,* 17–18.

22. Melvyn Bragg, *Richard Burton: A Life,* 90.

23. Dane Kennedy, *The Highly Civilized Man: Richard Burton and the Victorian World,* 1–4

24. Edward Rice, *Captain Sir Richard Francis Burton: A Biography,* 268.

25. Ibid., 273.

26. James Clifford, "Notes on Travel and Theory" from *Inscriptions 5* (1989), www2.ucsc.edu/culturalstudies/PUBS/Inscriptions/insc_ top1.html

27. Edward Rice, *Captain Sir Richard Francis Burton: A Biography,* 119.

28. Toni Morrison, *Playing in the Dark: Whiteness and the Literary Imagination,* 6–7.

29. Ibid., 38.

30. Thomas Crow, "Saturday Disasters: Trace and Reference in Early Warhol" in *Andy Warhol,* 54–55.

31. Mary L. Dudziak, *Cold War Civil Rights: Race and the Image of Democracy,* 153.

32. Lenore Manderson, "The Pursuit of Pleasure and the Sale of Sex," in *Sexual Nature, Sexual Culture,* 310.

33. There were three hundred extras present dressed as slaves. See J. Randy Taraborrelli, *Elizabeth,* 277–80 and his discussion of the shooting of Cleopatra's arrival and Burton's excitement. Upon viewing, not all of the extras visually code as Nubian slaves, particularly the ones in long shots pulling the Sphinx. But the sedan carriers who have more camera time and are photographed in tighter medium shots are Black performers playing Nubian slaves.

34. Edward W. Said, *Orientalism,* 1–3.

35. Scott Trafton, *Egypt Land: Race and Nineteenth-Century American Egyptomania,* 24–27.

36. Penny von Eschen, *Race Against Empire: Black Americans and Anti-Colonialism, 1937–1957,* 18–20, 171.

37. See Francesca T. Royster, *Becoming Cleopatra,* 63 and her readings of early silent film representations of Egypt that are situated in those terms, especially the film *The Haunted Curiosity Shop* (1896).

38. Ella Shohat, *Taboo Memories, Diasporic Voices,* 168.

39. Arthur Goldschmidt, Jr., *Modern Egypt: The Formation of a Nation State*, 94–95.

40. See entry "Muhammad Ali" the Albanian Ottoman viceroy of Egypt (1769–1749) in Arthur Goldschmidt, Jr., *Biographical Dictionary of Modern Egypt*, 135.

41. Ella Shohat, *Taboo Memories, Diasporic Voices*, 186–89.

42. Ibid., 190.

43. *Cleopatra Jones* (1973) directed by Jack Starrett, Jr. is a Blaxploitation film. Blaxploitation is Junius Griffin's portmanteau of the terms "Black" and "exploitation" that names a cycle of films that emerges in the late 1960s to entertain Black audiences and is used by mainstream Hollywood to try to entice those viewers to theaters en masse in an attempt to save itself while in the throes of a devastating industrial crisis. Blaxploitation films whose imagery is often problematic in terms of race and gender did typically valorize Black characters as primary protagonists while villainizing whites, both as an explicit filmic acknowledgment of the oppressiveness of racism and as a reflection of a shift in racial-cultural values that emerge with the arrival of the Black Power Movement. While these low-budget films fall under various genres that include drama, horror, comedy, capers, musicals, coming of age, crime, detective, and plantation films, they are often set in the inner city and usually demonstrate much lower production values than other Hollywood films.

44. William J. Mann, *How to Be a Movie Star: Elizabeth Taylor in Hollywood*, 263.

45. Sam Kashner and Nancy Schoenberger, *Furious Love: Elizabeth Taylor, Richard Burton, and the Marriage of the Century*, 173.

46. See bell hooks, "Eating the Other Desire and Resistance" from her *Black Looks Race and Representation*, 29.

47. See Sam Kashner and Jennifer MacNair's "Bell, Book and Scandal: Kim Novak and Sammy Davis, Jr.," 210 which discusses their relationship which Novak had previously denied and includes mentions of an alleged marriage license for the stars.

48. See *Photo By Sammy Davis, Jr.* (2007).

49. See Francesca T. Royster, *Becoming Cleopatra*, 102–103.

50. Brenda Maddox, *Who's Afraid of Elizabeth Taylor*, 163–65.

51. Alexander Walker, *Elizabeth: The Life of Elizabeth Taylor*, 228–31.

52. It bears noting that the *Cleopatra* was the top-grossing hit of 1963, earning $15.3 million dollars at the box office, $2 million more than rival sword and sandal epic *Spartacus* (1960). Fifty-three percent of viewers in a public opinion poll deemed *Cleopatra* excellent, 29 percent said it was good, and only 18 percent rated it fair or poor. See William Mann, *How to Be a Movie Star*, 332.

53. See Debora L. Spar and Briana Huntsburger, "The Business of Birth Control." *Harvard Health Policy Review*, Spring 2005, 6. When the birth control pill was first introduced in 1960, it set off a major boom in the pharmaceutical industry.

54. Donald Bogle, *Dorothy Dandridge: A Biography*, 457.

55. See the website *Taylor Tribute* under "The Cleo Craze," www.elizabethtaylorthelegend.com/Retrieved 6.1.22.

56. Melani McAlister, *Epic Encounters Culture, Media and U.S. Interests in the Middle East, 1945–2000*, 22–23.

57. Scott Trafton, *Egypt Land,* 19–20.

58. Ibid., 36–37.

59. DVD commentary of the film *Cleopatra* (2006), quoted from assistant on set, Christopher Mankiewicz, son of the director.

60. Michael T. Taussig, *The Devil and Commodity Fetishism in South America,* 25–29.

61. Sam Kashner and Nancy Schoenberger, *Furious Love,* 194–95.

62. Michael T. Taussig, *The Devil and Commodity Fetishism in South America,* 26.

63. William J. Mann, *How to Be a Movie Star,* 4.

64. See William J. Mann, *How to be a Movie Star,* 4.

65. Ibid., 360.

66. Ibid., 757.

67. Kitty Kelly, *The Last Star,* 147.

68. When filming *Butterfield 8,* Taylor tells the press that she "hates the girl I play—I hate what she stands for—the men, the sleeping around." See Kitty Kelly, *The Last Star,* 150.

69. Bette Davis's battles with the Warner Brothers Studio are well accounted for in Ed Sikov's *Dark Victory: The Life of Bette Davis,* 92. Davis's case is listed as *Warner Bros. Pictures, Inc., v. Nelson* (1937). She lost her case, much of her income and returned to Hollywood to resume her career.

70. Actor Alec Guinness noted that messages and gifts on numerous occasions never reached Burton but were routed through the Taylor–Burton entourage. Melvyn Bragg, *Richard Burton: A Life,* 404.

71. Alexander Walker, *Elizabeth: The Life of Elizabeth Taylor,* 292, 313–16

72. Ibid., 336.

Chapter 4

The Most Beautiful Woman Saves the World

Capitalism, the Maternal Melodrama, and the Meaning of Elizabeth Taylor's AIDS Activism

When asked in a televised interview for PBS's *Great Performances* series in 2001 about her famed AIDS activism, Elizabeth Taylor recalls her hospital visits to comfort sufferers that coincided with the promotional tour for her perfume, White Diamonds, in the early 1990s. With the formidable passion so often attributed to her, she asserts that her activism began even before she learned that her dear friend and costar Rock Hudson was afflicted with the disease. Her voice breaks as she relays to viewers how Hudson's doctor confirmed to her, "Rock had no chances" and she sighs deeply. She continues by saying, "I asked the patients what they wanted, what *they* needed. They said, we just want somebody to put their arm around us. We aren't contagious."

In this chapter, I read Elizabeth Taylor, an icon of bodily and capitalist excess as an effective agent of positive social change. I theorize that Taylor's well-known AIDS activism is a successful form of embodied emotive politics. This refers to her political activism that hinges on masterful gestural performances that fulfills the affective needs of patients as well as an audience not afflicted with the illness within a politicized affective register that brings to light the numerous lacks of the initial US federal response to AIDS while providing care to patients on the ground. Her activism is an iteration of neoliberal white privilege, an evolution of postcolonial white power anchored by global citizenship that affirms her ability to initiate political change through the open flow of capitalism. Her activism models how social change can be produced under American Pragmatism, a philosophy itself easily congruous to capitalism which asserts that "truth is probabilistic and socially determined and that men are mutable and improvable." Not unproblematically, American Pragmatism claims that social injustices are essentially logistical problems that can be overcome, in part through the mobilization of participatory democracy, insisting that individuals can no longer appeal to institutions for moral authority or ethical truths and must work with fellow citizens to produce solutions to social problems.[1]

Robert J. Lacey notes that Bertrand Russell was highly critical of Pragmatism and what he perceived as its hubris and obsession with methods. Pragmatists believe that man is capable of infinite self-improvement and can therefore achieve perfection. Russell found its rejection of absolute truth existing outside of human experience objectionable and led to the actual "worship of force" rather than the redistribution of power from the few to the many. When there is no absolute truth, what is true is actually what is most "expedient" as they assume that the concentration and mobilization of the correct means (the scientific method) would automatically yield good results. This in turn leads to a reversal of the Machiavellian motto of the "ends justify the means" to contend that the "means justify the ends."[2]

While the tenets of American Pragmatism and its spirit of practicality and logistical application helped inspire the rise of the New Left in the 1960s including the writing of the Port Huron Statement by the Students for a Democratic Society in 1962, no viable longstanding model for direct participatory democracy exists in the United States mostly, it has been theorized, because voter apathy prevents acts of deliberate political action.[3] Certainly American Pragmatism does not provide a perfect model for democracy open to all, because the securing of social justice through the eradication of its multiple root causes cannot be diminished or simplified as a set of logistical concerns. Nevertheless, I argue that Elizabeth Taylor's AIDS activism is so successful because of its unapologetically practical use of capitalism as a medium for social change and because Elizabeth Taylor has masterfully deployed her affective prowess to perform in an engrossing maternal melodrama of white noblesse oblige to fight against voter apathy. Her work to secure funding to help people with AIDS models a form of participatory democracy that neither Charles Peirce, William James, John Dewey, nor the Students for a Democratic Society anticipated. But because Elizabeth Taylor was unwavering in her convictions that the AIDS epidemic in Reagan America was exacerbated by virulent homophobia and is a form of social injustice, her honest performance of compassion for the sick and her open expressions of abhorrence toward their discrimination gave her the moral authority in the eyes of spectators and lawmakers to fight on their behalf.

Elizabeth Taylor is also at the forefront of celebrity diplomacy, a phenomenon of the culture industry that enables what Néstor García Canclini describes as "consumer citizenship" which favors markets over states and helps reconfigure national cultures within transnational exchanges. Her global influence as an AIDS activist allows the theorization of the role of affect in political mobilization under the conditions of neoliberalism, in which the state has abdicated the job of caring for its citizens. Taylor's affective labor in her fight against AIDS produces icons and melodramatic narratives that serve to spur political action and shows how the centrality of emotion mediated by cultural symbols spurs political activity and brings about social change. While consumer citizenship's affirmation of capitalism is contradictory as a means of overcoming inequalities because capitalism depends upon their reproduction, the presentation of AIDS as a neoliberal social problem is a persuasive example of how capitalism still ameliorates the problems produced by social injustice through the delivery of pragmatic and logistical solutions.

As a very successful fundraiser until her death in 2011, Elizabeth Taylor directly helps generate donations amounted to $275 million illuminating her unparalleled ability to stimulate capitalism through her symbolism as a mostly reformed sexual voluptuary. I trace Taylor's AIDS activism as it is inspired by her professional and interpersonal relationships with gay white men to examine how her passionate voice above others helped to redefine global perceptions of AIDS, particularly in its first wave as a US white gay male health crisis, initially obscuring the African history and neocolonial global dimensions of the medical epidemic. I assert that Elizabeth Taylor's genius as an affective laborer is evidenced through her management of the timely self-disciplining of her body through her dramatic weight loss, her treatment for drug addiction at the Betty Ford Center, and her marriage to teamster Larry Fortensky that she uses to sanitize her extensive history of extraordinary maladies and sexual excessiveness in the popular imaginary. She thus transforms herself into a figure through which viewers can safely encounter the disease. Her efforts elicit the viewer's compassion for people with AIDS and help to reroute the US federal response from indifference to obligation toward the AIDS body as she works for its begrudged reincorporation into the nation.

Deploying the work of Marxist theorists Michael Hardt and Antonio Negri I put focus here on affective labor to explain that in the last decades of the twentieth century, industrial labor loses its hegemonic hold and, in its place, emerges "immaterial labor" which they describe as work that creates immaterial products such as knowledge, information, communication, relationships, and emotional responses.[4] It exists in two forms: The first form recognizes labor that is primarily intellectual or linguistic such as problem solving, symbolic and analytic tasks, codes, texts, linguistic figures, and other such products. The second form of immaterial labor, which is affective labor, produces or manipulates feelings of well-being and ease. The examples often used to illustrate this include the work of flight attendants, nurses, and fast-food servers and the adage: "Service with a smile." In actuality, immaterial labor is the meshing of the two formations.

The exemplary model of affective labor, which produces symbolic meaning, feelings of intimacy, and an emotional response from subjects is the work of the star who is well remunerated and celebrated for it. For Elizabeth Taylor, AIDS activism is a means through which she can perform the level of engrossing affective labor symmetrical to her film acting, mobilizing her charisma and her earnestness to compel viewers to give money. Her ontology as a star, icon, and as a historical figure in the world hinges on her ability to feel and to emote in compelling and inspirational ways that produce the affective tones that stimulate a specific emotive response from an audience. In her estimation, her fight against AIDS gives her the opportunity to play her greatest role, that of an unfaltering advocate possessing real agency, to produce change anchored in the actualities of the social world. When receiving the Jean Hersholt Humanitarian Award from the Academy of Motion Pictures Arts and Sciences for her efforts against AIDS in 1992, Taylor is asked about the difference between her work as an actor and her work as an activist. She begins her response by saying, "This is for what I have done with my own life."

> Reporter: "What are you getting back from people regarding your work with AIDS?"
>
> Elizabeth Taylor: "AIDS is real life, movies are make-believe and that's the difference."
>
> R: "The difference between what you get back from people?"
>
> ET: "Yes."[5]

Since Elizabeth Taylor stops making hit movies at age thirty-five in 1967, her AIDS activism becomes the principle medium that allows her to produce highly nuanced performances that reach an international audience. As a woman who is the archetypal beautiful dark woman and feminine object of desire in American cinema for two decades, her work as a leading lady of romantic melodramas types her as the Dream Girl or the colonial bride, parts which become greatly diminished in quantity and quality in her mid-thirties. Not only does she play beautiful women in films, she stands as a figuration of Beauty Incarnate, a form of labor already tittering on a ledge of the somewhat impossible and a type of work with a finite timeline. Furthermore, the arrival of New Hollywood filmmaking in the late 1960s puts greater critical focus and audience interest on the production of male-centered narratives of discontent. As someone who is so closely associated with the studio system, her unapologetic glamour and long institutional history with studio system filmmaking makes her seem like an anthemia to masculine New Hollywood.[6]

With the breakup of the studios' vertical integration and the end of their monopoly on labor, Elizabeth Taylor is no longer subject to the ironclad studio contract and is allowed to secure her own deals and choose her own costars and directors. But while Taylor's career as a film actor reaches it critical apex when she wins her second Academy Award for *Who's Afraid of Virginia Woolf* in 1966 at the age of thirty-four, almost every film she makes after that year is not a box-office hit nor critically acclaimed. By 1969 films like *Midnight Cowboy* and *Easy Rider* announce the New Hollywood phase in American cinema, with its heavy focus on masculinities in crisis and veers away from Elizabeth Taylor. She as a signifier of hyperfemininity and more importantly as a woman film worker does not have the institutional support of the studio system to produce the types of films, in regard to genre and in the level of production value, for which she is best suited.

Because Elizabeth Taylor's film career spans the shift from Fordist to post-Fordist modes of work in Hollywood that reorganizes the studio system through the elimination of star contracts and assembly-line film production in the early 1960s, she experiences the transformation of the production of labor that informs both the tail end of her career as a film actor as well as her AIDS activism. The terms Fordism and post-Fordism are used to mark the shift from an economy characterized by long-term employment typical of factory workers which Hollywood actors of her era are (although highly paid ones), to one marked by flexible, mobile, and precarious labor relations. These workers are flexible because they must adapt to different tasks, mobile because they have to move frequently between jobs and precarious because no long-term contracts guarantee stable, extended employment.[7] Flexibility for Elizabeth Taylor as a professional actress means remaking herself and building a new and different career to counter this industrial crisis. This leads to her performing off screen. Instead of acting solely in movies, she conveys her actual emotions directly to a still hungry audience first through her tabloid-driving globetrotting adventures of accumulation with husband and frequent costar Richard Burton and then through her exacting and almost immediate response to the AIDS crisis, which begins in the early 1980s.

AIDS theorist and activist Cindy Patton explains the AIDS pandemic as the result of the chasm between a transnational disease and a deficit international response which is the pivotal factor in the failures of AIDS prevention and care initiatives.[8] As HIV's propensity to completely trespass national borders and remake identities facilitate the development and connecting of a new kind of NGO, AIDS activism becomes a kind of global identity politics that creates communities based on serostatus (meaning the presence or absence of sub-stances in blood) in a world in which communities are more incorporeal and abstract than based on direct and interpersonal contact. Through multimedia performances of precise, earnest compassion Elizabeth Taylor's fight against AIDS gives her a new culturally recognizable identity as an activist through the performance of emotionally charged gestures of caring and intimate physical contact, primarily between the advocate/herself and the sufferer/patient. This is her platform to express her mastery as a communicator and producer of engrossing affect that parallels her most acclaimed film work particularly when as a younger actress viewers and critics were sometimes distracted by her extraordinary beauty which diminished their estimations of her actual performative abilities.

According to Susan Sontag, while war is being declared on the plague of AIDS in the 1980s and 1990s, AIDS had actually banalized cancer, since the misunderstanding of cancer as an epidemic and plague was receding while fear for AIDS was metastasizing.[9] The war that is declared to fight this plague was a set of battles specifically against the bodies of gay men in the United States. As a counterstrategy, Elizabeth Taylor uses the language of the universal to openly, passionately argue for the dignity of gay men fighting and dying from AIDS. Through a politics of the personal, she uses her recognition of the labor of gay men in the industrialization of aesthetics of which Hollywood filmmaking is an epicenter to fight for their care. In no uncertain terms she initially frames the proliferation of AIDS amongst gay film workers as an industrial crisis within Hollywood—as film workers such as Rock Hudson are losing their lives—both valorizing American cinema through the impulse of nostalgia at a moment of danger while presenting herself as an unequivocally white American star, a stable white subject operating within the basic machinery of US politics that runs on and fuels capitalism.

At an early AIDS fundraiser, Elizabeth Taylor declares that art is forever, meaning that the contributions of gay men to the arts are invaluable and immeasurable to American culture and as such, sick gay men should not be made into social outcasts but given compassion and help. Up to the point of that speech and until the rest of her life, she enjoys celebrated friendships with many notable gay men, melding her signification as a gay icon with theirs. She is closely associated with Montgomery Clift, her costar in three films whose life she saves in a devastating car crash in 1956. When Clift begins choking on his two front teeth, he survives because Taylor crawls into the wreck and sticks her hand down his bleeding throat to retrieve them. And, of course, her friendship with Rock Hudson, her on-screen husband in the film *Giant* (1958), is thought to be at the heart of her AIDS activism and further catapults her status as a beloved gay icon. Hudson's public death from AIDS makes a grotesque spectacle out of his once beautiful face and body that are decimated by the disease. Her activism means to diffuse the pathologization of his decades of closeted homosexuality brought about by the spectacularization of his annihilated body. She continuously reaffirms Hudson's status as both a movie star and a friend deserving of her love and loyalty by repetitively citing her glamorous personal and professional history with him as her work to fight AIDS becomes the primary focal point of her performative life soon after.

As a cult figure amongst gay men she has always happily accepted their affection and chooses to fight against their sexual demonization and medical discrimination by becoming a founding member of the American Foundation for AIDS Research known as amFAR in 1985. In 1991 she establishes the Elizabeth Taylor AIDS Foundation and through her efforts helps donate an estimated $12 million during her lifetime to hundreds of AIDS care organizations and facilities across the United States and throughout the globe. She funds care centers in Canada, Mexico, Honduras, Haiti, Ireland, Romania, China, India, Thailand, the Philippines, Malawi, Ghana, Uganda, South Africa, and Mozambique. Taylor's activist efforts in the last decade of her life also help highlight AIDS's presence as both a US problem, particularly amongst African Americans, as well as an international medical crisis of the neocolonial world.[10] During the immediate aftermath of the botched federal response to Hurricane Katrina, Taylor in partnership with Macy's, gives $40,000 to the New Orleans AIDS Task Force and commissions the building of a care van equipped with X-ray machines and examination tables drawing attention to AIDS's explosion outside its initial documented discovery within American communities of affluent urban gay white males. Through the AIDS Healthcare Foundation, based in Los Angeles, she insists that the freezers of AIDS care facilities that receive support through her fundraising always be stocked with rainbow sherbet ice cream.[11]

Figure 4.1. Elizabeth Taylor and Betty Ford at the Commitment for Life benefit dinner in Los Angeles raising AIDS awareness. Source: Bettmann/Getty Images.

BECOMING THE SAFE BODY

As a woman who realizes her sexuality in the very socially and political conservative early 1950s and who becomes a singular icon of liberalized feminine sexuality in the early 1960s, notably as cinema's most famous and seductive Cleopatra, Elizabeth Taylor's public and rampant vilification for her erotic exploits arguably makes her an appropriate figure to stand up for gay men whose sexual practices are represented as virulent and deadly in the 1980s. But her numerous body adventures cannot be categorized only under the sexual or erotic. Discourses about her body throughout her public life seem to suggest that she is always already in the throes of a medical crisis. Sadly, in the spring of 2011, Elizabeth Taylor is last hospitalized at Cedars-Sinai Medical Center in Los Angeles for treatment of symptoms linked to congestive heart failure and dies during her six-week stay at the facility at age seventy-nine. But even as a twenty-six-year-old woman, physically incapacitated and publicly struggling after the death of third husband, producer Mike Todd, magazine writers fear for her health, pondering openly about her actual mortality, not necessarily the longevity of her film career. [12]

Elizabeth Taylor is famously a medical spectacle for most of her public life. Some of her well-documented medical interventions include operations for her three difficult pregnancies and for her bad back, a hysterectomy, three hip replacement surgeries, the removal of a benign brain tumor, and procedures to replace a leaky heart valve. She reportedly undergoes thirty major operations in her lifetime and is hospitalized an estimated seventy times; her most publicized medical incident being an emergency tracheotomy during the filming of *Cleopatra* in London when Taylor's pneumonia escalates into a coma. While fans hold vigils for her and after newspapers falsely report her death she wakes from her coma and asks that the famed hairdresser Alexandre of Paris style her hair into an up-do called the "Artichoke." After being released from the hospital, she emerges to greet her public wearing a sable coat and a long white scarf wrapped around her neck to hide her tracheotomy scar. In archival newsreel footage she is seen boarding a private plane to Hollywood to fully recuperate.

The scar remains with Taylor for a time, and she sometimes refers to it during interviews, saying, "I've earned that." Until her actual death she enjoys being perceived as a survivor with an invincible body—someone who consistently beat the medical odds and lived—an able manager of numerous maladies who seems always sick but strong enough to still be living, mirroring how the conditions AIDS is often imagined after the sustained success of antiviral drugs in postindustrial nations after the initial outbreak of the epidemic. In the First World, AIDS is now considered a chronic disease that weakens the body but through the taking of proper precautions can be ably managed. In fact, in 2011 US medical doctors and federal health officials call for an amendment of the National Organ Transplant Act, supporting the repeal of a provision that bans the organs of HIV-positive donors for use in transplants of other HIV patients, arguing that the virus is currently more treatable than organ failure. [13]

The containment of Elizabeth Taylor's physical excesses particularly her widely reported treatment for drug abuse at the Betty Ford Center expresses a willingness for self-discipline that turns her formerly volatile corporeal self into a safe body through which viewers could encounter AIDS. During the second of Taylor's two rehabilitation stints at the Center she also meets her seventh husband, Larry Fortensky. While achieving sobriety Taylor pairs her abstinence from drug use with her last attempt at domesticity and monogamy tempering her once legendary volatile sexuality in exchange for a chance at keeping a well-managed hearth and home.

But the visible evidence necessary to prove that Elizabeth Taylor is both a safe and capable body is produced when she successfully utilizes a low-carbohydrate high protein diet to reshape her form to its 1950s dimensions, the ultimate sign of mastery and control over her dangerous and derailing physical desires.[14] After dieting, she once again has a hand-span waist as she did during her studio days as the circumference of her narrow midsection looks at most to be twenty-one inches. By negotiating the 1980s in a body so visually analogous to her 1950s corporality, the reclamation of her former physicality provides a visual signifier for the gender and sexual repression of both decades, thirty years apart as Taylor is forced to defeat her troublesome needy body that had for years branded her as both an insatiable sexual libertine and uncontrollable eater. In order to claim her political agency during the Reagan era in which misfit bodies and behaviors are continuously remade or made invisible to suit the needs of the state, Taylor reclaims her thin body in pursuit of her own needs and what she desires most—to be a culturally relevant star who can mobilize useful social-political action that assuages the fears of the nation towards AIDS.

Elizabeth Taylor's able management of her formerly uncontrollable and insatiable body and its repositioning within the flows of capitalism helps her become an effective political activist and also helps build her perfume empire. By 2011, she sells one billion dollars worth of her White Diamonds perfume simply because women want to be like her, a relentless pursuer of pleasure and an exacting fulfiller of dreams. By then she realizes all of her desires: lavish fortune, global renown, and political power. Through her, the viewer moves closer to the possibility of fulfilling her yearnings for accolades, monetary success, amorous exploits, and global adventure. In a thirty-one-second-long black-and-white television ad campaign produced in 1998 that is as ethereal as perfume itself, Taylor appears like an exquisite phantom, dressed in white and bursting through a set of wooden doors. She takes off her diamond earrings and declares, "These have always brought me luck," as two men, who code as game hunters are engrossed in a high stakes game of cards, a scenario that seems too common amongst rich idle whites. Here, her body and beauty, which decades before are considered excessive and uncontrollable while still sumptuous, are made ideal again.

In a televisual exotic wilderness that codes as Africa the continent once again becomes a space of Taylor's renewal and recalibrates her glamorous persona for spectators as the singular white woman whose desires for adventure still knows no geographical bounds as it cites her extended six-week visit to Chobe National Park in Botswana, the venue for her second wedding to Richard Burton. Through Taylor's perfume ad, spectators can envision how a former colonial site remains a playground for white subjects seeking pleasure, love, reinvigoration, and magic, as Africa still exists in the white imaginary solely for its desires to be fulfilled. This commercial is also an ode to her film work as a Hollywood plantation mistress and doubly erases Native oppression under colonialism by making Africa once again a white paradise, this time in an effort to sell perfume that negates both the African origins of AIDS as well as its unchecked devastation on the continent through the continual forced erasure of Black subjects and Black people with the disease in popular media.[15] This erasure is symptomatic of the white neocolonial control of Africa as underserving interventions for African people with AIDS mimic other older systems of white occupation and control.

Wearing a white gown, her face and figure visually blanched in the overexposed black-and-white photography, Taylor is made not only to look very white but *made white again*, as her global image as the jet-setter is domesticated for American television audiences, an essential element in the process of her US repatriation as the legendary white American movie star. This is a maneuver that she begins after marrying and campaigning for US Senator John Warner in the early 1970s which she completes through her 1980s and 1990s AIDS activism that secures her formerly precarious whiteness of the 1960s. She becomes not only a global humanitarian but an American citizen of the first order, having been awarded the Presidential Citizen's Medal by Bill Clinton in 2001 for her work.

The media's focus on Elizabeth Taylor's capitalist-fueled activism allows a closer examination of the political economy of AIDS care and its neocolonial tendencies in which power is overwhelming aligned with white Western nations. Cindy Patton in her investigation of First World interventions of AIDS in the developing world presents a sobering assessment about white power. She notes that the pseudoscientific label of "African AIDS" or its WHO's classification "Pattern Two," while detailing the spread of disease where heterosexual sex seemed to predominate, recirculated old racist ideas of unchecked and uncontrollable Black sexuality, in turn having a devastating effect on local activism in Africa and North America.[16] In her criticism of transnational efforts of which multinational drug companies, First World intervention policies, and the World Health Organization are all complicit in their circumvention of care in the African AIDS epidemic, she uses an example based on the disparity of funding for AIDS treatment in the United States versus Zaire (now Congo) in the late 1980s. While estimating the amount allotted for care is $20,000 per person in the United States and only a few hundred dollars a year in the latter country, she writes,

> Well-researched analysis of these administrative practices reveals the basic logic on which global resources planning rests: the rich get health and the poor are seen as expendable . . . Instead of revealing how little it would cost rich countries to buy health and life for people in poor countries, such analyses reinforce the idea that poor countries are already lost to the epidemic.

Indeed, it seems that the largest portion of monies for AIDS research and treatment goes to only the most privileged, as WHO's division of the world into six administrative regions still reflect colonial and neocolonial cessions to individual nations and the power in them, which has undergirded the organization since it was established in 1948. The World Health Organization's spatial logic of world regions is reflective of European and American imperialist forays that insisted on a moral view of the world that former colonial powers espoused. As such, the whole of the Western hemisphere is grouped under the Pan American Health Organization headed in Washington, D.C., and replicates nineteenth century isolationism which guarantees US domination over other regions including Latin America and Africa through exclusionary policy-making. Returning to the lack of direct and forceful interventions to fight AIDS in Africa Patton concludes,

> Economic analysis cannot help us recognize that AIDS *in* Africa is a symptom of Black people's history of exclusion from global prosperity and economic dependency enforced by lack of control over either local or global resources.[17]

The whiten-ing of effective AIDS treatment in which the white First World receives and initiates the mammoth share of treatment on its own behalf at the exclusion of Africa is emblematic of the continent's literal whiten-ing in visual media through the reblanching of the world's foremost AIDS activist in her White Diamonds commercial. As White Diamonds is "The fragrance dreams are made of," viewers can continue to dream of the white control of Africa and rest assured that postwar America's greatest star is unequivocally white.[18] Selling a perfume that promises encounters with this neocolonial white utopia then seems not difficult at all. In his essay, "Advertising: The Magic System, " Raymond Williams references the paradox at the core of advertising by stating,

> Advertising, in its modern forms, then operates to preserve the consumption ideal from criticism inexorably made of it by experience. If consumption of individual goods leaves the whole area of human need unsatisfied, the attempt is made, by magic, to associate consumption with human desires to which it has no real reference. You do not buy an object; you buy social respect, discrimination, health, beauty, success, power to control your environment.[19]

As White Diamonds's phenomenal sales numbers attest, its short film successfully evokes the enticing notion of capturing and mobilizing Taylor's seductive femininity and now stable whiteness to meet their needs and yearnings. These include the dream of a white Africa without AIDS made possible through the concerted efforts of the mythical figure whose noblesse oblige allows her to single-handedly take the helm of the AIDS fight. And just as magically, the commercial disappears into the ether of ever-present televisual flow only to reappear every year around Christmas, wrapping Taylor's activism with the pleasure of consumption into one tidy parcel.

As Elizabeth Taylor's initial AIDS activism occurs during the Reagan administration, it is forced to function through a circuit of her American repatriation and the blanching of her image in her White Diamonds campaign since Ronald Reagan transfuses exclusionary 1950s political and social values to American political life for the sole benefit of wealthy white voters. Also because Reagan was previously the oldest American president ever elected, his virility and masculinity must be put on display. As Susan Jeffords demonstrates, the health of the symbolic American body politic is so closely tied to the physical health of the body of the Commander-in-Chief that its status, whether it is spotted, frail, and elderly is of utmost concern.[20] When Reagan's body codes as less than virile and healthy, steps are taken to harden his body through a performative and visual remasculinization. During Reagan's photo opportunities with the press, props including a cowboy hat, an ax, and a horse are used to represent the elderly president as an able outdoorsman who enjoys horseback riding and chopping his own firewood.

THE WELFARE QUEEN VS. THE AIDS MOTHER

Before Ronald Reagan adapted images of the great American outdoorsman to connote white masculine power and help secure a second term in office, he deftly mobilizes images of the "welfare queen," during his presidential run in 1976, a political construction many falsely believe frauds the US welfare system, a figure perceived as one who burdens the state and forces the unnecessary expansion of the American welfare apparatus which in turn is believed to result in a perpetuation of a culture of nonwork and criminality. Tales of welfare queens continue to gain traction in popular media from the late seventies onward as they are used by Reagan and the rising New Right to end the social welfare programs of the 1960s. This helps secure their partnerships with corporations and the votes of angry and fearful working-class white constituents who believe social welfare undercuts poor whites. A contrived political tool used to demonize the poor, the welfare queen is an enemy of the state whose gender and racial dimensions often conflate the age-old stereotypes of women's uncontrollable sexuality and African American laziness into one monstrous body that then must be punished for the sanctity of the United States.[21] The welfare queen is a powerful and anxiety-producing figure through which discourses of the impossibilities of welfare reform are often configured, even more so as the questionable public identity of the welfare queen as an African American unwed mother has never been challenged, largely because Senator Daniel Patrick Moynihan's quasi-sociological readings of Black poverty remain hegemonic. [22]

The welfare queen continues to signify as an improperly feminine and monstrous mother, and is not afforded the compassion and funding that the AIDS mother such as Jeanne White, the mother of fallen AIDS activist Ryan White, elicits. Pointedly, this is so even as the welfare queen who is overwhelmingly imagined to be a Black woman, is now statistically at the highest risk of contracting AIDS, as her rate of infection is five times higher than the US national estimate.[23] The African American woman with AIDS becomes an example who then points to the racial and class markers which dictate whose AIDS body can be reclaimed by the state. A frighteningly contagious disease that has tied gay male sex to death now conflates AIDS with poverty and nonwhite impropriety. And while the upper-class gay male body has been officially recognized by the nation, the Black woman with AIDS is still in dire need of federal acceptance and care.[24]

As a counterpoint to the US model, the constitutional monarchy of Denmark with its high tax rates and nationalized health care system serves as the primary example of a relatively well-functioning social welfare state in the industrialized, capitalist Western hemisphere. It is a rather unique example. Danish citizens of average income were taxed at the rate of 33 percent in 2010. A high-income earner in Denmark is expected to pay over 50 percent in taxes. These funds are used to provide free healthcare, childcare, job training, and generous support for the unemployed. Monies are used to even sustain clubs organized around leisure activities and common interests for members of the private sector.[25] A reasonable theory that explains the success of the Danish welfare state is one that outlines the comparatively ethnic and religious homogeneity of the Danish population.[26] The Danish case suggests that people are collectively willing to pay high taxes to benefit those in need who are very much like themselves.[27] According to Henning Jørgensen, Denmark's state-building process has long been characterized by a fundamental stability, continuity, and homogeneity. This is largely due to the cultural, linguistic, and ethnic homogeneity of its population that has made a historical absence of religious and ethnic violence possible and, "a unique congruence between the nation and the state." Perhaps not incidentally, the number of people with AIDS is Denmark is estimated at 5,300 in 2009, with fewer than 100 deaths.

While US income taxes are at about 11 percent, there is not yet a working system of nationalized free healthcare. While American big business is taxed at the highest rate in the world, at 35 percent, because of loopholes in the tax code, it is not actually paying those taxes.[28] The US population of over 330 million is also ethnically, racially, religiously, and economically diverse. Indexes of identity are used to sustain categories of difference that maintain social and economic inequality as figures such as the Black welfare queen are constructed and deployed to link poverty and fraud to the lazy nonwhite body that obstruct federal interventions to aid the American poor. Therefore, subjects living in America, both official citizens and nonlegal residents must fend for themselves for healthcare, higher education, childcare, and job training. What helps the heterogeneous US populace to cohere to itself is capitalism. Simply, everyone shops. As the Elizabeth Taylor AIDS activism case attests, the pleasures tied to consumption intimately align consumers with capitalism and charts the ways the open markets of neoliberalism are fueled by numerous affects including compassion.

Néstor García Canclini considers the exercise of citizenship in the United States not only through its relations to rights tied to state institutions bestowed to those born within its territorial purview but the various cultural practices that produce a sense of belonging, confer a sense of difference and enable a satisfaction for people who possess knowledge of a given language and organize themselves in certain ways.[29] For Canclini, consumer citizenship is a conceptual model to revise the juridical-political sense of citizenship in which the state once provided the means and forms to participate in public life.

Currently, the market provides the framework for engaging in the public sphere through the form of consumption, which reconfigures the very terrain of citizenship.[30] Canclini asserts that citizenship and consumerism have always been linked and that the practice of citizenship is always associated with the accumulation of commodities and the ways of using them.[31] State-sponsored citizenship is by default closed to multicultural diversity as both the US and Danish models suggest. While critical work on cultural citizenship in the United States strives to legitimate members of minority groups whose practices are based on racial, sexual, gender, linguistic, and economic differences, Canclini wishes for the affirmation of difference to be used to reform the state, to accept the development of diverse communities and to allow equal access to the resources brought by globalization.[32]

What is referred to as the public sphere emerges from the political discourse of eighteenth-century continental Europe. Participants within the public sphere would collectively discuss and decide the matters that were important to them. Ideally, a site in which democratic, rational critique is used to establish an equalitarian culture, engaging those concerned with the common interest is limited to those who had entry to bourgeois salons and the ability to communicate through and understand writing.[33] Access to the public sphere then was rather prohibitive and available only to the educated, literate, and the prosperous owners of property and labor power.

Furthermore, according to Grace Kyungwon Hong, US citizenship is invented to protect the right to accumulation, and infuses American identity with an inalienable notion of self-possession and freedom, often realized through the subject's temporary breaking away from constricting societal structures. These themes are frequently narrated in American literature including Huck Finn's turning away from society and consequent brief revelatory liberation.[34] American citizenship is initially restricted to free white male property owners and excludes Blacks, slaves, Indigenous peoples, and women. American citizenship at the moment of its inception is exclusive and cordoned off to the disenfranchised and held by an elite class, capable of exercising political power. The American citizen is an evolution of the possessive individual who himself first arises in the seventeenth century Enlightenment discourse of liberal Europe that advocates the triumph of reason, science, human freedom, and achievement. The rights of the enlightened individual, initiated into nation-state based citizenship and guaranteed by the state belong only to him and to others very much like him—a free, white, male property holder. Inspired by the work of John Hobbes, political philosopher C.B. Macpherson's theory of possessive individualism is seminal to the idea of American citizenship and reiterates that man's power is defined by the "eminence" of his ability over other men, not by his natural ability, nor his strength or prudence on its own.[35, 36]

Subjects who participate alongside Elizabeth Taylor in her AIDS activism are modern possessive individuals endowed with the powers once derived only through formal citizenship and only created for the security of self-interest. These modern subjects whose primary practice of consumption overrides the strictures of the US state can help provide services and care for AIDS sufferers whose bodies are often invisible to the nation, as the social welfare state in the United States remains to be realized. Donations to the Elizabeth Taylor AIDS Foundation come from consumers who not only enter a circuit of affect, whether it is compassion, empathy, love, outrage, frustration, desperation, or hope but also reorganize citizenship and relocate the public sphere in late capital through the terms of an inclusive agency that they calibrate for themselves. This is particularly meaningful because it operates alongside the US nation-state's dual imperatives of whiteness and property ownership.

Elizabeth Taylor is a legendary exemplar of the possessive individual whose public life is an archive of the pursuit of pleasure. The celebration of her self-possession through her open expressions of her sexuality hinges on her unabashed desire for the collecting of affective adventures most pointedly through her adoption of new identities including her conversion to Judaism in the 1950s, her insistence on maintaining dual American and British passports in the 1960s and 1970s and finally her role as a world-renown activist in the 1980s. She models the pleasurable and practical facets of accumulation to a global audience through her well-known generosity to both close friends and those she considers the downtrodden. She also bristles against the monetary entreaties of the nation state as a postcolonial white subject trotting around the world in part to avoid paying British taxes within a geopolitical new world order that avowedly is not a social welfare state.

Through Elizabeth Taylor's example, people know, to quote the star herself that, "money is fun." But more than that, money empowers and pays for medical research, treatment, direct interpersonal care, buys ad time for the airing of television public service announcements, and can even purchase prestige as the money Taylor raises at galas also raises the media profile of AIDS intervention as a formidable social cause worthy of public interest and concern. And with some money, even with the disposable dollars a consumer could spend to buy a bottle of White Diamonds perfume or a screening of an Elizabeth Taylor movie, anyone can join the fight she spearheaded to help end the AIDS plague.

Willing consumer citizens under neoliberalism can use portions of their disposable incomes to help subjects cut off from the benefits of proper citizenship including poor African Americans, whose rate of HIV infection is highest of all racial groups.[37] This fundamental shift in the racial profile of people with AIDS is also reflected in the Elizabeth Taylor AIDS Foundation website which features a photograph of its founder beaming and surrounded by Black children.[38] As a First World, industrialized nation the United States comes into being through the tenets of European liberal democracy while its infrastructure was being built by laboring Black and Native slaves and its very philosophies of freedom were defined against and in the closest proximity to those very bodies it has forced into bondage. Therefore, the United

States bestows citizenship, its guarantees of freedom and self-possession to a select few through the disenfranchisement and oppression of many. Social, political, and economic inequalities are maintained in the US state through racial formations in which subjects are given agency in accordance to their proximity to whiteness. Therefore, racial difference and the disadvantages that accompany them in the dominant subject's (white, male, and hetero-sexual) encounters with the world of the racial Other are not imagined or illusionary but real.

This being the case, the remaking of fat and old bodies during the ini-tial AIDS crisis of the 1980s are examples which disavow the presence of non-normative corporealities in the United States during an extremely politi-cally and sexually conservative era. The fears that forcibly sanitize the gay male body, whether it is achieved through the utter desexualization on film of Rock Hudson in light romantic comedies and the onscreen/off screen images of meticulous self-comportment that earn him the moniker "gentle giant" in the 1950s, exist alongside fears of Reagan's frail presidential body. His regressive social and economic policies and the discourses that celebrate the separation of gay men from the pleasures of sex exemplify the melancholia and moralism brought by AIDS in the 1980s. It is first theorized and decried by art scholar Douglas Crimp who voices his strong criticism for comments made by the politically conservative HIV-positive pundit Andrew Sullivan who states unflinchingly that

> Before AIDS, gay life—rightly or wrongly—was identified with freedom from responsibility, rather than with its opposite. Gay liberation was most commonly understood as liberation from the constraints of traditional norms, almost a dispensation that permitted homosexuals a lack of responsibility in return for an acquiescence in second-hand citizenship. . . . But with AIDS, responsibility became a central aspect of imposing gay life. . . . People who thought they didn't care for one another found out they could.[39]

Crimp explains that Sullivan is unable to recognize the intractability of homophobia because of his melancholic identification with the homophobe's repudiation of him. His moralism against gay men is his clearest symptom.[40]

Certainly, the condemnation of gay men for what Sullivan argues as the hedonism that is unleashed after Stonewall does not alter the social or psy-chological structure of homophobia. His embrace of a punitive narrative of AIDS pushes what he perceives as the inevitable consequence of sex among active gay men—death. It is not a remedy against the fear of homosexual difference but an example of homophobia itself.[41] Sullivan tries to mobilize the language of the universal in his assessment of AIDS, meaning the bad homosexuals will be punished for their sexual sins and in the end make good gays for capitalism and the state, a fantasy he presents as the final equalizer under liberalism. Clearly his is not a discourse of empathy or compassion or even practical as his criticisms do not halt the spread of the illness.

GAY IDENTITY AND CAPITALISM

Historically, the prevailing reason for the federal government's reluctance to respond immediately to the AIDS crisis in the 1980s and duly noted by Elizabeth Taylor herself is homophobia stemming from the fear that homosexuality threatens the patriarchal capitalist structure of the United States.[42] Because gay sex historically has not reproduced new laborers for capital through procreation, gay subjects are prohibited from the proper protections and privileges of US citizenship by the state itself, producing political inequality and social injustice. That being so, John D'Emilio in his discussion of gay identity's relationship to capitalism reveals the irony of the free-labor system that allows for men and women to "see themselves as part of a community, to organize politically on the basis of that identity, that gays have not always existed but are a product of history and emerged through the historical development of capitalism."[43]

John D'Emilio asserts that the relationship between capitalism and family is incongruous and contradictory. While capitalism continuously weakens the material foundation of family life and allows gay and lesbian identities to develop as individuals who live outside the family, it still needs the family long enough to push men and women to procreate to reproduce the next generation of workers. Most importantly, D'Emilio masterfully argues that the ideological eminence of the family assures the reproduction of children for capitalism but also heterosexism and homophobia.[44] This being so, the reassertion of gay bodies within the family unit through the melodramatic drive of Elizabeth Taylor's AIDS activism thrives on the ideological symbolism of the inalienable bond between a mother and an ailing child that reappropriates the ideological power of the family for gay use.

THE NEED FOR ICONICITY IN ACTIVISM

In fact, the labor of homosexuals particularly that of gay men has been an integral part of the commercial sphere of US aesthetics especially in the industries of film, fashion, and high art during the twentieth century. This allows gay subjects and their advocates to imagine and use capitalist solutions to the problems tied to AIDS perceived as a First World white, gay, male disease during its first global cycle. As Susan Sontag accounts for the cultural contribution of gay men to Western aesthetics in her essay, "Notes on Camp," she also maps the codes of a hegemonic self-legitimizing gesture, a predominantly gay male sensibility in the arts that has been widely adopted to allow the cultivation of new forms of taste in the name of pleasure.[45]

The launching of the AIDS ribbon is a product of gay men's labor as well as an object of exchange in the open markets of neoliberalism reifying the inextricability of gay male labor from capitalism. As the prevalent symbol of AIDS activism in the 1990s that circulated widely in various media, the red ribbon adorned the gowns and lapels of stars at televised awards shows. Elizabeth Taylor herself is seen wearing one when she copresents the Best Picture Oscar to the producers of *The Silence of the Lambs* with Paul Newman in 1991. The ribbon is also replicated as part of a US postage stamp, and worn annually during World AIDS Days around the world.

As a disease abounded in metaphors, the image of a plague being the central one, the red ribbon logo is created by gay painter Frank C. Moore II of the Visual AIDS Artist Caucus of New York in 1991 as a tool to raise awareness, elevate consciousness towards AIDS, and allow wearers to show their solidarity with sufferers.[46] Conceived during the first Gulf War when yellow ribbons are emblematic of US nationalism and for supporting the US military's aggression in the Middle East, the AIDS red ribbon is created in response, to make visible the waves of gay men that are battling their bodies as an indifferent federal government seems blind to the many who are dying. The AIDS ribbon is a political object created to draw attention to AIDS as a national issue, according to Visual AIDS Director Patrick J. O'Connell. However, John Weir, a gay writer and vocal critic of the ribbon, asserts that, "People who are truly living with or dying of AIDS or caring for sick lovers or friends do not need gentle reminders about their situation."[47] The red ribbon, criticized by both gay and heterosexual observers, is a principle icon of AIDS that also becomes a commercial product, which can be read as a testament to its success as a compelling symbol to consumers as they locate themselves within the logic of accumulation that turns AIDS into as neoliberal social problem with a capitalist solution.[48]

Still others including the well-known AIDS activist group ACT UP are wary of the ribbon's potentially normalizing effect, thinking that the wearing of it inspires complacency instead of action. In various rebuttals they create posters reading, "AIDS Is Not a Fashion Statement. It Is Genocide, Take Another Step. *Act Up.*" Critical of the US Postal Service's circulation and commodification of the ribbon, they also create posters that read, "You Can't Lick a Stamp When You're Dead! *Complacency Kills.*"[49] Exactly what the AIDS red ribbon signifies to whom in what historical moment remains rather dynamic and compels academic and AIDS activist Simon Watney to write:

Rather that blaming red ribbons for not explaining everything that by now ought
to be more widely understood about HIV/AIDS, we should strive to make public
discussion of HIV/AIDS clearer and better informed. Let's campaign to make
red ribbons indeed emblematic of injustice in the AIDS crisis.[50]

The ambiguity of the AIDS red ribbon presents the possibilities of it being
a depoliticized blank signifier pointing to its commandeering by American
federal institutions or its relegation as a passing 1990s fashion trend. But its
ubiquity also alludes to how political activism must to be played on the platform of the symbolic through the mobilization of icons. While the red ribbon
may signify solidarity with AIDS sufferers and AIDS injustice, or may have
sanitized the disease and made being aware of its devastation fashionable,
it still stands for in a fundamental capacity, AIDS and AIDS's existence in
the world.

The utilization of the red ribbon by AIDS activists elucidates how state
sponsored projects or those conducted in the name of state reformation
require the utilization of icons that are recognizable and negotiable and that
deliver messages which operate through the emotive register of spectators
who have the agency to produce the outcomes of movements. Closely associated with Eastern Orthodox Christianity, whose use and variety were widened
particularly in Russia, icons were originally religious images that represented
and stood in for the divine. They are also symbols that stand in for an object
by virtue of its resemblance or analogy to it.[51] In late capital, icons operate
beyond the dimensions of any religious denomination and have compelling
affective values that operate in the world to present numerous secular ideas
that may have not have been elevated into the realm of the spiritual, but do
make various concepts seem at least ubiquitous.

According to political scientist David O. Sears, objects, acts, and people
can serve as powerful symbols, or *icons* I posit, to rally and mobilize emotions to initiate political events and social change. He ponders why individuals en masse become so involved in abstract political events with only
remote personal cost and benefit to themselves as they participate in the most
significant political, social, and religious conflicts in the history of the United
States. He examines the crucial role of affect in politics and proposes a theory
of individual psychology as actually a theory of symbolic politics.[52]

Sears begins by defining a political symbol as an "affectively charged element in a political attitude object." Attitude itself is a concept from psychology that provides a representational construct that marks an individual's like
or dislike of something, in this case, a political idea.[53] This means that a subject's feelings about political ideas are tied to various symbols that circulate
alongside them as those symbols can be framed and utilized to elicit specific
emotional responses.

Simply, this theory of symbolic politics contends that people acquire stable affective responses to specific symbols through basic conditioning from rather early in life. In American politics, the strongest most persistent dispositions that survive to adult life are symbolic dispositions, these include party identification, political ideology, and racial prejudice. The adult individual has a number of symbolic dispositions, that is, having developed affective responses which are attached to particular symbols, the subject as voter is able to then react specifically to political events. This theory of politics is useful in that it evaluates and foregrounds the power of affect in the making of individual political choices and determines the subject's participation in political movements. Elizabeth Taylor, as an icon, a persuasive affective laborer and as a figure of fantasy produces the various structured affective responses to her image and performances from viewers that enable her to initiate and sustain the intervention she desires for people suffering from AIDS.

Currently viewers have instant access to decades of discursive information about Elizabeth Taylor whose death in March 2011 became a global multimedia event. This assures that the present generation of spectators who may have not seen a Taylor film can still have discursive awareness of her and can understand the ways she operates as a specific symbol in popular culture. Narratives that neatly surmise her life's work as a film actor, as the greatest woman star of postwar American film—the Queen of Hollywood epithet circulating freely—recognize her as an international exemplar of American glamour and stardom, and credit her work as a globalizer of American celebrity and mass culture in the Third World during the 1960s. She is framed as an earnest, generous, and steadfast activist who worked to help humanize AIDS suffers which not only honor her but elicit positive responses toward her and her numerous extraordinary labors. She is now a continuously circulating, citational symbol of white American hyperfeminine, maternal, loving compassion. Audiences young and old, well versed in the Taylor legend and neophytes who have encountered Taylor as icon more recently, are attaching affects to her. And through her example they learn that the culturally vetted and official universally acceptable response to sufferers of AIDS is a basic respect for their humanity, and if possible to contribute monetary funds in a collective effort to treat, comfort, and heal the sick.

THE UNIVERSAL MOTHER

By evoking compassion and shame in viewers witnessing the AIDS epidemic in mass media, including public service announcements on television, in newspapers, and in books, Elizabeth Taylor coaxes them to take action by contributing money to two of the funding bodies that she helps establish to aid in research, treatment and education.[54] When she declares with great indignation, "President Bush, Mr. Quayle, Senator Helms, your policy on AIDS is wrong . . . dead wrong," her statement is televised and widely aired. She ignites the passion of viewers who agree to donate sums to help AIDS patients who are unable to receive support from the federal government.

Coinciding with Elizabeth Taylor's public criticism of the Bush administration's apathy towards AIDS, the disease is finally federally acknowledged as a growing medical, social, and national crisis, and the state symbolically reclaims the AIDS body in 1990. By then the number of Americans with AIDS is estimated at about eight million people that year alone, an astronomical figure from the first five cases of the illness reported by the Centers of Disease Control in 1981.[55] In a belated national response, president George H. W. Bush approves an emergency aid package of $882 million dollars to help sixteen cities affected by the epidemic, including Washington, D.C., which was one of the urban areas most devastated by the disease.[56]

The US government also initiates HRSA, the Health Resources and Services Administration, the primary federal agency that aims to improve access to health services for those who are uninsured, isolated, and underserved. The HAB, the HIV/AIDS Bureau, is then formed under HRSA, a part of the US Department of Health and Human Services. Finally, legislation on the Ryan White HIV/AIDS Program begins on May 16, 1990, with the Senate voting 95 to 4 to enact it. Coming to the floor with sixty-six cosponsors, there is enough bipartisan support to block a filibuster attempt by Senator Jesse Helms. It is the largest federal program focused solely on HIV/AIDS care with a budget of $2.1 billion dollars in 2008. Its main function is to fund primary health care and support services for people with AIDS.

According to Michael Iskowitz, Senator Edward Kennedy's chief medical counsel on HIV from 1986 to 1992, Elizabeth Taylor is present in the US Capitol during these proceedings, and unlike other stars who venture to Washington solely for personal publicity, she follows through on all AIDS bills and even the amendments. In her guise as the once and always Hollywood star, she dazzles and persuades many reluctant Congressional members, including the star-struck conservative senator from Utah, Orrin Hatch, to vote for the bill. She speaks to the senators directly or sends them personalized letters on her signature violet-colored lavender-scented stationary to accompany detailed information about AIDS that they previously had no intention of reading.[57]

Just a day before, the Senate votes to name the bill in honor of Ryan White, who dies five weeks before the passing of the bill. An Indiana teenager and a hemophiliac, White himself becomes an AIDS activist, having contracted the disease from a blood transfusion and dies after six years of fighting. After his exposure, even though doctors try to assure parents that he poses little if any danger to other students, White is expelled from his middle school in Kokomo, Indiana. While being home-schooled over the telephone for seven weeks, he legally wins the right to attend public school in the neighboring town of Cicero. Having contracting HIV through a gross medical error, he helps change the national perceptions of AIDS proving that the disease does not only afflict homosexual men.

The example of Ryan White's discrimination by the Indiana public school system re-educates Americans, allowing them to feel differently for AIDS patients, to consider the sick as actual victims and worthy of sympathy.[58] Because he comes in contact with AIDS not through gay sex or intravenous drug use, Ryan White is the iconic AIDS martyr who could, unlike Rock Hudson, be perceived as an absolute innocent.[59] He is even described by Thomas Brandt, the spokesman for the National Commission on AIDS at the time of his death, as "a fine and loving and gentle person" and his image is the one the federal government chooses to use to rally itself during its first official, delayed response to the crisis. Most significantly, this is because this "fine and loving and gentle person" is also somebody's child.

Ryan White's mother Jeanne comes to Capitol Hill to garner support for the bill three weeks after her son's death while Elizabeth Taylor appears before the Senate during the bill's introduction in early March and speaks to the gathered assembly in its support. Their concerted effort strongly suggests that the kind of successful AIDS activism that enacts laws through the making of new legislation, the generating of hundreds of millions in funding by the federal government as well as from its citizens willing to donate what they wish happens through the receptive performance of a symbolic politics that elicit feelings of remorse, anguish, shame, and hope. This yearning for hope and the unshakable belief in Elizabeth Taylor and Jeanne White's entitlement to live free in a better world is based on the white subject's historical and continued access to the privileges and inalienable rights of proper American citizenship secured by their whiteness. This access including the opportunity to directly interface with the US federal legislative body and testify in front of Congress is a right that is not guaranteed to the Black mother.

Jeanne White and Elizabeth Taylor prove that AIDS activism from its onset depends on social actors who ably perform through the sanitized body in the universal form of the loving mother whose devotion makes the caring of the sick an inalienable right and duty under humanism. The loss of Jeanne White's child, who is considered one of AIDS's innocent victims, makes her that kind of mother. Elizabeth Taylor's extraordinary ability to express pure love in cinema and to her audience, makes her that kind of mother as well— as many of the AIDS patients she visited in hospitals called her "Mom." Her role as the accepting, understanding, sensitive, and loving mother of Jordan II (Dennis Hopper) considered improperly masculine by his gruff father (Rock

Hudson) in *Giant* filmically foreshadows Taylor work as an AIDS activist made possible through her evolution as a symbol of the universal mother capable of performing and being read as a figure of unconditional love.

Still, Elizabeth Taylor's deep sense and projections of maternal love are in tension with her hypersexualized image as a young star, which previously worked to obscure the aspects of her lived reality as a devoted working mother. But Taylor's loving maternity is well documented in various photographs taken during the 1950s, 1960s, and 1970s and the television specials that documented her milestones and celebrated her many achievements in the 1980s, 1990s, and 2000s in which she was accompanied by her children. But it is best expressed in photos shot during the filming of *Cleopatra* that picture her with her three school-aged children on set. While often dressed as the Egyptian queen, she is surrounded by her kids who are mostly seen laughing, smiling, and gazing in wonder or lovingly at her as she beams back at them. She also finalizes the adoption of her daughter Maria during this period, a process which she undertakes with great zeal and which is widely reported.[60] Recalling the hey-day of Taylor's globetrotting during the 1960s and 1970s, Vicky Tiel, a member of her entourage, asserts that the star cared little about film work but focused her attention in procuring delicious food, free alcohol, gossip on the other stars, and being a nurturing earth mother to her family and friends who traveled with her.[61] Her storied public battles with addiction, weight, divorce, and illness inspired her to often muse that she was Mother Courage, saying, "I've survived it all."

In fact, Elizabeth Taylor's literal status as a mother is fetishized at the time of her death as her work as an activist for AIDS sufferers operates through her image as a loving mother and reiterates her symbolism as a healer, a set of significations that Taylor works to project during the last twenty-five years of her life. The confirmation of her passing on March 23, 2011, in Los Angeles is a breaking news story on American network television as anchors Robin Roberts and David Muir, on the set of *Good Morning America*, announce that Taylor was surrounded by her four children at the time of death. *Muir* continues by saying that Taylor is survived by her ten grandchildren and four great grandchildren. He also reads the official statement from Taylor's family by Michael Wilding, Jr., her eldest child:

> My mother was an extraordinary woman who lived life to the fullest, with great passion, humor and love. Though her loss is devastating to those of us who held her so close and so dear, we will always be inspired by her enduring contribution to our world. Her remarkable body of work in film, her ongoing success as a businesswoman, and her brave and relentless advocacy in the fight against HIV/AIDS, all make us incredibly proud of what she accomplished. We know, quite simply, that the world is a better place for Mom having lived in it. Her

Figure 4.2. Loving working mom Elizabeth Taylor alongside her actual son Michael Wilding, Jr. and her costar Loris Loddi who plays her on-screen son Caesarion on the set of *Cleopatra.* **Source: Keyston Features/Hulton Archive/Getty Images.**

legacy will never fade, her spirit will always be with us, and her love will live forever in our hearts.

Spoken of with deep affection, love and gratitude, Taylor's family continues to shift her persona from a brazen sex symbol of the 1960s Sexual Revolution to a loving, caring, and brave modern mother, allowing the pleasure viewers feel when thinking of her work as a global humanitarian to eclipse their sense of titillation when imagining her legendary sexual exploits. [62]

AIDS WORK AS MATERNAL MELODRAMA

Elizabeth Taylor's considerable achievements as an AIDS activist and fundraiser are realized through her ability to rouse and hearten viewers, powers she first harnesses as a performer of Hollywood melodramas. As audiences once felt invigorated by her moral indignation, triumphs, and her exhilaration in falling in love on and off screen, now they can feel her compassion for the sick through the same emotional power that made her an incandescent star on the silver screen. Shortly after her death, a stirring tribute video memorializing her and valorizing her AIDS battles is featured on the amfAR website designed to elicit the emotional responses that Taylor ably produced from viewers through her activism and her film work which unlike Andrew

Sullivan's 1980s AIDS condemnations succeeds through a melodramatic mode of celebratory melancholia.

The video is narrated by Vanessa Redgrave, the mother of the late actress, Natasha Richardson, who is a former amfAR trustee. As an AIDS worker and fundraiser,[63] Richardson doubly codes as an innocent victim after she dies from head injuries sustained during a ski lesson in March 2009 and as a devoted daughter and caregiver to her father, the British New Wave filmmaker Tony Richardson who died of AIDS-related causes in 1991. Redgrave's performance here is an act of considerable generosity because it shines a brighter light on Taylor's AIDS work instead of her daughter's, even as Richardson activism is imbricated in the video through her mother's voice. The video allows Elizabeth Taylor's activism to be a space for experiencing a number of affects including loss, nostalgia, appreciation, comfort, and noblesse. Not only are Taylor's strength and courage lovingly highlighted but it is Redgrave's gravelly voice and the marked absences of Richardson and Taylor that provide the pathos for the viewer.

As she sets aside the grief of the loss of her own daughter to honor Elizabeth Taylor, Vanessa Redgrave, who for the majority of her public life since the 1960s presented herself as a leftist radical is here, transformed as her status as the parent of a fallen AIDS activist overrides and suspends other facets of her public identity and turns her like Jeanne White and Elizabeth Taylor, into a universal mother, deserving of compassion and forgiveness for any past transgressions that marked her as unruly or improperly feminine. This is especially moving since she has been represented as a negligent mother in popular media in the past. She was a former anti-Vietnam War activist who had unsuccessfully run for British Parliament on the Communist Workers' Revolutionary Party ticket twice. She was also a vocal advocate of the Palestine Liberation Organization, having produced and narrated a television documentary supporting Palestine, called *The Palestinian* (1977), that she financed through the selling of the home she shared with her daughters Natasha and Joely Richardson. Most famously she was accused of anti-Semitism for denouncing those she referred to as "Zionist hoodlums" in her acceptance speech for the Best Supporting Actress Academy Award for her performance in *Julia* (1977). Her dogged devotion to her political views and work for social justice took her away from her children, particularly Natasha who at age six asked her mother to spend more time at home. When Redgrave tries to console her daughter by telling her that others in the world desperately need her help and that she would spend more time with her later, Natasha reported told her mother that she needs her now, not when she is older. Redgrave later admits that, "the children certainly suffered" due to her absence.[64]

Through the intertextual, extrafilmic history between mother and daughter that is already embedded in the video, Vanessa Redgrave is finally *present* for her daughter, standing in for her through her role as the narrator, as she continues her daughter's fight against AIDS while her disembodied but recognizable voice guides the viewer to feel compassion for people with the disease and to feel the triumph of imminent victory in order to enlist new fighters. The video is made up of a visual collage of the numerous victorious moments in the fight against AIDS that feels like high melodrama but works to actualize itself as a visual document historicizing a significant political and social movement. Through the inclusion of photographs of Taylor at various vigils and Congressional meetings, the video suggests that participating in the battle against AIDS provides the emotional closures that rival any well-crafted Hollywood melodrama, through its themes of personal redemption and returns to innocence.

For the nation turning a blind eye to AIDS and for Taylor and Redgrave whose AIDS work functions through their performances of proper mothering, whiteness, and femininity, their celebration and success reveal the extremely narrow parameters of what constitutes effective and sanctioned women's activism. Vanessa Redgrave's performance as a devoted mother who is forced to live through the death of her child and her choice to continue on with her daughter's AIDS work shows how AIDS activism demands personal sacrifice, copious generosity, the conquest of tragedy through survival, and most importantly, expressions which code as contrition. The video invites the viewer to experience the very emotional and cathartic release that accompanies the afterglow of the activist's achievement by pairing Vanessa Redgrave and Elizabeth Taylor whose work against AIDS helps redeem their past transgressions of unpopular radical stances, domestic negligence, sexual, and corporeal excesses to universal inalienable motherhood.

This exposure of the delimitations of women's political agency, even those of famous, rich, white women who had starred in several film melodramas that made them rich and famous in the first place brings to mind the generic limitations of the melodrama itself, a pervasive cinematic mode most closely associated with women through its female characters and its intended female audience. It valorizes moral courage and produces pleasure through the temporary triumph of the good against evil. But victories in melodramas are often only moral ones which while "revealing the wish-fulfilling impulse for the achievement of justice that gives American popular culture its appeal," do not provide the rights which would accompany the forceful realignment of the justice and legislative systems to compensate the disenfranchised, embolden the weak, and right that social wrongs that exploit the poor to guarantee lives of comfort for the rich.[65] In movie melodramas, "doing the right thing," that is, making a painful personal sacrifice that results in the happiness of another person, ensures a moral victory, as Stella Dallas does when she gives up her daughter in order for her child to enter high society. But this selflessness, often on the part of the woman protagonist cannot make or initiate the collective social change that makes such a sacrifice superfluous.

Elizabeth Taylor herself has several filmic rehearsals to project her desire to live in a world based on social equity and acceptance. In a stirring scene from one of her earlier films for MGM, a splashy screen adaptation of Sir Walter Scott's *Ivanhoe* (1952), she plays a Jewish healer named Rebecca persecuted by the anti-Semitic Norman court of Prince John (Guy Rolfe). For helping the Saxon Ivanhoe, she is accused of being an infidel and a witch. She speaks out against her persecution by saying,

> It is true that I was taught healing from Miriam of Manassas. But I have always used this skill in the service of man, to ease his suffering. If that makes me guilty of witchcraft and with me my people, then may God have mercy on your soul. I am innocent.

Her jilted suitor, the Norman knight De Bois-Guilbert (George Sanders), begs her to confess and to renounce her faith and save herself. She refuses and hopes that her "people are not ashamed of the way [she] dies." She declares,

> I will not live in the world that you offer. It has no sun nor moon, nor air to breathe. No faith, no love, no honor.

As a subject occupying a minority position and considered the Other by the Christian Saxons and Normans, Rebecca is the magical Jew who is not permitted to love the Christian Ivanhoe and condemned to an interminable loneliness. Rebecca's trial ends with her inevitable rescue by the titular knight but hers is a fleeting victory that serves to display her moral goodness when she gives up all romantic claims to Ivanhoe because she cannot secure her equal rights under English law to love, marry, or worship without persecution.

Elizabeth Taylor's portrayal of Rebecca marks her first cinematic foray into representing difference, which she continues to do throughout the fifties and sixties, including her roles in *Giant* and *Cleopatra* and culminates in her voice over work in the Holocaust documentary *Genocide* (1982). Not unproblematically, as a performer, Elizabeth Taylor is a figure through which white film audiences in the United States and the world can encounter an iteration of exceptional whiteness, a mutable iteration of a singular white minority position and aberrant body which I discussed in detail in chapter 1. Whether as a white colonial subject outside the imperial metropole (*Elephant Walk*), a white social progressive standing alone against a regressive political and racial majority (*Giant*), or as a white misfit (*Cleopatra*), she stars in many

Hollywood melodramas that are emotionally enriching, entertaining, and engrossing but whose pleasures are regrettably and almost always imbricated in the failure of social justice, even for the deserving white minority in the specific case of Taylor's Rebecca. But her embodiment of a singular white subjectivity on screen as well as her past sexual indiscretions also allow her to ably stand in for the white gay sick minority exiled from social justice and sexual equality.

According to Christine Gledhill, American melodrama operates on the polarization of good and evil as the innocent, virtuous protagonist cannot use the powers available to the villain and in accordance to her nature must become the victim. Her inaction is legitimated by a range of devices as her undeserved and prolonged suffering produces pleasure through pathos for the audience.[66] Because this is so, Elizabeth Taylor's work fighting the AIDS epidemic and its transcendence of the fundamental limitations of the filmic melodrama provides the emotional relief, satisfaction and joy that comes from the making of a better social world beyond the screen.

Elizabeth Taylor's AIDS work mobilizes people to bring lasting political and social change, by inspiring the culture around a political issue to shift from indifference to a new understanding and acceptance. According to Raymond Williams, in *Keywords* he notes that the term *culture,*

> In all its early uses was a noun of the process of the tending *of* something, basically crops or animals . . . This provided a further basis for the important next stage of meaning, by metaphor. From the early sixteenth century the tending of natural growth was extended to a process of human development . . .[67]

Her work contributes to the development of the gradual cultivation of a new cultural sensibility about AIDS by the US federal government and US subjects. As billions of dollars are raised, donated, earmarked, and distributed to help people with AIDS through a mixture of symbolic performance, radical thinking, and federal intervention, AIDS is framed as a series of social problems that can find solutions through what is still further revealed as the racial logics of capital, as white noblesse oblige is spectacularized and commodified through Taylor's hypermediated performances of compassion.

While on a trip to Bangkok, Thailand, in 1989 Elizabeth Taylor is photographed shaking hands with an AIDS patient and the image is printed in newspapers all over Southeast Asia. This is significant because the rate of HIV infection is high in the country, a global hub of sex work, sex traffic, and sexual tourism. While extending her hand helps to humanize the Thai AIDS sufferer immeasurably, Taylor's gesture of compassion is also used to demonize Thailand's perceived apathy toward the disease and its hatred toward its sufferers while concurrently representing the AIDS humanitarian as white and American through Taylor's image. This obscures the fact that legions of white Americans travel to Thailand annually specifically for sex and are complicit in the proliferation of violence and exploitation of Thai sex workers and children, of which the outbreaks of Thai AIDS are a symptom.[68] On World AIDS Day in 1996 Elizabeth Taylor appeals to the General Assembly of the United Nations to urge all nations to join together to fight HIV/AIDS through the making of a vaccine.[69] This in turn also allows viewers to automatically assume that the United States has taken an effective leadership role in the global AIDS fight, particularly in Africa and by extension skewing perceptions of the U.S.'s greater authority in the United Nations as largely based in humanitarian concerns. This is untrue as U.S global interventions are always pursued to protect American interests.

Still better known is Elizabeth Taylor's participation in Kenneth Cole's "We All Have AIDS" photo campaign and art installation produced in honor of World AIDS Day in 2005. Shot in panorama style by photographer Mark Seliger and featuring other prominent figures such as President Nelson Mandela, Archbishop Desmond Tutu, singer-actor Harry Belafonte, HIV-positive Olympic gold medalist Greg Louganis, and actors Whoopi Goldberg and Tom Hanks, the panoramic photo was featured in its 8" x 11½" panel form in over 200 magazines including *Vogue* and *Vanity Fair* with the section featuring Elizabeth Taylor, who while not standing in the center of the actual panoramic photo is now repositioned and centered in the folded panel. Barefoot, like all of the other subjects beside her, Taylor is framed against Mandela, Tutu, and Belafonte, iconic political activists who have fought for decades in valiant efforts to win Black freedom in South Africa and the United States. The inclusion of Mandela, Tutu, Belafonte, and Goldberg acknowledges that AIDS is both an African and African American epidemic, but Taylor's recentering in the photo suggests that the actual power to fight the disease comes from white American noblesse and its unequalled ability to spur capitalism through both its consumer power and its own sense of elevated value that privileges white images over Black ones.

While the savvy Kenneth Cole company tries to argue that the photo is not an advertisement for shoes but is in fact an example of political art by having its subjects be barefoot, it was still commissioned by a shoe manufacturer that also sold T-shirts reading "We All Have AIDS" to various high-end retailers including Barneys New York in conjunction with the photo campaign.[70] The racial dimensions of AIDS care and proper AIDS activism is clear—white funds which initially helped white patients in AIDS's first international cycle now are used to help fight the global battle in Africa as white activists such as Elizabeth Taylor and Kenneth Cole receive the lion's share of publicity and accolades. Elizabeth Taylor's millennial AIDS activism is so successful precisely because it produces white pleasure by showing how postcolonial neoliberal whites can help fight the neocolonial problem of African AIDS while suggesting that capitalism is both redemptive and redeemable. Her prominence as an AIDS activist also presents a larger fascinating polemic— the political economy of money's moral value to produce positive political and social change.

AFFECTIVE GENIUS

The two Elizabeth Taylor films that most astound viewers and critics are *National Velvet* and *Who's Afraid of Virginia Woolf,* her first and last major film performances, the bookends of her fabled onscreen career. They show her explosive power as a cinematic wonder which confirms that this acting prodigy did grow, thrive, and learn to not only act exceedingly well in films but remake the cultures of performance and celebrity in foundational and ingenious ways. Elizabeth Taylor's affective genius expands the purview of stardom and star power to bring greater understanding of how mediated performative acts as a set of affective modes can fundamentally organize subjective and collective experiences and knowledges about identity. In her work she visualizes once invisible human feelings through the hyperprojection of unguarded, open human emotion that melds with the inner world through optical and aural registers that form new interconnected spheres of emotive experiences. As a film actor and an activist, she is a performer who is more than an "erotic legend"[71] and an ultimate object of beauty who "has no bad angles"[72] who as a "natural" knows the camera so intimately well that she describes it as an all-seeing eye that is tied to her with an invisible umbilical cord.[73] More than the greatest architect of postwar fame and celebrity, which she undoubtedly is, she is an affective genius who on film charms, entices, and makes empathetic every character she has ever played. She uses her various abilities to make a controversial medical crisis worthy of empathy, providing a culturally acceptable emotive grounding for a political cause that profoundly resonates with mainstream, nonqueer Americans who now understand how to feel about people with AIDS.

Elizabeth Taylor's ability to electrify and elicit pleasure through viewer empathy, removes any distance between the screen and the spectator, the filmic character, and the viewer. She becomes the conduit through which a fundamental understanding between the viewer and the character allows an engrossing, transcendent, and revelatory experience to occur, passing through and beyond the flat dimensions of the screen. Her undiminished power and unwavering ability to elicit a specific emotional response from the viewer, including compassion for her plights and delight in her triumphs also make her a genius. Her ability to engender those feelings through her filmwork, her perfumes, and her AIDS activism confirms this. As the knowing performer who accepts the limited imagination of her audience she willingly makes her body safe in order to mobilize millions of people in her fight against HIV/ AIDS. She teaches the world what the appropriate response is to the most menacing medical crisis of the twentieth century through the performance of her earnest feelings which no political opponent can diminish.

Not only does Elizabeth Taylor live long enough to see promising trials for an AIDS vaccine called RV144 which are conducted in 2009, the US medical community also documents the case of Timothy Ray Brown in 2011, whom they name the "Berlin Patient," the first man given a "functional cure" for HIV through a stem cell transplant. While seeking treatment for his leukemia he receives stem cells from a donor possessing an HIV immunity gene that puts his HIV in remission. Diagnosed with the disease in 1995 and residing in the Bay Area of California, Brown is considered the first person to be cured of HIV/ AIDS.[74] Dr. Jay Levy, one of the foremost researchers of AIDS who is credited with codiscovering the HIV virus, says Brown's success "opens the door to cure research."[75] Living long enough to see an AIDS cure is one of Taylor's greatest wishes and it seems it has in a way, come true. Unquestionably her efforts to help people with the disease makes HIV/AIDS a topic of continuing social interest and concern worldwide. Her activism helps spur American federal funding for care and research, which in turn makes trials of successful AIDS vaccines possible. During her life she encourages transnational pharmaceutical firms to make treatment drugs more accessible to people with AIDS in the Third World. Finally, her work with the US government gives media attention to federal funding which then becomes a global model for AIDS intervention as other First World nations as Great Britain, Germany, the Netherlands, France, and Denmark have also set aside monies for AIDS care both at home and abroad, particularly in sub-Saharan Africa.[76]

Elizabeth Taylor's AIDS activism, like her filmwork, reveals the power of iconicity to change culture. The overwhelmingly positive receptions of her AIDS work suggest that performative and affective genius ably operates within the circuits of human pulchritude, visual pleasure, and erotic capital. And as the cultural model for the beautiful woman as an affective genius, she shows how she is not just an object within the firmament of fame, or merely the master of the feminized arts of seduction and masquerade, but a performer who made the cinematic more magical, love feel more transcendent, and one who proves that the pursuit of pleasure is a proper organizing principle for living.

By communicating her compassion for gay men and other people sick with AIDS and by signifying as an empathetic body for the sick as well as the surviving, Elizabeth Taylor performs a symbolic politics that allows spectators to openly and passionately express compassion and empathy for the sick as subjects with fundamental rights deserving of care. These viewers as consumers donate the hundreds of millions of dollars that have and continue to fund direct care to those in need on the ground across the world. The response of donors to Elizabeth Taylor and her work points to the possibilities for compassion to fuel the open market of neoliberalism and bring lasting social change. Elizabeth Taylor's activism shows how the star as an embodiment and maker of meaning and the producer of affects can help change the world.

Elizabeth Taylor is the world's most celebrated and famous AIDS activist because of her performance of stable white maternity and her formidable ability to reach out to a global audience including members of national and international legislative bodies while temporarily connecting the millions of people who have AIDS in the United States and around the globe to others who do not. She modeled the proper behavior of a compassionate advocate for AIDS sufferers in a series of loving and respectful gestures toward people with AIDS that continue to circulate across media. She used her voice and her image to perform an AIDS advocacy that is intimately interpersonal and universal and simultaneously enveloping engrossing and transnational.

Ultimately Elizabeth Taylor is a successful activist because she globalizes her inalienable sense of personal power to expect progress, showing the multitude that passion and constancy do bring about permanent social change, highlighting the stability of white authority. While doing so, she reveals the truths of both the racial logic of American citizenship and its ability to exercise political power. She also exposes the racial logic of capitalism and its redemptive potential that over values white subjectivity and consumption. Finally, she demonstrates the very narrow parameters of effective women's activism which functions through performances of proper femininity and motherhood. Elizabeth Taylor is all the more extraordinary because she contends with and adapts herself to these caveats to produce the political response to AIDS that she desires, once again proving her genius for getting exactly what she wants.

NOTES

1. Robert J. Lacey, *American Pragmatism and Democratic Faith*, 9.
2. Ibid., 13.
3. Ibid., 7.
4. Michael Hardt and Antonio Negri, *Multitude: War and Democracy in the Age of Empire*, 108.
5. From the pressroom of the 65th Academy Awards after Elizabeth Taylor is given the Jean Hersholt Humanitarian Award in 1992.

6. This is so even as Taylor's tenure as a full-fledged movie star begins in the 1950s when the major studios are being forced to relinquish their vast holdings through successful anti-trust litigation by the US government often referred to as the Paramount Decree that comes into effect in 1948 making her a member of the last generation of MGM's screen goddesses. *United States v. Paramount Pictures, Inc.* 334 US 131.

7. Michael Hardt and Antonio Negri, *Multitude: War and Democracy in the Age of Empire,* 112.

8. Cindy Patton, *Globalizing AIDS,* 28.

9. Susan Sontag, *Illness as Metaphor and AIDS and Its Metaphors,* 132.

10. As noted from the Elizabeth Taylor AIDS Foundation website www .elizabethtayloraidsfoundation.org/ retrieved 3.1.11.

11. From an anecdote of a cohort whose brother received care for AIDS in a facility sponsored by Elizabeth Taylor.

12. Shooting of *Cat on a Hot Tin Roof* is halted so Taylor can emotionally recover while Rabbi Max Nussbaum who later oversees her conversion to Judaism visits her frequently, concerned for her well-being. Kitty Kelley, *The Last Star,* 128.

13. Pam Belluck, "New Push to Let HIV Patients Accept Organs That Are Infected," *The New York Times,* published and retrieved 4.11.11. http://www.nytimes .com/2011/04/11/us/11hiv.html?pagewanted=1&emc=eta1

14. Elizabeth Taylor, *Elizabeth Takes Off,* 15.

15. Jacques Pepin, *The Origin of AIDS,* 7.

16. Cindy Patton, *Globalizing AIDS,* xii.

17. Ibid., 31.

18. From a White Diamonds print ad, Elizabeth Arden Fragrances, 1991.

19. Raymond Williams, "Advertising: the Magic System," from *The Cultural Studies Reader*, 422.

20. Susan Jeffords, *Hard Bodies: Hollywood Masculinities in the Reagan Era,* 25.

21. Ange-Marie Hancock, *The Politics of Disgust: the Public Identity of the Welfare Queen,* 55.

22. Ibid., 59.

23. ICAP at Columbia University's Mailman School of Public Health has released studies that assert that the rate of infection amongst African American women in certain parts of the United States is five times greater than overall estimate of the rate of infection of Black women provided by the Centers of Disease Control.

24. Anna Marie Smith, *Welfare Reform and Sexual Regulation,* 172.

25. Jeff Stinson, "Denmark a Unique Mix of Welfare, Economic Growth," *USA Today,* 3.8.07 retrieved 5.2.11, http://www.usatoday.com/momey.2007-03-06 -denmark-usat_N.htm.

26. See Henning Jørgensen's *Consensus, Cooperation, and Conflict: The Policy Making Process in Denmark,* 27.

27. Ninety-five percent of Danes identify as Evangelical Lutherans and 3 percent as members of other Christian denominations (Roman Catholic and Protestant). There is also a Jewish population in Denmark. While the ethnic makeup of Denmark includes people who are Scandinavians, Inuits (from Greenland which has been a Danish colony since 1814), Faroeses (a Norse people who settled in Denmark in the tenth

century), Germans, Turks, and Somalis, statistics indicate that a majority of the five and a half million contemporary Danes trace their heritage to the Iron Age Germanic tribes which include Scandinavians and Germans.

28. David Kocieniewski, "US Business Has High Tax Rates But Pays Less," *The New York Times* published 5.3.11.

29. Nestor García Canclini, *Consumers and Citizens,* 20.

30. Ibid., 22.

31. Ibid., 15.

32. Ibid., 21.

33. Ibid., 22.

34. Grace Kyungwon Hong, *The Ruptures of American Capital,* 5–9.

35. C.B. Macpherson, *The Political Theory of Possessive Individualism Hobbes to Locke,* 3.

36. Ibid., 263–64.

37. This is according to the Centers for Disease Control and Prevention, under "Basic Statistics." Retrieved from the CDC website www.cdc.gov/hiv/topics .surveillance/basic.htm 5.12.11.

38. See www.elizabethtayloraidsfoundation.org/ retrieved 5.12.11.

39. Douglas Crimp, *Melancholia and Moralism,* 5

40. Ibid., 8.

41. Ibid., 7.

42. Elizabeth Taylor affirms that she believes that the delayed response by the US government to AIDS sufferers is based on the belief that the majority of those sick with AIDS in the United States are gay men during a press conference in which she fields the question about homophobia from a child.

43. John D'Emilio, "Capitalism and Gay Identity," 270.

44. Ibid., 274.

45. Susan Sontag, "Notes on Camp," 290.

46. Simon Watney, "Signifying AIDS: 'Global AIDS,' Red Ribbons and Other Controversies," 175.

47. Ibid., 175, I use Watney's quoting of Weir here from "The Red Plague: Do Red Ribbons Really Help in the Fight Against AIDS?" *The Advocate,* May 4, 1993, 38.

48. Read Watney's account of the various contradictions of the global commercialization of the AIDS red ribbon to consider its often precarious shifts as a symbol in the above article.

49. Read Marita Sturken's larger discussion of the ambiguity of the AIDS ribbon as a signifier in *Tangled Memories: The Vietnam War, the AIDS Epidemic and the Politics of Remembering.* ACT UP Posters, 174

50. Simon Watney, "Signifying AIDS: 'Global AIDS,' Red Ribbons and Other Controversies," 178.

51. Alfredo Tradigo, *Icons and Saints of the Eastern Orthodox Church,* 6–9.

52. David O. Sears, "The Role of Affect in Symbolic Politics, 15–16.

53. Ibid., 16.

54. The number of stories about AIDS including television news stories, numbered about 3,500 compared to 1,200 stories for heart disease during the same time,

1980—1998, even while the death toll for AIDS, approximately fourteen million lives lost is about the same number of those who died of heart disease. These statistics are found in Peter Conrad's *The Sociology of Health and Illness,* 136.

55. Michael Gottlieb, "Pneumocystos Pneumonia—Los Angeles 1981."

56. As noted in the HAB HRSA website, hab.hrsa.org/ retrieved 4.15.11.

57. Sam Kashner, "Elizabeth Taylor's Closing Act," 202.

58. Dirk Johnson, "Ryan White Dies of AIDS at 18; His Struggle Helped Pierce Myths," *New York Times* Obituary, published on April 9, 1990.

59. Ryan White's struggle with AIDS was dramatized for television in the ABC movie *The Ryan White Story,* featuring Lukas Haas as White in 1989.

60. Alexander Walker, *Elizabeth: The Life of Elizabeth Taylor,* 253.

61. Vicky Tiel, *It's All about the Dress,* 43.

62. Around the time of Rock Hudson's infection, Taylor's former daughter-in-law, the oil heiress Aileen Getty, who was once married to her son, Christopher, also contracts the disease, and receives the star's full support as she seeks treatment and learns to manage her illness. In 2005, she remarries and is in good health.

63. From the In Memoriam page dedicated to Elizabeth Taylor on the amfAR website www.amfar.org/community/article.aspx?id=6810 retrieved 4.25.11.

64. From Tim Adler's *The House of Redgrave*, online abridged extract, retrieved 5.8.11. www.dailymail.co.uk.

65. Linda Williams, "Melodrama Revised," 48.

66. See Christine Gledhill, *Home Is Where the Heart Is: Studies in Melodrama and the Woman's Film,* 30.

67. Raymond Williams, *Keywords,* p. 87.

68. Ryan Bishop and Lillian S. Robinson, *Night Market: Sexual Cultures and the Thai Economic Miracle,* 44–49.

69. From the amfAR Elizabeth Taylor Memorial page, "amfAR Mourns the Passing of Dame Elizabeth Taylor" retrieved 5.12.11, http://amfar.org/page,aspx?id=9588.

70. The "We All Have AIDS" T-shirts sold for $35 at Barneys. See Eric Wilson, "From Kenneth Cole a New Solidarity" *The New York Times,* printed December 1, 2005.

71. Named as such by Richard Burton in his diaries, Ellis Amburn, *The Most Beautiful Woman in the World,* 221.

72. Claimed by a photographer at MGM. Ruth Waterford, *Elizabeth Taylor*, 60. According to Hollywood lore, actress Claudette Colbert, a fellow cinematic Cleopatra, believes she has a bad side, and insists on always being photographed on her left side. From David Niven's memoir, *Bring on the Empty Horses*, 286.

73. Elizabeth Taylor describes the camera to Johnny Carson in such a way during her only appearance on *The Tonight Show* in February 1992.

74. See Donald G. McNeil, Jr., "For the First Time, AIDS Vaccine Shows Some Success," published in *The New York Times* September 24, 2009. Retrieved 5.12.11 from http://www.nytimes.com/2009/09/25/health/research/25aids.html.

75. Televised local news report, CBS 5 San Francisco, "Apparent Immunity Gene 'Cures' Bay Area Man of AIDS." Dated 5.16.11, retrieved 5.17.11, sanfranciscolocal. cbs.com.

76. From advert, a UK-based AIDS charity using references from UNAIDS reports. Retrieved from www.avert.org/aids-funding.htm, 5.12.11.

Conclusion

Elizabeth Taylor by the Numbers: The Political Economy of White Singularity

Testifying to the phenomenological effects of Elizabeth Taylor's image, Andy Warhol once said, "It would be very glamorous to be reincarnated as a great big ring on Liz Taylor's finger," articulating his wish to live out a new life alongside the most famous woman in the world in order to share in her excessive body adventures and exhilarating affective experiences. It seems that Warhol's fantasy of living vicariously through Taylor is not a unique one, as the phenomenal success of Christie's auction of Elizabeth Taylor's collection of jewelry, fine art, clothing, and memorabilia attests.

"The Collection of Elizabeth Taylor" was comprised of 1,778 lots and generated tens of thousands of bids across the globe, including over fifty-seven thousand bids online from fans who could not spend millions to own a piece of Taylor jewelry or art but could spend hundreds on a number of quirky Taylor trinkets, namely her costume jewelry and handbags. Every lot was sold, often at five, ten, or fifty times its estimated price and generated $156.75 million. This final number sums up her allure in US dollars in the hearts and minds of fans and investors who have bought into Elizabeth Taylor's legend as the iconic star of American Empire. She is the magical figure of the twentieth century who best simultaneously glamorized capitalism and romanticized imperialism through Hollywood cinema which works in part by promoting US capitalism and American nationalist interests across the world.[1] Warhol also proclaimed that "It's the movies that have really been running things in America ever since they were invented. They show you what to do, how to do it, when to do it, how to feel about it, and how to look how you feel about it."

Every item up for bids that once belonged to the cultural figure best emblematic of American Empire at the apex of its power and who is also often called the last great American movie star is not only a commodity fetish as discussed in chapter 3, but an anthropological fetish as well. These items are the mystical objects whose new owners believe will imbue them with Elizabeth Taylor's power as a performer. Her extracinematic charisma, beauty, and innate and sublime sense for affect and pleasure help account for her stardom, which since her death has become a global celebration of her performative genius.[2] Through Taylor's things, spectators around the globe understood simply why and how she is the most shimmering body in the constellation of stars past and present: her iconicity signified the inherent pleasure of power bestowed on subjects by both capitalism and whiteness but she also unfailingly managed to contour those privileges with an undeniable humanism. She is the one star who best represents the formidable power of American Empire to accumulate material goods, spur capitalism, and protect and secure the white American subject's desire for global mobility in the various pursuits of what that subject deems worthy and desirable. But through her many significations including the meaning of her capacity to express love and feel passion, she endowed the act of accumulation with noblesse oblige that compelled her to use her performative prowess to help people with AIDS, showed the possibilities of the redemptive aspects of capitalism, and the ways compassionate consumption has a legitimate place in the open markets of neoliberalism.

There is a real tension between Elizabeth Taylor's signification of imperial excess and the urges to redeem her which she herself encouraged through her authorship of her AIDS activism that allows us to have her both ways. Elizabeth Taylor as the forthright imperial figure is most compelling as a performer, as a social actor, and a cinematic dream, when she embodies compassion for others and invites viewers to consider the potential of capitalism to change the world in positive ways. This is ultimately the key to understanding her performance of global citizenship and why this formulation is so enticing for white viewers who view her as not only an aspirational figure but now as a hallowed icon of exceptional whiteness who seems to have turned the contradictory notion of benevolent capitalism into the realization of a pragmatic neoliberal utopia. Here the movements of positive social change actually work because whites feel good about wielding their power and working on behalf of their own affective needs and politicized interests to practice good citizenship to those made invisible by the state.

The continuous global economic downturn of the post Great Recession of 2008 did not hamper the bidding or infuse the auction with a staid culture of austerity. Far from it, as members of the 1 percent possessing and controlling the world's wealth and political power as well as working-class and middle-class bidders purchased Taylor's items. This was a striking reminder of the star's ability to continuously fuel capitalism in face of the concurrent explosion of Arab revolutions in the Middle East, the weakness of the euro, and the ailing US economy. Perhaps this is because Elizabeth Taylor's capacity to consume no longer demonizes her as it once did in the 1970s. She worked during the last quarter of her life to complete her hagiography through her performances as a global humanitarian, which functions best through collective and massive acts of consumption. Now Taylor's stardom ultimately commemorates a life of staggering achievement. Favorable reassessments of her film work and the success of her AIDS activism make previous camp readings of her pernicious desires and ruptured body outmoded.

Elizabeth Taylor's collection of prized treasures toured the globe even before it landed on the auction block in New York, traveling without their mistress to London, Paris, Los Angeles, Hong Kong, Moscow, and Dubai becoming her final act, exposing the truth about whiteness through her extra-cinematic image of globalized glamour. Elizabeth Taylor reveals whiteness as an exclusive political formation defined by and reified through the performance of global citizenship that is based on a fantasy of white exceptionalism that is then used to argue that whiteness is deserving of those privileges. As these rights are guaranteed by the power of American Empire, whiteness refuses to be contained and tied to the territorial borders of one nation state and operates through an expansive globalism that contends that whites can live freely and happily anywhere in the world.

In the past scholars have previously defined whiteness to be, amongst other things, a compensatory wage, a possessive investment, and as an unmarked category with a visual hegemony in media culture. Labor historian David R. Rodieger asserts that it should be read as a psychological and public wage that gives whites public deference and free admittance to all spaces. These wages conferred through race make amends for exploitative and alienating class relationships for poor whites who then use these wages to define their class position as not Black.[3] For fellow historian George Lipsitz, whiteness is a form of an "investment in white supremacy that denies communities of color opportunities for asset accumulation and upward mobility." He theorizes that as a social construction, whiteness almost always possesses white people themselves unless they themselves divest in white supremacy.[4] For cultural studies scholar Richard Dyer, whiteness is powerful because it is the default category, writing, "There is no more powerful position than that of being 'just' human."[5] With that claim, whiteness is everything and nothing, an unnamed category that is diffuse and invisible. It can also claim to speak to the "commonality of humanity" as all other identity formations exist as the "Other" to it while being forced to locate its very power through whiteness itself. Roediger, Lipsitz, and Dyer have ably examined whiteness through its constructions against specific historical phenomena such as immigration, twentieth-century racial politics, and through its representations in Hollywood cinema as beautiful and morally superior with extensive focus on the notion of whiteness as a form of property, noting its continuous accruing value.

My investigation of whiteness as an ideological imaginary builds from and adds to their work considering how whiteness remains powerful as institutions that guarantee white global authority must recalibrate themselves after decolonization through its discursive representation, expressly cinema and its ancillary products that elevate it as a prodigious formation through Elizabeth Taylor's strange beauty. Certainly, her various on-screen and off-screen jaunts locate whiteness as being nowhere and everywhere at once in which the only viable civilization is established by the whites who have settled those places. I looked to Elizabeth Taylor's imperial iconicity and her signification of white singularity to argue that whiteness gives its subjects the singular privilege they do not discuss. Through Taylor's performing a fantasy of a magical whiteness secured by her beauty that justifies white global citizenship and helps explain the continuation of imperial power, I put focus on Taylor's imbrication within various media representations that frame white subjectivity as an exceptional formation deserving of love and the fulfillment of all its dreams.

More significantly, my investigation of Elizabeth Taylor's white beauty reminds readers that feminine beauty is ideologically rich and complex, and that beauty indeed matters. It should not be dismissed as superficial, superfluous, or illusionary. After all, so much of postwar and contemporary visual and media culture is anchored and spurred by the spectacularization of the beautiful woman as she can be framed as a figuration of various and sometimes contradictory ideologies or even present herself as Elizabeth Taylor has done as a maker of profound meaning.

As Elizabeth Taylor's treasures were displayed in a series of gallery installations in Christie's showroom in Rockefeller Center in the US financial capital, the fact that her storied collection toured the globe should not be surprising. This is so firstly because Elizabeth Taylor as well as her collection which stands as her proxy signify how white power follows a logic of American globalism that protects unencumbered mobility marking its control in which all other nations are imbricated in the US struggle for power. Secondly, Taylor was prescient in her understanding of what the ravenous public always desired from her most: direct and intimate access to her and her allure. The tour was a rousing success in all cities including in Moscow, the greatest of former communist strongholds, as thousands of Muscovites gathered in the underground mall beneath the Kremlin to stare at Taylor's jewels and gowns. As the greatest star during the period in which the Cold War was at its most strident, Taylor had visited Moscow with producer Mike Todd, who boasted, "What impressed the Russians the most was that a bum like me could grow up in America and become Elizabeth Taylor's husband which is a helluva better job than being President of the United States!"[6]

Her collection's positive reception in Moscow reminds us that her image of conspicuous consumption and the fantasy of capitalism's capacity to secure upward mobility has circulated in global media for decades as even the Iron Curtain was permeable to her glamour. Taylor's beautiful objects were also sent to Dubai in the United Arab Emirates. Built as a sanctuary of capitalism, luxury, and leisure within the Middle East, a haven from fundamentalist revolution, this city of gold is being constructed by a migrant underclass of workers who labor to build everything within the nation's borders at the accelerated pace demanded by capitalism, and whose working conditions and lack of agency still mean they are more slaves than builders.[7] This final visit to Dubai cites Elizabeth Taylor's continuous and intimate proximity to slavery which has always enveloped her image through her work as Hollywood's plantation mistress of the 1950s and 1960s, her ignoble status as the Western world's most insatiable maneater who enslaved and destroyed men, and lastly through the love of her devoted fans who are tied to her through an unbreakable set of diamond-encrusted chains.

The United States and American Empire have historically been political formations made possible by slave labor, whose conspicuous accumulation and extension of territorial and discursive power were effects to prove its exceptionalism to its citizens and to the world. It is appropriate that the objects that signify the extensions of Elizabeth Taylor's star power complete a final imperial metaphor by not only connecting her to the capitals of glamour but also to the geographical linchpins where capitalism has steadily and assuredly defeated all other models. In Dubai in particular, capitalist power ignites the strict organization, discipline, and censure of bodies that must labor at its behest.

Elizabeth Taylor's performance of white American identity and global citizenship as beholden to no other authority than its own, as an indomitable and fantastical identity with a boundless purview is signaled through the beautiful objects she left behind. Her projection of American subjectivity as a form of white exceptionalism was best expressed through her capacity to hunger for and experience new pleasures. This carte blanche of white modernity for liberation and adventure is reconfirmed by countless white subjects each time they travel beyond their national borders using their American, Commonwealth, or EU passports. These travelers simply practice their global citizenship in the pursuit of pleasure with the ease bestowed upon them by their racialized juridical formal identities that both ties them to the nation-state and imbricates them within the community of nations and its imperative of white power that organizes contemporary geopolitics.

This white imbrication in the world is reflected in a cycle plantation films, in which the spectacle of Elizabeth Taylor's whiteness is used to regiment and celebrate white identity through the discipline of her lavish body and excessive femininity. This cultivation of whiteness often leads to further white fulfillment and greater access to physical and spiritualized white liberation. The three films that make up the official cycle, *Elephant Walk, Giant,* and *Raintree County,* are didactic texts and do the necessary work of genre by presenting viewers with filmic encounters of social problems that are then solved through imaginative solutions. These films address the white problems and anxieties tied to race brought about as the results of postcolonialism namely new nationalisms, the building of new enclosures, and new liberation movements. Through these films whites are given the dual definitions of citizenship which in turn helped determine what whiteness as a formation would become after the death of empire and what it remains today.

In *Elephant Walk* after an elephant stampede destroys their Ceylonese tea plantation, Ruth and John Wiley come to realize that their power is actually not tied to the plantation itself, but that their whiteness always already bestows upon them the privileges of global citizenship and a newfound mobility to search for greater adventures across the world. In *Giant,* the Texas oil boom brings about petro-modernity and with it the new luxury of racial tolerance as rich whites such as the Benedicts are further ennobled by their cultivation of a noblesse oblige towards Mexicans with whom they live alongside. Their acceptance of Mexicans makes the Benedicts good citizens and valorizes their paternalism and justifies the power they practice as a white dynasty. In *Raintree County,* it becomes clear that for white power to remain intact it must be protected against the threats to whiteness posed by miscegenation. The dangers of desegregation are laid out while the burdens of race and fears of Blackness are forcibly contained in the South as the cultural designated site of national racial trauma in order that race and racism remain wholly Southern rather than Northern problems. In these three narratives, Elizabeth Taylor's plantation mistress is regimented through filial femininity to come into proper whiteness. This is so even in *Raintree County,* as her Southern belle is finally tamed after her racial liminality demands that she be destroyed for the sanctity of Southern white identity and its logic of racial domination.

Cleopatra is a plantation film dressed up like a sword and sandal epic, the genre's direct masculine counterpart, in which films such as *The Fall of the Roman Empire* released one year after Taylor's own epic use male-centered narratives of heroic bodies laboring in the securing of nations and the building of empires against the dangerous barbarism posed by nonwhite others, and cinematically romanticizes the *pax romana,* the global peace resulting in Rome's benevolent rule of the world. Cleopatra's body as projected by Taylor becomes the object in a war fought to secure white masculine power and to constrict and control the parameters of proper whiteness as a political identity and cultural practice precisely as whiteness comes into greater power and reestablishes its global authority in the immediate postcolonial world outside the screen. But it is through her performance of Cleopatra that Taylor fully glorified her steadfast pursuit of pleasure as the Oriental in whiteface, a white figure whose orientalist-inspired sexual liberation and propensity for conspicuous consumption made her an unparalleled superstar and cemented her imperial iconicity allowing her stardom to reach its greatest heights that would no longer need Hollywood films to directly promote her image. Taylor's body adventures with drugs, food, sex, and money helped normalize excess with viewers as her personal life which she played out in public was symmetrical to Cleopatra's battle for her political authority. Elizabeth Taylor's coming to full ascendance as a star at this time is metaphorical of the rewards tied to the zenith of power guaranteed by whiteness itself which she expressed through her transnational mobility and unapologetic relationship to capitalism.

Elizabeth Taylor's unquestionable love of capitalism also inspires her to launch her AIDS activism through the flexible and racially inflected circuits of capital. She performs in a riveting maternal melodrama that colors American whiteness with a sense of largesse that becomes globally recognized as the most legible form of good white citizenship, as evidenced by her universal celebration as an AIDS humanitarian. By aiding the disenfranchised not formally recognized by the nation-state—referencing her role as the loving, politically progressive Leslie Benedict in *Giant,* Taylor's AIDS activism is so successful because it reveals the redemptive potential of capitalism through its delivery of practical solutions, compelling so many others not just whites to both glimpse at and invest in the hope subjects purchase through capitalist consumption.

Arguably Elizabeth Taylor is now more admired for being an AIDS activist that for being a film goddess because her AIDS work imbues her now eternally glamorous image with an unwavering humanism that is even more ideologically powerful than her considerable physical beauty. While signifying exceptional whiteness whose ubiquity and media dominance as a star were emblematic of American Empire at the height of its power, she provides a compelling epistemology of that power through a captivating and fascinating performance of earnest compassion that is astounding as it hinges on Virginia Woolf's maxim, "The beautiful seem right by the force of beauty, and the feeble wrong because of weakness." And Elizabeth Taylor does all of this while sparkling like no other celestial body before or after her.

NOTES

1. Moira Forbes, "Elizabeth Taylor Auction: A Fitting Remembrance," *Forbes*, printed December 11, 2011. Retrieved 5.25.12. <www.forbes.com/sites/moiraforbes /2011/12/14/elizabeth-taylor-auction-a-fitting-rememberance/.

2. See Stella Bruzzi, "Desire and the Costume Film" and her discussion of the anthropological fetish as symbolic and embodying the deity, 249.

3. David R. Roediger, *The Wages of Whiteness: Race and the Making of the American Working Class*, Revision Edition, 12–13.

4. George Lipsitz, *The Possessive Investment in Whiteness: How White People Profit from Identity Politics*, viii.

5. Richard Dyer, *White*, 2.

6. Kitty Kelley, *The Last Star*, 117.

7. Pardis Mahdavi, *Gridlock: Labor, Migration, and Human Trafficking in Dubai*, 43–46.

Bibliography

Adas, Michael. *Machines as Measures of Men: Science, Technology and Ideologies of Western Dominance*. Ithaca, NY: Cornell University Press, 1989.

Adler, Tim. *The House of Redgrave: The Secret Lives of a Theatrical Dynasty*. London: Aurum Press Ltd, 2011.

Adorno, Theodoro and Max Horkheimer. "The Culture Industry: Enlightenment as Mass Deception" in *The Cultural Studies Reader, Second Edition*, ed., Simon During, 31–41. New York and London: Routledge, 1999.

Alexander, Paul. *Boulevard of Broken Dreams: The Life, Times, and Legend of James Dean*. New York: Viking Adult, 1994.

Amburn, Ellis. *The Most Beautiful Woman in the World: The Obsessions, Passions, and Courage of Elizabeth Taylor*. New York: HarperEntertainment, 2000.

AmfAR.org. "Dame Elizabeth Taylor Founding International Chairman." 7.9.22 www.amfar.org/about/dame-elizabeth-taylor/.

Anderson, Karen. *Little Rock: Race and Resistance at Central High School*. Princeton: Princeton University Press, 2009.

Anger, Kenneth. *Hollywood Babylon II*. New York: E.P. Dutton, 1984.

Bahktin, M.M. *The Dialogic Imagination: Four Essays*. ed., Michael Holquist. Translated by Vadim Liapunov. Austin: University of Texas Press, 1982.

Balibar, Etienne, and Immanuel Wallerstein. *Race, Nation, Class: Ambiguous Identities*. London: Verso, 1992.

Banner, Lois W. *American Beauty: A Social History . . . Through Two Centuries of the American Idea, Ideal, and Image of the Beautiful Woman*. Los Angeles: Figueroa Press, 1983.

Barthes, Roland. *Mythologies*. New York: Farrar, Straus and Giroux, 1972.

Bayer, David. L "Urban Peru: Political Action as Sellout," In *Peruvian Nationalism: A Corporatist Revolution*. Ed. David Chaplin, 226–240. New Brunswick, NJ: Transaction Inc, 1976.

Beaton, Cecil, and Hugo Vickers. *The Unexpurgated Beaton: The Cecil Beaton Diaries as He Wrote Them, 1970–1980*. New York: Knopf, 2003.

Belluck, Pat. "New Push to Let HIV Patients Accept Organs That Are Infected." *The New York Times*, April 11, 2011.

Berg, Charles Ramirez. "Manifest Myth-Making: Texas History in the Movies." In *The Persistence of Whiteness Race and Contemporary Hollywood Cinema.* ed. Daniel Bernardi, 3–27. New York and London: Routledge, 2007.

Berlant, Lauren and Michael Warner. "Sex in Public." In *the Cultural Studies Reader,* ed. Simon During, 334–70. New York and London: Routledge, 2001.

Berridge, Virginia, and Griffith Edwards. *Opium and the People: Opiate Use in Nineteen-Century England.* New York: St. Martin's Press, 1983.

Bhabha, Homi K. *The Location of Culture.* London and New York: Routledge, 1994.

Bishop, Ryan, and Lillian S. Robinson 1998. *Night Market: Sexual Cultures and the Thai Economic Miracle.* New York and London: Routledge, 1998.

Bogle, Donald. *Toms, Coons, Mammies, Mulattoes, and Bucks: An Interpretative History of Blacks in Films.* New York: Viking Press, 1973.

———. *Dorothy Dandridge: A Biography.* New York: Amistad, 1999.

Bordo, Susan. *Unbearable Weight: Feminism, Western Culture and the Body.* Berkeley: University of California Press, 1993.

Bosworth, Patricia. *Montgomery Clift: A Biography.* New York: Harcourt Brace Jovanovich, 1978.

Bowles, Paul. *Their Heads Are Green and Their Hands Are Blue: Scenes from the Non-Christian World.* New York: Random House, 1963.

Bragg, Melvyn. *Richard Burton: A Life.* New York: Little Brown, 1987.

Britton, Andrew. "Stars and Genre." In *Stardom: Industry of Desire,* ed. Christine Gledhill, *Entertainment.* Austin: University of Texas Press, 1991.

Brode, Douglas. *Multiculturalism and the Mouse: Race and Sex in Disney Entertainment.* Austin, TX: University of Texas Press, 2006.

Bruzzi, Stella. *Undressing Cinema: Clothing and Identity in the Movies.* Oxfordshire: Routledge, 1997.

Canclini, Néstor García. *Consumers and Citizens: Globalization and Multicultural Conflicts.* Translated by George Yúdice. Minneapolis: University of Minnesota Press, 2001.

CBS 5 San Francisco "Apparent Immunity Gene 'Cures' Bay Area Man of AIDS" 5.16.11 www.cbsnews.com/sanfrancisco/news/apparent-immunity-gene-cures-bay -area-man-of-aids/.

Cdc.gov "Basic Statistics." 5.12.11. www.cdc.gov/hiv/topics.surveillance/basic.html.

Chion, Michel. *The Voice in Cinema.* Translated by Claudia Gorbman. New York: Columbia University Press, 1991.

Christies.com "Andy Warhol (1928–1987): The Collection of Elizabeth Taylor. Diamond Dust Candy Box." 12.15.11. https://www.christies.com/en/lot/lot -5503128.

Classen, Steven D. *Watching Jim Crow: The Struggles over Mississippi TV, 1955– 1969.* Durham, NC, and London: Duke University Press, 2004.

Clifford, James. "Notes on Travel and Theory" *Inscriptions 5* (1989). 5.29.11. www.2 .ucsc.edu/culturalstudies/PUBS/Inscriptions/vol_5/clifford.html.

Conrad, Peter. *The Sociology of Health and Illness.* New York: Worth Publishers, 1991.

Corliss, Richard. "Elizabeth Taylor Dies at 79; Actress Defined Modern Fame." *Time*, March 23, 2011.

Crimp, Douglas. *Melancholia and Moralism: Essay on AIDS and Queer Politics.* Cambridge: The MIT Press, 2002.

———. AIDS Cultural Analysis, Cultural Activism, in *AIDS Cultural Analysis/ Cultural Activism.* ed. Douglas Crimp, Cambridge (MA): The MIT Press, 1988.

Crow, Thomas. "Saturday Disasters: Trace and Reference in Early Warhol." *October Files Andy Warhol.* Ed. Annette Michelson, 49–68. Cambridge: MIT Press, 2001.

Crowther, Bosley. "The Screen in Review: 'Elephant Walk' Opens at Astor Theater." *New York Times*, April 22, 1954.

Cumings, Bruce. *The Korean War: A History.* New York: Modern Library, 2010.

Davidson, Bill. *Jane Fonda: An Intimate Biography.* New York: Dutton Adult, 1990.

De León, Arnoldo. *Mexican Americans in Texas.* Wheeling, IL: Harlan Davidson, 1993.

Deleuze, Gilles, and Felix Guattari. *Anti-Oedipus: Capitalism and Schizophrenia* Trans. Robert Hurley. New York: Viking Adult, 1997.

D'Emilio, John. "Capitalism and Gay Identity," In *The Lesbian and Gay Studies Reader.* eds., Henry Abelove, Michéle Aina Barale, and David M. Halperin, 467–76. New York and London: Routledge, 1993.

Dickens, Charles. *Hard Times* (Mass Market Paperback). New York: Simon & Schuster, 2007.

Dirks, Nicholas. B. *Castes of the Mind: Colonialism and the Making of Modern India.* Princeton: Princeton University Press, 2001.

Dudziak, Mary L. *Cold War Civil Rights: Race and the Image of American Democracy.* Princeton and Oxford: Princeton University Press, 2000.

Dyer, Richard. *Stars.* London: British Film Institute, 1979.

———. *Heavenly Bodies: Film Stars and Society.* London: St. Martin's Press, 1986.

———. *White: Essays on Race and Culture.* New York and London: Routledge, 1997.

Elizabethtayloraidsfoundation.org "Our Story." "Our Work." 7.9.22, elizabethtaylo-raidsfoundation.org/story.

Englis, Basil G. "The Role of Affect in Political Advertising: Voter Emotional Responses to the Nonverbal Behavior of Politicians." In *Attention, Attitude and Affect in Response to Advertising.* Eds. Eddie M. Clark, Timothy C. Brock, and David W. Stewart, 223–50. Hillsdale, NJ: Lawrence Erlbaum Associates, Inc, 1994.

Epstein, David Mark. *Nat King Cole.* New York: Farrar Straus Grioux, 1999.

Epstein, Jean. 1993. "Magnification." In *French Film Theory and Criticism, Vol. 1.* Ed., Richard Abel, 235–39. Princeton: Princeton University Press, 1993.

Esseks, John D. "Political Independence and Economic Decolonization: Ghana Under Nkrumah." *Western Political Quarterly* 24.1 (1971): 59–64.

Etcoff, Nancy. *Survival of the Prettiest The Science of Beauty.* New York: Anchor Books, a Division of Random House, 1999.

Forbes, Moira. "Elizabeth Taylor Auction: A Fitting Remembrance." *Forbes Magazine.* 12.11.14. www.forbes.com/sites/moiraforbes/2011/12/14/elizabeth-taylor-auction -a-fitting-rememberance/.

Gabbard, Krin. *Black Magic: White Hollywood and African American Culture.* New Brunswick: Rutgers University Press, 2004.

Genovese, Eugene D. *The Political Economy of Slavery: Studies in the Economy and Society of the Slave South.* Middletown, CT: Wesleyan University Press, 1961.

Gledhill, Christine. *Home Is Where the Heart Is: Studies in Melodrama and the Woman's Film.* London: British Film Institute, 1987.

Goldschimdt, Arthur Jr. *Modern Egypt: The Formation of a Nation State.* Second Edition. Boulder, CO: Westview Press, 2004.

———. *Biographical Dictionary of Modern Egypt.* New York: Lynne Rienner Publishing, 2000.

Gottlieb, Michael. "Pneumocystos Pneumonia—Los Angeles 1981." *American Journal of Public Health* 96, no.6 (2006): 90–91.

Gramsci, Antonio. *Selections from the Prison Notebooks.* Eds. Quintin Hoare and Geoffrey Nowell Smith. London: International Publishers, 1971.

Griffith, Nancy. "The 'Thriller' Diaries." *Vanity Fair* 599 (July 2010): 60–79.

Guerrero, Ed. *Framing Blackness: The African American Image on Film.* Philadelphia: Temple University Press, 1993.

Hall, C. Michael, and Hazel Tucker. eds., *Tourism and Postcolonialism: Identities and Representations.* Oxfordshire: Routledge, 2004.

Hall, Stuart. "The Work of Representation." In *Representations: Cultural Representations and Signifying Practices.* ed. Stuart Hall, 13–74. London: Sage Publishing, 1997.

———. *Encoding and Decoding in Television Discourse.* Birmingham (UK): University of Birmingham Press, 1974.

Hallowell, John. "Don't Put the Blame on Me Boys." *The New York Times,* October 25, 1970.

Hardt, Michael, and Antonio Negri. *Multitude: War and Democracy in the Age of Empire.* New York: Penguin (Non-Classics), 2004.

Heussner, Ki Mae. "Elizabeth Taylor: The Science Behind Her Beauty." ABC News, March 23, 2011. https://abcnews.go.com/Technology/elizabeth-taylor-science-great-beauty/story?id=13203775.

Hevesi, Dennis. "Warren Leslie Dies at 84; Wrote Book That Rankled Dallas." *The New York Times,* July 23, 2011.

Holden, Anthony. *Laurence Olivier: A Biography.* London: Random House Value Publishing, 1991.

Hong, Grace Kyungwon. *Ruptures of American Capital: Women of Color Feminism and the Culture of Immigrant Labor.* Minneapolis: University of Minnesota Press, 2006.

hooks, bell. *Black Looks: Race and Representation.* Boston: South End Press, 1992.

Icap.columbia.edu. "HIV Rates for African American Women in Parts of the US Much Higher Than Previously Estimated." 3.10.12 icap.columbia.edu/news-events/hiv-rates-for-african-american-women-in-parts-of-the-u-s-much-higher-than-previously-estimated/

Jacobson, Matthew Frye. *Barbarian Virtues: The United States Encounters Foreign Peoples at Home and Abroad, 1876–1917.* New York: Hill and Wang, 1991.

———. *Whiteness of a Different Color European Immigrants and the Alchemy of Race.* Cambridge and London: Harvard University Press, 1998.

Jeffords, Susan. *Hard Bodies: Hollywood Masculinities in the Reagan Era.* New Brunswick: Rutgers University Press, 1994.

Jones, Richard O. . . . *Natural (The Beautiful "N" Word): Breaking the Psychological Bondage of the American Standard of Beauty.* Lincoln, NE: iUniverse, 2007.

Jørgensen, Henning. *Consensus, Cooperation, and Conflict: Policy-Making Process in Denmark.* Gloucestershire (UK) and Southampton (MA): Edward Elgar Publishing, 2002.

Kamp, David. "When Liz Met Dick." *Vanity Fair*, April 1998: 366–88, 393–94. Print.

Kanfer, Stefan. *Somebody: The Reckless Life and Remarkable Career of Marlon Brando.* New York: Knopf, 2008.

Kant, Immanuel. *Critique of the Power of Judgment.* Translated by Paul Guyer and Eric Matthews. Cambridge: Cambridge University Press, 2000.

Kaplan, Amy. *The Anarchy of Empire and the Making of US Culture.* Cambridge: Harvard University Press, 2003.

Kaplan, Lawrence, S. *NATO Divided, NATO United: The Evolution of an Alliance.* Westport, CT: Praeger Publishers, 2004.

Kashner, Sam, and Jennifer MacNair. "Bell, Book, and Scandal: Kim Novak and Sammy Davis Jr." In *The Bad & The Beautiful Hollywood in the Fifties.* New York: W. W. Norton & Company, 2003.

Kashner, Sam, and Nancy Schoenberger. *Furious Love: Elizabeth Taylor, Richard Burton, and the Marriage of the Century.* New York: Harper, 2010.

Kelen, Christopher. "Hymns for and from White Australia." In *Postcolonial Whiteness.* ed. Alfred J. Lopez, 201–30. Albany: State University of New York Press, 2005.

Kelley, Kitty. *Elizabeth Taylor the Last Star.* New York: Simon and Schuster, 1981.

Kennedy, Dane. *The Highly Civilized Man: Richard Burton and the Victorian World.* Cambridge and London: Harvard University Press, 2005.

Kiernan, Thomas. *Jane Fonda: Heroine for Our Time.* New York: Putman Group, 1982.

Kocieniewki, David. "US Business Has High Tax Rates but Pay Less" *Newsweek,* May 3, 2011.

Lacey, Robert J. *American Pragmaticism and Democratic Faith.* DeKalb: Northern Illinois University Press, 2007.

Lefebrve, Henri. *The Production of Space.* Trans. Donald Nicholson-Smith. London: Blackwell Publishers, 1991.

Levy, Shawn. *Paul Newman: A Life.* New York: Harmony Books, 2009.

Limón, José E. *American Encounters: Greater Mexico, the United States, and the Erotics of Culture.* Boston: Beacon Press, 1998.

Lindstrom, Pia. "Alzheimer Fight in Her Mother's Name." *The New York Times,* February 23, 1997.

Lipsitz, George. *The Possessive Investment in Whiteness: How White People Profit from Identity Politics.* Philadelphia: Temple University Press, 1998.

Lovell, Alan. "The Western." In *Movies and Methods 1,* ed. Bill Nichols, 164–76. Berkeley: University of California Press, 1976.

Macpherson, C. B. 1962. *The Political History of Possessive Individualism Hobbes to Locke.* Oxford and London: Oxford University Press, 1962.

Maddox, Brenda. *Who's Afraid of Elizabeth Taylor?* New York: Jove, 1978.

Mahdavi, Pardis. *Gridlock: Labor, Migration, and Human Trafficking in Dubai.* Stanford: Stanford University Press, 2011.

Mailer, Norman. "The White Negro: Superficial Reflections on the Hipster." In *Advertisements for Myself,* 337–58. Cambridge: Harvard University Press, 1959.

Manderson, Leonore. "The Pursuit of Pleasure and the Sale of Sex." In *Sexual Nature, Sexual Culture.* eds. Paul R. Abramson and Steven D. Pinkerton, 305–29. Chicago: University of Chicago Press, 1995.

Mann, William J. *How to Be a Movie Star: Elizabeth Taylor in Hollywood.* Boston and New York: Houghton Mifflin Harcourt, 2009.

Marks, Lara V. *Sexual Chemistry: A History of the Contraceptive Pill.* New Haven: Yale University Press, 2001.

Mask, Mia. *Divas on Screen: Black Women in American Film.* Champaign: University of Illinois Press, 2009.

McAlister, Melani. *Epic Encounters Culture, Media, and US Interests in the Middle East, 1945–2000.* Berkeley and Los Angeles: University of California Press, 2001.

McCusker John J., and Russell R. Menard. *The Economy of British America, 1607–1789 with Supplementary Bibliography.* Chapel Hill: University of North Carolina Press, 1985.

McIntrye, W. David. *The Commonwealth of Nations: Origins and Impact, 1869–1971.* Minneapolis: University of Minnesota Press, 1978.

McLean, Adrienne L. *Being Rita Hayworth: Labor, Identity, and Hollywood Stardom.* New Brunswick: Rutgers University Press.

McNeil, Donald G. "For First Time, AIDS Vaccine Shows Some Success." *The New York Times,* September 24, 2007.

McPherson, Tara. *Reconstructing Dixie: Race, Gender, and Nostalgia in the Imagined South.* Durham and London: Duke University Press, 2003.

Meyer, Richard. "Rock Hudson's Body." In *Inside/ Out Lesbian Theories, Gay Theories.* ed. Diana Fuss, 259–90. New York and London: Routledge, 1991.

Michaud, Michael Gregg. *Sal Mineo: A Biography.* New York: Crown Archetype, 2010.

Montejano, David. *Anglos and Mexicans in the Making of Texas, 1836–1986.* Austin: University of Texas Press, 1987.

Morrison, Toni. *Playing in the Dark Whiteness and the Literary Imagination.* New York: Vintage Books, 1993.

Mulvey, Laura. "Visual Pleasure and Narrative Cinema." *Screen* 16, no. 3 (Autumn 1975), 6–18.

Munn, Michael. *Richard Burton: Prince of Players.* New York: Skyhorse Publishing, 2008.

Münsterberg, Hugo. *Hugo Müsterberg on Film: The Photoplay: A Psychological Study and Other Writings.* Ed. Allan Langsdale. New York and London: Routledge, 2001.

Niven, David. *Bring on the Empty Horses.* New York and London: Putnam, 1977.

Oliver, Kelly. "The Crisis of Meaning." In *The Kristeva Critical Reader.* Eds. John Lechte and Mary Zournazi, 36–54. Edinburgh, UK: Edinburgh University Press, 2003.

Ondaatje, Christopher. 2005. *Woolf in Ceylon An Interpretative Journey in the Shadow of Leonard Woolf 1904–1911.* Toronto: Harper Collins Ltd., 2005.

Patton, Cindy. *Globalizing AIDS (Theory out of Bounds)*. Minneapolis: University of Minnesota Press, 2002.

Paul, Tessa. *Handbags: The Ultimate Accessory*. New York: Chartwell Books 2010.

Pepin, Jacques. *The Origins of AIDS*. Cambridge: Cambridge University Press, 2011.

Pérez-Torres, Rafael. *Mestizaje: Critical Uses of Race in Chicano Culture*. Minneapolis: University of Minnesota Press, 2006.

Phillipson, Robert. *Linguistic Imperialism*. Oxford: Oxford University Press, 1992.

Pitman, Joanna. *On Blondes*. New York and London: Bloomsbury, 2003.

Rice, Edward. *Captain Sir Richard Francis Burton: A Biography*. New York: Da Capo Press, 1990.

Rinehart, James. "Transcending Taylorism and Fordism? Three Decades of Work Restructuring" In *The Critical Study of Work: Labor Technology and Global Production*. Eds. Rick Baldox, Charles Koeber, and Philip Kraft, 179–95. Philadelphia: Temple University Press, 2001.

Rives, George Lockhart. *The United States and Mexico, 1821–1848: A History of the Relations between the Two Countries from the Independence of Mexico to the Close of the War with the United States, Volume 2*. New York: Charles Scribner's Sons, 1913.

Roediger, David R. *Wages of Whiteness: Race and the Making of the American Working Class*. Revised Edition. London and New York: Verso, 1991.

Rogin, Michael. *Blackface, White Noise: Jewish Immigrants in the Hollywood Melting Pot*. Berkeley: University of California Press, 1996.

Rosaldo, Renato. *Culture and Truth: The Remaking of Social Analysis*. Boston: Beacon Press, 1989.

Ross, Steven. J. *Hollywood Left and Right: How Movie Stars Shaped American Politics*. Oxford: Oxford University Press, 2011.

Royster, Francesca T. *Becoming Cleopatra: The Shifting Image of an Icon*. New York: Palgrave MacMillan, 2003.

Ruby, Robert H., and John Arthur Brown. *The Cayuse Indians: Imperial Tribesmen of Old Oregon*. Norman: University of Oklahoma Press, 1972.

Ryanwhite.hrsa.org "Who Was Ryan White?" 7.9.22. https://ryanwhite.hrsa.gov/about/ryan-white.

Said, Edward W. *Orientalism*. New York: Pantheon Books, 1979.

Sampson, Robert D. *John L. O'Sullivan and His Times*. Kent: Kent State University Press, 2003.

Schatz, Thomas. "From Genre and the Genre Film." In *Film Theory and Criticism (Fifth Edition)*. eds. Leo Braudy and Marshall Cohen, 642–53. Oxford and New York: Oxford University Press, 1999.

———. *The Genius of the System: Hollywood Filmmaking in the Studio Era*. New York: Pantheon Books, 1998.

Schiller, Lawrence. "A Splash of Marilyn." *Vanity Fair* 622 (June 2012): 128–39, 192–94.

Sears, David, O. "The Role of Affect in Symbolic Politics." In *Citizens and Politics: Perspectives from Political Psychology*. Ed. James H. Kuklinski, 14–40. New York: Cambridge University Press, 2001.

Sedgwick, Eve Kosofsky. *Between Men: English Literature and Homosocial Desire.* New York: Columbia University Press, 1985.

———.1993. *Tendencies.* Durham and London: Duke University Press, 1993.

Shaw, Andrea Elizabeth. *The Embodiment of Disobedience: Fat Black Women's Unruly Bodies.* Lanham, MD.: Lexington Books, 2006.

Shaw, Timothy M. *Commonwealth: Inter- and Non-State Contributions to Global Governance.* London and New York: Routledge, 2008.

Shohat, Ella. *Taboo Memories, Diasporic Voices.* Durham and London: Duke University Press, 2006.

Shohat, Ella, and Robert Stam. *Unthinking Eurocentrism: Multiculturalism and Media.* London and New York: Routledge, 1994.

———. (eds). *Multiculturalism, Postcoloniality, and Transnational Media* (Rutgers Depth of Field Series). New York and London: Rutgers University Press, 2003.

Shwadran, Benjamin. *Middle East Oil: Issues and Problems.* Cambridge, MA: Schenkman Publishing Company, 1977.

Sikov, Ed. *Dark Victory: The Life of Bette Davis.* New York: Holt Paperbacks, 2008.

Smith, Anna Marie. *Welfare Reform and Sexual Regulation.* Cambridge: Cambridge University Press, 2007.

Smith, Neil. *American Empire: Roosevelt's Geographer and the Prelude to Globalization.* Berkeley: University of California Press, 2003.

Smyth, J. E. "Jim Crow, Jett Rink and James Dean: Reconstructing Edna Ferber's *Giant.*" *American Studies* 48, no. 3 (Fall 2007): 5–27.

Sontag, Susan. "Notes on Camp." In *Queer Aesthetics and the Performing Subject: A Reader.* Ed. Fabio Cieto, 53–64. Ann Arbor, MI: University of Michigan Press, 1997.

———. *Illness as Metaphor and AIDS and Its Metaphors.* New York: Peter Smith Publisher, 1995.

Spar, Debora L., and Briana Huntsburger. "The Business of Birth Control." *Harvard Health Policy Review* 6, no. 1 (2005): 6–18.

Spoto, Donald. *A Passion for Life: The Biography of Elizabeth Taylor.* New York: Harper Collins, 1997.

———. *Enchantment: The Life of Audrey Hepburn.* New York: Harmony, 2006.

———. *High Society: The Life of Grace Kelly.* New York: Crown Archetype, 2009.

Steyn, Melissa. "White Talk: White South Africans and the Management of Diasporic Whiteness." In *Postcolonial Whiteness.* Ed. Alfred J. Lopez, 119–36. Albany: State University of New York Press, 2005.

Stinson, Jeff. "Denmark: A Unique Mix of Welfare and Economic Growth." *USA Today,* March 8, 2007.

Sturken, Marita. *Tangled Memories: The Vietnam War, the AIDS Epidemic, and the Politics of Remembering.* Berkeley: University of California Press, 1997.

Taraborelli, Randy J. *Elizabeth.* New York and Boston: Warner Books, 2006.

Taussig, Michael T. *The Devil and Commodity Fetishism in South America.* (Thirtieth Anniversary Edition with a New Introduction by the Author). Chapel Hill, NC: The University of North Carolina Press, 2009.

Taylor, Elizabeth. *Elizabeth Takes Off: On Weight Gain, Weight Loss, Self-Image, and Self- Esteem.* New York: Putnam, 1989.

Taylor, Paul C. "Malcolm's Conk and Danto's Colors; or, Four Logical Petitions Concerning Race, Beauty, and Aesthetics," In *Beauty Matters,* Ed. Peg Zeglin Brand, 57–64. Bloomington and Indianapolis: Indiana University Press, 2000.

Thomas, Robert Mcg, Jr. "George Masters Magician of Styling and Makeup Dies at 62." *New York Times* Obituary, dated April 26, 1998.

Tiel, Vicky. *It's All about the Dress: What I Learned in Forty Years about Men, Women, Sex, and Fashion.* New York: St. Martin's Press, 2011.

Tradigo, Antonio. *Icons and Saints of the Eastern Orthodox Church.* Los Angeles: John Paul Getty Trust, 2006.

Trivette, Alan "The Cleo Craze." 6.1.22, http://www.elizabethtaylorthelegend.com.

Trafton, Scott. *Egypt Land Race and the Nineteenth-Century American Egyptomania.* Durham and London: Duke University Press, 2004.

Tudor, Andrew. "Genre and Critical Methodology." In *Movies and Methods 1,* ed. Bill Nichols, 118–25. Berkeley: University of California Press, 1976.

Tugwell, Franklin. *The Energy Crisis and the American Political Economy: Politics and Markets in the Management of Natural Resources.* Stanford: Stanford University Press, 1988.

UNAIDS.org "Press Centre" 7.9.22

www.unaids.org/en/resources/presscentre/pressreleaseandstatementarchive/2022/june/20220622_financial_support_AIDS.

US Department of Defense.org. "United States Department of Defense Fiscal Year 2011 Budget Request." 8.8.11. comptroller.defense.gov/Portals/45/Documents/defbudget/fy2011/FY2011_Budget_Request_Overview_Book.pdf.

Vera, Hernan, and Andrew Gordon. "Sincere Fictions of the White Self in the American Cinema: The Divided White Self in Civil War Films." In *Classic Hollywood, Classic Whiteness.* Ed. Daniel Bernardi, 263–80. Minneapolis and London: University of Minnesota Press, 1991.

Vermilye, Jerry, and Mark Ricci. *The Films of Elizabeth Taylor.* Secaucus, NJ: Citadel Press, 1976.

Von Eschen, Penny Marie. *Race against Empire: Black Americans and Anticolonialism, 1937–1957.* Ithaca, NY: Cornell University Press, 1997.

Walker, Alexander. *Elizabeth: The Life of Elizabeth Taylor.* New York: Grove Public Relations, 1991.

Waterbury, Ruth. *Elizabeth Taylor: Her Life, Her Loves, Her Future.* New York: Appleton Century, 1964.

Watney, Simon. *Policing Desire: Pornography, AIDS, and the Media.* Minneapolis and London: University of Minnesota, 1997.

———. *Imagine Hope: AIDS and Gay Identity.* New York and London: Routledge, 2000.

Watson, Mary Ann. "Nat 'King' Cole Show." In *Encyclopedia of Television, Volume 1.* Second Edition. Ed. Horace Newcomb, 1593–96. New York and London: Routledge, 2004.

Williams, Linda. "Melodrama." Revised in *Refiguring American Film Genres*. Ed. Nick Browne, 42–88, Berkeley: University of California Press, 1998.

Williams, Raymond. "Advertising: The Magic System." In *The Cultural Studies Reader*. Second Edition, Ed. Simon During, 410–26. New York and London: Routledge, 1980.

———. *Keywords: A Vocabulary of Culture and Society*. Oxford and London: Oxford University Press, 1976.

Wilson, Eric. "From Kenneth Cole a New Solidarity." *The New York Times*, December 1, 2005.

Woodward, Ian. *Audrey Hepburn: Fair Lady of the Screen*. London: St. Martins Press, 1984.

Young, Iris Marion. *Throwing Like a Girl and Other Essays in Feminist Theory and Social Philosophy*. Bloomington: Indiana University Press, 1990.

Index

abstract places, 51–52

Academy Awards, 73, 107, 113, 125

accumulation, 160, 163; American Empire metaphor and, 31; life of, 12, 110, 125; logic of, 3, 139; practical facets of, 136; right to, 135. *See also* consumption

acousmêtre, 82

admirable face-object, 26

affective genius, 151–53

affective labor: AIDS activism and, 124; embodiment of, 4; fantasy and, 2; genius and, 1

African Americans, 51; AIDS and, 127, 133, 136, 150; civil rights movement, 4–5, 31, 79, 83; identity, 101; queer culture, 108

Africanism, 97–98

Afrocentrism, 9

AIDS: African Americans and, 127, 133, 136, 150; AIDS mother, 132–38; Hudson as victim, 121, 126–27; Ryan White HIV/AIDS Program, 142; World AIDS Day, 150

AIDS activism, 5, 98; affective genius in, 151–53; affective labor and, 124; AIDS red ribbon in, 139–40; appeal to government, 142–43, 155n42; awards for, 124; capitalism and, 165; Elizabeth Taylor AIDS Foundation, 127, 136; as embodied emotive politics, 121, 126; foundation funding, 127; gay identity and capitalism in, 138; iconicity and, 138–41, 152; as maternal melodrama, 145–51; overview, 121–27; performative prowess in, 160; photo campaign, 150–51; safe body and, 128–30; shame and compassion evoked in, 141–42, 149; success in, 10, 122, 153, 165; as symbolic politics, 152–53; through multimedia performances, 126; universal mother and, 141–45; vaccine development, 152; video tribute, 145–47; welfare queen compared to AIDS mother, 132–38

alcohol abuse, 95

American Dream, 27; American Dream Girl, 41, 101–2

American Empire metaphor, 2, 165; accumulation and, 31; American exceptionalism in, 23; beauty in, 15–16; body and, 43–44; consumption in, 31; darkness at center, 31; dreams of, 51; evoking American imperial power, 4; icon

177

welfare queen, 132–38
Welles, Orson, 29–30
White (Dyer), 31
White, Jeanne, 133, 143, 146
White, Ryan, 142–43
white American identity, 163
White Diamonds perfume, 121, 129,
    131–32, 136
white exceptionalism, 37, 163;
    fantasy of, 161
whiteface oriental: in Burton romantic
    pairing, 97–107; Cleopatra character
    as, 7, 18, 32
whiteness, 160; beauty and, 5;
    blondeness and, 18, 31, 33; Burton
    romantic pairing and, 90; dark visual,
    19; defined, 161; as ideological
    imaginary, 162; as imperial beauty,
    37–41; imperialism and, 11, 91;
    justification for, 23–24; moral
    goodness linked to, 31; off-screen,
    104; ownership and, 136; as political
    identity, 165; probationary whiteness,
    75; as sanctuary, 111; stardom and,
    16; studies, 11; as transnational,
    45; as unstable, 16; visual, 31–32,

39; white freedom, 3. *See also*
    postcolonial whiteness
white orientalism, 108, 110, 165
white power, 121, 130, 162; Black
    freedom impeding, 110; elite, 8, 53;
    extension of, 90, 94; loss of, 51, 89;
    protecting, 164; threats to, 12
white supremacy, 161
WHO. *See* World Health Organization
Who's Afraid of Virginia Woolf (film),
    115, 125, 151
Wiegman, Robyn, 11
Wilder, Billy, 30
Wilding, Michael, Jr. (son), 62, 144–45
Wilding, Michael, Sr. (husband), 63
Williams, Linda, 70
Williams, Raymond, 4, 132, 149
Wofford, Harris, 94
Workers' Revolutionary Party, 146
World AIDS Day, 150
World Health Organization
    (WHO), 130–31

Yankovic, Al, 42
Young, Iris Marion, 54–55

About the Author

Gloria Shin is a full-time instructor in film, TV, and media studies in the School of Film and Television at Loyola Marymount University in Los Angeles. She is a media consultant whose work has been featured in NPR and the *Los Angeles Times*.